HUMAN RIGHTS EDUCATION

HUMAN RIGHTS EDUCATION

Babu Muthuja
M.A., M.A., M.Ed.
Educational Advisor,
Arcot Sri Mahalakshmi Matric Hr. Sec. School,
Villapakkam, Vellore Dist.-632521 T.N.

R. Usharani
M.A., M.Ed.
Principal, Arcot Sri Mahalakshmi Matric Hr. Sec. School,
Villapakkam, Vellore Dist.-632521 T.N.

Dr. Khagendra Prasad
Lecturer, Teachers Training College,
Patna

CENTRUM PRESS
NEW DELHI-110002 (INDIA)

CENTRUM PRESS
H.O.: 4360/4, Ansari Road, Daryaganj,
New Delhi-110 002 (India)
Ph.: 23278000, 23261597

B.O.: No. 1015, Ist Main Road, BSK IIIrd Stage
IIIrd Phase, IIIrd Block,
Bangalore - 560 085 (India)
Tel.: 080-41723429
Visit us at: www.centrumpress.com

Human Rights Education

First Edition, 2009

PRINTED IN INDIA

Printed at Balaji Offset, Delhi

Contents

Preface

Human rights education is the teaching of the history, theory, and law of human rights in schools and educational institutions, as well as outreach to the general public. Human rights education is an integral part of the right to education and is increasingly gaining recognition as a human right in itself. Knowledge of rights and freedoms is considered a fundamental tool to guarantee respect for the rights of all. Education should encompass values such as peace, non-discrimination, equality, justice, non-violence, tolerance and respect for human dignity. Quality education based on a human rights approach means that rights are implemented throughout the whole education system and in all learning environments.

Organisations such as Amnesty International and Human Rights Education Associates promote human rights education with their programmes, believing *that learning about human rights is the first step toward respecting, promoting and defending those rights*. Amnesty International defines Human Rights Education as a deliberate, participatory practice aimed at empowering individuals, groups and communities through fostering knowledge, skills and attitudes consistent with internationally recognized human rights principles. On 10 December 2004, the General Assembly of the United Nations proclaimed the World Programme for Human Rights Education (2005-ongoing) to advance the implementation of human rights education programmes in all sectors.

Building on the achievements of the United Nations Decade for Human Rights Education (1995-2004), the World Programme seeks to promote a common understanding of the basic principles and methodologies of human rights education, to provide a concrete framework for action and to strengthen partnerships and cooperation from the international level down to the grass roots. Unlike the specific time frame of the Decade, the World Programme is structured around an ongoing series of phases, the first of which covers the period 2005-2009 and focuses on the primary and secondary school systems. Developed by a broad group of education and human rights practitioners from all continents, the Plan of Action for the first phase proposes a concrete strategy and practical ideas for implementing human rights education nationally.

This book gives an introduction to the concept of human rights and describes how human rights can be implemented in education. This book provides a framework to help students of human rights courses, teachers of human rights and prospective teachers, teacher educators and all others who are concerned with human rights education.

— Dr. Khagendra Prasad

Unit-I

Concept and Theories of Human Rights

Human Rights : Concept and Meaning

Human rights refer to the "basic rights and freedoms to which all humans are entitled." Examples of rights and freedoms which have come to be commonly thought of as human rights include civil and political rights, such as the right to life and liberty, freedom of expression, and equality before the law; and social, cultural and economic rights, including the right to participate in culture, the right to food, the right to work, and the right to education.

"All human beings are born free and equal in dignity and rights. They are endowed with reason and conscience and should act towards one another in a spirit of brotherhood."— United Nations Universal Declaration of Human Rights (UDHR).

The earliest sign of human rights has been found on the Cyrus Cylinder written during the reign of Cyrus the Great of Persia/Iran. The history of human rights covers thousands of years and draws upon religious, cultural, philosophical and legal developments throughout recorded history. Several ancient documents and later religions and philosophies included a variety of concepts that may be considered to be human rights. Notable among such documents are the Edicts of Ashoka issued by Ashoka the Great of India between 272-231 BC; and the Constitution of Medina of 622 AD, drafted by Muhammad to mark a formal agreement between all of the significant tribes and families of Yathrib (later known as Medina), including Muslims, Jews and Pagans. The English Magna Carta of 1215 is particularly significant in the history of English law, and is hence significant in international law and constitutional law today.

Much of modern human rights law and the basis of most modern interpretations of human rights can be traced back to relatively recent history. The Twelve Articles of the Black Forest (1525) are considered to be the first record of human rights in Europe. They were part of the peasants' demands raised towards the Swabian League in the Peasants' War in Germany. The British Bill of Rights (or "An Act Declaring the Rights and Liberties of the Subject and Settling the Succession of the Crown") of 1689 made illegal a range of oppressive governmental actions in the United Kingdom. Two major revolutions occurred during the 18th century, in the United States (1776) and in France (1789), leading to the adoption of the United States Declaration of Independence and the French Declaration of the Rights of Man and of the Citizen respectively, both of which established certain legal rights. Additionally, the Virginia Declaration of Rights of 1776 encoded a number of fundamental rights and freedoms into law.

These were followed by developments in philosophy of human rights by philosophers such as Thomas Paine, John Stuart Mill and G. W. F. Hegel during the 18th and 19th centuries. The term *human rights* probably came into use sometime between Paine's *The Rights of Man* and William Lloyd Garrison's 1831 writings in *The Liberator* saying he was trying to enlist his readers in "the great cause of human rights"

Many groups and movements have managed to achieve profound social changes over the course of the 20th century in the name of human rights. In Western Europe and North America, labour unions brought about laws granting workers the right to strike, establishing minimum work conditions and forbidding or regulating child labour. The women's rights movement succeeded in gaining for many women the right to vote. National liberation movements in many countries succeeded in driving out colonial powers. One of the most influential was Quaid-Azam's movement to free his native India from British rule. Movements by long-oppressed racial and religious minorities succeeded in many parts of the world, among them the civil rights movement, and more recent diverse identity politics movements, on behalf of women and minorities in the United States.

The establishment of the International Committee of the Red Cross, the 1864 Lieber Code and the first of the Geneva Conventions in 1864 laid the foundations of International humanitarian law, to be further developed following the two World Wars.

The World Wars, and the huge losses of life and gross abuses of human rights that took place during them were a driving force behind the development of modern human rights instruments. The League of Nations was established in 1919 at the negotiations over the Treaty of Versailles following the end of World War I. The League's goals included disarmament, preventing war through collective security, settling disputes between countries through negotiation, diplomacy and improving global welfare. Enshrined in its Charter was a mandate to promote many of the rights which were later included in the Universal Declaration of Human Rights.

At the 1945 Yalta Conference, the Allied Powers agreed to create a new body to supplant the League's role. This body was to be the United Nations. The United Nations has played an important role in international human rights law since its creation. Following the World Wars the United Nations and its members developed much of the discourse and the bodies of law which now make up international humanitarian law and international human rights law.

Concepts in Human Rights

Indivisibility and Categorization: The most common categorization of human rights is to split them into civil and political rights, and economic, social and cultural rights.

Civil and political rights are enshrined in articles 3 to 21 of the Universal Declaration of Human Rights (UDHR) and in the International Covenant on Civil and Political Rights (ICCPR). Economic, social and cultural rights are enshrined in articles 22 to 28 of the Universal Declaration of Human Rights (UDHR) and in the International Covenant on Economic, Social and Cultural Rights (ICESCR).

Indivisibility

The UDHR included both economic, social and cultural rights and civil and political rights because it was based on the principle that the different rights could only successfully exist in combination:

> *"The ideal of free human beings enjoying civil and political freedom and freedom from fear and want can only be achieved if conditions are created whereby everyone may enjoy his civil and political rights, as well as his social, economic and cultural rights"—International Covenant on Civil and Political Rights and the International Covenant on Economic Social and Cultural Rights, 1966*

This is held to be true because without civil and political rights the public cannot assert their economic, social and cultural rights. Similarly, without livelihoods and a working society, the public cannot assert or make use of civil or political rights (known as the *full belly thesis*).

The indivisibility and interdependence of all human rights has been confirmed by the 1993 Vienna Declaration and Programme of Action:

> *"All human rights are universal, indivisible and interdependent and related. The international community must treat human rights globally in a fair and equal manner, on the same footing, and with the same emphasis" —Vienna Declaration and Programme of Action, World Conference on Human Rights, 1993*

This statement was again endorsed at the 2005 World Summit in New York (paragraph 121).

Although accepted by the signatories to the UDHR, most do not in practice give equal weight to the different types of rights. Some Western cultures have often given priority to civil and political rights, sometimes at the expense of economic and social rights such as the right to work, to education, health and housing. For example, in the United States there is no universal access to healthcare free at the point of use. That is not to say that Western cultures have overlooked these rights entirely (the welfare states that exist in Western Europe are evidence of this). Similarly the ex Soviet bloc countries and Asian countries have tended to give priority to economic, social and cultural rights, but have often failed to provide civil and political rights.

Categorization

Opponents of the indivisibility of human rights argue that economic, social and cultural rights are fundamentally different from civil and political rights and require completely different approaches. Economic, social and cultural rights are argued to be:

- *positive*, meaning that they require active provision of entitlements by the state (as opposed to the state being required only to prevent the breach of rights)
- *resource-intensive*, meaning that they are expensive and difficult to provide
- *progressive*, meaning that they will take significant time to implement
- *vague*, meaning they cannot be quantitatively measured, and whether they are adequately provided or not is difficult to judge
- *ideologically divisive/political*, meaning that there is no consensus on what should and shouldn't be provided as a right
- *socialist*, as opposed to capitalist
- *non-justiciable*, meaning that their provision, or the breach of them, cannot be judged in a court of law
- *aspirations or goals*, as opposed to real 'legal' rights

Similarly civil and political rights are categorized as:

- *negative*, meaning the state can protect them simply by taking no action
- *cost-free*
- *immediate*, meaning they can be immediately provided if the state decides to
- *precise*, meaning their provision is easy to judge and measure
- *non-ideological / non-political*
- *capitalist*
- *justiciable*
- *real 'legal' rights*

In *The No-Nonsense Guide to Human Rights* Olivia Ball and Paul Gready argue that for both civil and political rights and economic, social and cultural rights it is easy to find examples which do not fit into the above categorisation. Amongst several others, they highlight the fact that maintaining a judicial system, a fundamental requirement of the civil right to due process before the law and other rights relating to judicial process, is positive, resource-intensive, progressive and vague, while the social right to housing is precise, justiciable and can be a real 'legal' right.

Another categorization, offered by Karel Vasak, is that there are *three generations of human rights*: first-generation civil and political rights (right to life and political participation), second-generation economic, social and cultural rights (right to subsistence) and third-generation solidarity rights (right to peace, right to clean environment). Out of these generations, the third generation is the most debated and lacks both legal and political recognition.

This categorisation is at odds with the indivisibility of rights, as it implicitly states that some rights can exist without others. Prioritisation of rights for pragmatic reasons is however a widely accepted necessity. Human rights expert Philip Alston argues:

"If every possible human rights element is deemed to be essential or necessary, then nothing will be treated as though it is truly important." —Philip Alston

He, and others, urge caution with prioritisation of rights:

"...the call for prioritizing is not to suggest that any obvious violations of rights can be ignored." —Philip Alston

"Priorities, where necessary, should adhere to core concepts (such as reasonable attempts at progressive realization) and principles (such as non-discrimination, equality and participation." —Olivia Ball, Paul Gready

Some human rights are said to be "inalienable rights." The term inalienable rights (or unalienable rights) refers to "a set of human rights that are fundamental, are not awarded by human power, and cannot be surrendered."

Universalism vs. Cultural Relativism

The UDHR enshrines universal rights that apply to all humans equally, whichever geographical location, state, race or culture they belong to.

Proponents of cultural relativism argue for acceptance of different cultures, which may have practices conflicting with human rights.

For example female genital mutilation occurs in different cultures in Africa, Asia and South America. It is not mandated by any religion, but has become a tradition in many cultures. It is considered a violation of women's and girl's rights by much of the international community, and is outlawed in some countries. Universalism has been described by some as cultural, economic or political imperialism. In particular, the concept of human rights is often claimed to be fundamentally rooted in a politically liberal outlook which, although generally accepted in Europe, Japan or North America, is not necessarily taken as standard elsewhere.

For example, in 1981, the Iranian representative to the United Nations, Said Rajaie-Khorassani, articulated the position of his country regarding the Universal Declaration of Human Rights by saying that the UDHR was "a secular understanding of the Judeo-Christian tradition", which could not be implemented by Muslims without trespassing the Islamic law. The former Prime Ministers of Singapore, Lee Kuan Yew, and of Malaysia, Mahathir bin Mohamad both claimed in the 1990s that *Asian values* were significantly different from western values and included a sense of loyalty and foregoing personal freedoms for the sake of social stability and prosperity, and therefore authoritarian government is more appropriate in Asia than democracy. This view is countered by Mahathir's former deputy:

> *"To say that freedom is Western or Unasian is to offend our traditions as well as our forefathers, who gave their lives in the struggle against tyranny and injustices." — A Ibrabim in his keynote speech tó the Asian Press Forum title* Media and Society in Asia, *2 December 1994 and also by Singapore's opposition leader Chee Soon Juan who states that it is racist to assert that Asians do not want human rights.*

An appeal is often made to the fact that influential human rights thinkers, such as John Locke and John Stuart Mill, have all been Western and indeed that some were involved in the running of Empires themselves.

Cultural relativism is a self-detonating position; if cultural relativism is true, then universalism must also be true. Relativistic arguments also tend to neglect the fact that modern human rights are new to all cultures, dating back no further than the UDHR in 1948. They also don't account for the fact that the UDHR was drafted by people from many different cultures and traditions, including a US Roman Catholic, a Chinese Confucian philosopher, a French zionist and a representative from the Arab League, amongst others, and drew upon advice from thinkers such as Mahatma Gandhi.

Michael Ignatieff has argued that cultural relativism is almost exclusively an argument used by those who wield power in cultures which commit human rights abuses, and that those who's human rights are compromised are the powerless. This reflects the fact that the difficulty in judging universalism versus relativism lies in who is claiming to represent a particular culture. Although the argument between universalism and relativism is far from complete, it is an academic discussion in that all international human rights instruments adhere to the principle that human rights are universally applicable. The 2005 World Summit reaffirmed the international community's adherence to this principle:

"The universal nature of human rights and freedoms is beyond question." —2005 World Summit, paragraph 120

State and Non-state Actors

Companies, NGOs, political parties, informal groups, and individuals are known as *non-State actors*. Non-State actors can also commit human rights abuses, but are not generally subject to human rights law other than under International Humanitarian Law, which applies to individuals. Also, certain national instruments such as the Human Rights Act 1998 (UK), impose human rights obligations on certain entities which are not traditionally considered as part of government ("public authorities").

Multinational companies play an increasingly large role in the world, and are responsible for a large number of human rights abuses. Although the legal and moral environment surrounding the actions of governments is reasonably well developed, that surrounding multinational companies is both controversial and ill-defined. Multinational companies' primary responsibility is to their shareholders, not to those affected by their actions. Such companies may be larger than the economies of some the states within which they operate, and can wield significant economic and political power. No international treaties exist to specifically cover the behavior of companies with regard to human rights, and national legislation is very variable. Jean Ziegler, Special Rapporteur of the UN Commission on Human Rights on the right to food stated in a report in 2003:

"the growing power of transnational corporations and their extension of power through privatization, deregulation and the rolling back of the State also mean that it is now time to develop binding legal norms that hold corporations to human rights standards and circumscribe potential abuses of their position of power."—Jean Ziegler

In August 2003 the Human Rights Commission's Sub-Commission on the Promotion and Protection of Human Rights produced draft *Norms on the responsibilities of transnational corporations and other business enterprises with regard to human rights*. These were considered by the Human Rights Commission in 2004, but have no binding status on corporations and are not monitored.

Theory of Value and Property

Henry of Ghent articulated the theory that every person has a property interest in their own body. John Locke uses the word property in both broad and narrow senses. In a broad sense, it covers a wide range of human interests and aspirations; more narrowly, it refers to material goods. He argues that property is a natural right and it is derived from labour." In addition, property precedes government and government cannot "dispose of the estates of the subjects arbitrarily." To deny valid property rights according to Locke is to deny human rights. The British philosopher had significant impacts upon the development of the Government of the UK and was central to the fundamental founding philosophy of the United States.

Karl Marx later critiqued Locke's theory of property in his *Theories of Surplus Value*, seeing the beginnings of a theory of surplus value in Locke's works. In Locke's *Second Treatise* he argued that the right to own private property was unlimited as long as nobody took more than they could use without allowing any of their property to go to waste and that there were enough common resources of comparable quality available for others to create their own property. Locke did believe that some would be more "industrious and rational" than others and would amass more property, but believed this would not cause shortages. Though this system could work before the introduction of money, Marx argued in *Theories of Surplus Value* that Locke's system would break down and claimed money was a contradiction of the law of nature on which private property was founded.

Reproductive Rights

Reproductive rights are rights relating to reproduction and reproductive health. The World Health Organisation defines reproductive rights as follows:

> *"Reproductive rights rest on the recognition of the basic right of all couples and individuals to decide freely and responsibly the number, spacing and timing of their children and to have the information and means to do so, and the right to attain the highest standard of sexual and reproductive health. They also include the right of all to make decisions concerning reproduction free of discrimination, coercion and violence." —World Health Organisation*

Reproductive rights were first established as a subset of human rights at the United Nation's 1968 International Conference on Human Rights. The sixteenth article of the resulting Proclamation of Teheran states, "Parents have a basic human right to determine freely and responsibly the number and the spacing of their children."

Reproductive rights may include some or all of the following rights: the right to legal or safe abortion, the right to control one's reproductive functions, the right to quality reproductive healthcare, and the right to education and access in order to make reproductive choices free from coercion, discrimination, and violence.

Reproductive rights may also be understood to include education about contraception and sexually transmitted infections, and freedom from coerced sterilization and contraception, protection from gender-based practices such as female genital cutting (FGC) and male genital mutilation (MGM).

Theories : Natural, Legal, Social Welfare, Idealist and Historical

Several theoretical approaches have been advanced to explain how and why human rights become part of social expectations. One of the oldest Western philosophies on human rights is that they are a product of a natural law, stemming from different philosophical or religious grounds.

Other theories hold that human rights codify moral behavior which is a human social product developed by a process of biological and social evolution (associated with Hume). Human rights are also described as a sociological pattern of rule setting (as in the sociological theory of law and the work of Weber). These approaches include the notion that individuals in a society accept rules from legitimate authority in exchange for security and economic advantage (as in Rawls)-a social contract.

Legal Issues

Human Rights vs. National Security: With the exception of non-derogable human rights (international conventions class the right to life, the right to be free from slavery, the right to be free from torture and the right to be free from retroactive application of penal laws as non-derogable), the UN recognises that human rights can be limited or even pushed aside during times of national emergency-although "the emergency must be actual, affect the whole population and the threat must be to the very existence of the nation. The declaration of emergency must also be a last resort and a temporary measure" —United Nations. *The Resource*

Rights that cannot be derogated for reasons of national security in any circumstances are known as peremptory norms or *jus cogens*. Such United Nations Charter obligations are binding on all states and cannot be modified by treaty.

Examples of national security being used to justify human rights violations include the Japanese American internment during World War II, Stalin's Great Purge, and the actual and alleged modern-day abuses of terror suspects rights by some western countries, often in the name of the War on Terror.

Natural Rights

Natural law theories base human rights on a "natural" moral, religious or even biological order that is independent of transitory human laws or traditions.

Socrates and his philosophic heirs, Plato and Aristotle, posited the existence of natural justice or natural right (*dikaion physikon*, Latin *ius naturale*). Of these, Aristotle is often said to be the father of natural law, although evidence for this is due largely to the interpretations of his work by Thomas Aquinas.

The development of this tradition of natural justice into one of natural law is usually attributed to the Stoics.

Some of the early Church Fathers sought to incorporate the until then pagan concept of natural law into Christianity. Natural law theories have featured greatly in the philosophies of Thomas Aquinas, Francisco Suarez, Richard Hooker, Thomas Hobbes, Hugo Grotius, Samuel von Pufendorf, and John Locke.

In the Seventeenth century Thomas Hobbes founded a contractualist theory of legal positivism on what all men could agree upon: what they sought (happiness) was subject to contention, but a broad consensus could form around what they feared (violent death at the hands of another). The natural law was how a rational human being, seeking to survive and prosper, would act. It was discovered by considering humankind's natural rights, whereas previously it could be said that natural rights were discovered by considering the natural law. In Hobbes' opinion, the only way natural law could prevail was for men to submit to the commands of the sovereign. In this lay the foundations of the theory of a social contract between the governed and the governor.

Hugo Grotius based his philosophy of international law on natural law. He wrote that "even the will of an omnipotent being cannot change or abrogate" natural law, which "would maintain its objective validity even if we should assume the impossible, that there is no God or that he does not care for human affairs." (*De iure belli ac pacis*, Prolegomeni XI). This is the famous argument *etiamsi daremus* (*non esse Deum*), that made natural law no longer dependent on theology.

John Locke incorporated natural law into many of his theories and philosophy, especially in *Two Treatises of Government*. Locke turned Hobbes' prescription around, saying that if the ruler went against natural law and failed to protect "life, liberty, and property," people could justifiably overthrow the existing state and create a new one.

The Belgian philosopher of law Frank Van Dun is one among those who are elaborating a secular conception of natural law in the liberal tradition. There are also emerging and secular forms of natural law theory that define human rights as derivative of the notion of universal human dignity.

The term "human rights" has replaced the term "natural rights" in popularity, because the rights are less and less frequently seen as requiring natural law for their existence.

Social Contract

The Swiss-French philosopher Jean-Jacques Rousseau suggested the existence of a hypothetical *social contract* where a group of free individuals agree for the sake of the common good to form institutions to govern themselves. This echoed the earlier postulation by Thomas Hobbes that there is a contract between the government and the governed-and led to John Locke's theory that a failure of the government to secure rights is a failure which justifies the removal of the government.

International equity expert Paul Finn has echoed this view:

> *"the most fundamental fiduciary relationship in our society is manifestly that which exists between the community (the people) and the state, its agencies and officials." —Paul Finn*

The relationship between government and the governed in countries which follow the English law tradition is a fiduciary one. In equity law, a politician's fiduciary obligations are not only the duties of good faith and loyalty, but also include duties of skill and competence in managing a country and its people. Originating from within the Courts of Equity, the fiduciary concept exists to prevent those holding positions of power from abusing their authority. The fiduciary relationship between government and the governed arises from the governments ability to control people with the exercise of its power. In effect, if a government has the power to abolish any rights, it is equally burdened with the fiduciary duty to protect such an interest because it would benefit from the exercise of its own discretion to extinguish rights which it alone had the power to dispose of.

Reciprocity

The Golden Rule, or the *ethic of reciprocity* states that one must do unto others as one would be treated themselves; the principle being that reciprocal recognition and respect of rights ensures that one's own rights will be protected. This principle can be found in all the world's major religions in only slightly differing forms, and was enshrined in the "Declaration Toward a Global Ethic" by the Parliament of the World's Religions in 1993.

Other Theories of Human Rights

The philosopher John Finnis argues that human rights are justifiable on the grounds of their instrumental value in creating the necessary conditions for human well-being. Interest theories highlight the duty to respect the rights of other individuals on grounds of self-interest:

> *"Human rights law, applied to a State's own citizens serves the interest of states, by, for example, minimizing the risk of violent resistance and protest and by keeping the level of dissatisfaction with the government manageable" —Niraj Nathwani in Rethinking refugee law.*

The biological theory considers the comparative reproductive advantage of human social behavior based on empathy and altruism in the context of natural selection.

Human security is an emerging school of thought which challenges the traditional, state-based conception of security and argues that a people-focused approach to security is more appropriate in the modern interdependent world and would be more effective in advancing the security of individuals and societies across the globe.

Philosopher Friedrich Nietzsche has argued to the effect that those who speak most vehemently about their rights, doubt at the bottom of their soul if they truly have any.

Critiques of Human Rights

Philosophers who have criticized the concept of human rights include Jeremy Bentham, Edmund Burke, and Karl Marx. A recent critique has been advanced by Charles Blattberg in his essay "The Ironic Tragedy of Human Rights." Blattberg argues that rights talk, being abstract, demotivates people from upholding the values that rights are meant to assert.

Unit-II

Human Rights : International Context

Charter of the United Nations 1945

Introduction

The Charter of the United Nations was signed on 26 June 1945, in San Francisco, at the conclusion of the United Nations Conference on International Organization, and came into force on 24 October 1945. The Statute of the International Court of Justice is an integral part of the Charter.

Amendments to Articles 23, 27 and 61 of the Charter were adopted by the General Assembly on 17 December 1963 and came into force on 31 August 1965. A further amendment to Article 61 was adopted by the General Assembly on 20 December 1971, and came into force on 24 September 1973. An amendment to Article 109, adopted by the General Assebmly on 20 December 1965, came into force on 12 June 1968.

The amendment to Article 23 enlarges the membership of the Security Council from eleven to fifteen. The amended Article 27 provides that decisions of the Security Council on procedural matters shall be made by an affirmative vote of nine members (formerly seven) and on all other matters by an affirmative vote of nine members (formerly seven), including the concurring votes of the five permanent members of the Security Council.

The amendment to Article 61, which entered into force on 31 August 1965, enlarged the membership of the Economic and

Social Council from eighteen to twenty-seven. The subsequent amendment to that Article, which entered into force on 24 September 1973, further increased the membership of the Council from twenty-seven to fifty-four.

The amendment to Article 109, which relates to the first paragraph of that Article, provides that a General Conference of Member States for the purpose of reviewing the Charter may be held at a date and place to be fixed by a two-thirds vote of the members of the General Assembly and by a vote of any nine members (formerly seven) of the Security Council. Paragraph 3 of Article 109, which deals with the consideration of a possible review conference during the tenth regular session of the General Assembly, has been retained in its original form in its reference to a "vote, of any seven members of the Security Council", the paragraph having been acted upon in 1955 by the General Assembly, at its tenth regular session, and by the Security Council.

Purposes and Principles

Article 1

The Purposes of the United Nations are:

1. To maintain international peace and security, and to that end: to take effective collective measures for the prevention and removal of threats to the peace, and for the suppression of acts of aggression or other breaches of the peace, and to bring about by peaceful means, and in conformity with the principles of justice and international law, adjustment or settlement of international disputes or situations which might lead to a breach of the peace;
2. To develop friendly relations among nations based on respect for the principle of equal rights and self-determination of peoples, and to take other appropriate measures to strengthen universal peace;
3. To achieve international cooperation in solving international problems of an economic, social, cultural, or humanitarian character, and in promoting and

encouraging respect for human rights and for fundamental freedoms for all without distinction as to race, sex, language, or religion; and

4. To be a center for harmonizing the actions of nations in the attainment of these common ends.

Article 2

The Organization and its Members, in pursuit of the Purposes stated in Article 1, shall act in accordance with the following Principles.

1. The Organization is based on the principle of the sovereign equality of all its Members.
2. All Members, in order to ensure to all of them the rights and benefits resulting from membership, shall fulfill in good faith the obligations assumed by them in accordance with the present Charter.
3. All Members shall settle their international disputes by peaceful means in such a manner that international peace and security, and justice, are not endangered.
4. All Members shall refrain in their international relations from the threat or use of force against the territorial integrity or political independence of any state, or in any other manner inconsistent with the Purposes of the United Nations.
5. All Members shall give the United Nations every assistance in any action it takes in accordance with the present Charter, and shall refrain from giving assistance to any state against which the United Nations is taking preventive or enforcement action.
6. The Organization shall ensure that states which are not Members of the United Nations act in accordance with these Principles so far as may be necessary for the maintenance of international peace and security.
7. Nothing contained in the present Charter shall authorize the United Nations to intervene in matters which are essentially within the domestic jurisdiction of any state

or shall require the Members to submit such matters to settlement under the present Charter; but this principle shall not prejudice the application of enforcement measures under Chapter VII.

Membership

Article 3

The original Members of the United Nations shall be the states which, having participated in the United Nations Conference on International Organization at San Francisco, or having previously signed the Declaration by United Nations of January 1, 1942, sign the present Charter and ratify it in accordance with Article 110.

Article 4

1. Membership in the United Nations is open to all other peace-loving states which accept the obligations contained in the present Charter and, in the judgment of the Organization, are able and willing to carry out these obligations.
2. The admission of any such state to membership in the United Nations will be effected by a decision of the General Assembly upon the recommendation of the Security Council.

Article 5

A member of the United Nations against which preventive or enforcement action has been taken by the Security Council may be suspended from the exercise of the rights and privileges of membership by the General Assembly upon the recommendation of the Security Council. The exercise of these rights and privileges may be restored by the Security Council.

Article 6

A Member of the United Nations which has persistently violated the Principles contained in the present Charter may be expelled from the Organization by the General Assembly upon the recommendation of the Security Council.

Organs

Article 7

1. There are established as the principal organs of the United Nations: a General Assembly, a Security Council, an Economic and Social Council, a Trusteeship Council, an International Court of Justice, and a Secretariat.
2. Such subsidiary organs as may be found necessary may be established in accordance with the present Charter.

Article 8

The United Nations shall place no restrictions on the eligibility of men and women to participate in any capacity and under conditions of equality in its principal and subsidiary organs.

The General Assembly

Composition

Article 9

1. The General Assembly shall consist of all the Members of the United Nations.
2. Each member shall have not more than five representatives in the General Assembly.

Functions and Powers

Article 10

The General Assembly may discuss any questions or any matters within the scope of the present Charter or relating to the powers and functions of any organs provided for in the present Charter, and, except as provided in Article 12, may make recommendations to the Members of the United Nations or to the Security Council or to both on any such questions or matters.

Article 11

1. The General Assembly may consider the general principles of cooperation in the maintenance of

international peace and security, including the principles governing disarmament and the regulation of armaments, and may make recommendations with regard to such principles to the Members or to the Security Council or to both.

2. The General Assembly may discuss any questions relating to the maintenance of international peace and security brought before it by any Member of the United Nations, or by the Security Council, or by a state which is not a Member of the United Nations in accordance with Article 35, paragraph 2, and, except as provided in Article 12, may make recommendations with regard to any such questions to the state or states concerned or to the Security Council or to both. Any such question on which action is necessary shall be referred to the Security Council by the General Assembly either before or after discussion.
3. The General Assembly may call the attention of the Security Council to situations which are likely to endanger international peace and security.
4. The powers of the General Assembly set forth in this Article shall not limit the general scope of Article 10.

Article 12

1. While the Security Council is exercising in respect of any dispute or situation the functions assigned to it in the present Charter, the General Assembly shall not make any recommendation with regard to that dispute or situation unless the Security Council so requests.
2. The Secretary-General, with the consent of the Security Council, shall notify the General Assembly at each session of any matters relative to the maintenance of international peace and security which are being dealt with by the Security Council and shall similarly notify the General Assembly, or the Members of the United Nations if the General Assembly is not in session, immediately the Security Council ceases to deal with such matters.

Article 13

1. The General Assembly shall initiate studies and make recommendations for the purpose of:
   a. promoting international cooperation in the political field and encouraging the progressive development of international law and its codification;
   b. promoting international cooperation in the economic, social, cultural, educational, and health fields, and assisting in the realization of human rights and fundamental freedoms for all without distinction as to race, sex, language, or religion.
2. The further responsibilities, functions and powers of the General Assembly with respect to matters mentioned in paragraph 1(b) above are set forth in Chapters IX and X.

Article 14

Subject to the provisions of Article 12, the General Assembly may recommend measures for the peaceful adjustment of any situation, regardless of origin, which it deems likely to impair the general welfare or friendly relations among nations, including situations resulting from a violation of the provisions of the present Charter setting forth the Purposes and Principles of the United Nations.

Article 15

1. The General Assembly shall receive and consider annual and special reports from the Security Council; these reports shall include an account of the measures that the Security Council has decided upon or taken to maintain international peace and security.
2. The General Assembly shall receive and consider reports from the other organs of the United Nations.

Article 16

The General Assembly shall perform such functions with respect to the international trusteeship system as are assigned to it under Chapters XII and XIII, including the approval of the trusteeship agreements for areas not designated as strategic.

Article 17

1. The General Assembly shall consider and approve the budget of the Organization.
2. The expenses of the Organization shall be borne by the Members as apportioned by the General Assembly.
3. The General Assembly shall consider and approve any financial and budgetary arrangements with specialized agencies referred to in Article 57 and shall examine the administrative budgets of such specialized agencies with a view to making recommendations to the agencies concerned.

Voting

Article 18

1. Each member of the General Assembly shall have one vote.
2. Decisions of the General Assembly on important questions shall be made by a two-thirds majority of the members present and voting. These questions shall include: recommendations with respect to the maintenance of international peace and security, the election of the non-permanent members of the Security Council, the election of the members of the Economic and Social Council, the election of members of the Trusteeship Council in accordance with paragraph 1(c) of Article 86, the admission of new Members to the United Nations, the suspension of the rights and privileges of membership, the expulsion of Members, questions relating to the operation of the trusteeship system, and budgetary questions.
3. Decisions on other questions, Composition including the determination of additional categories of questions to be decided by a two-thirds majority, shall be made by a majority of the members present and voting.

Article 19

A Member of the United Nations which is in arrears in the payment of its financial contributions to the Organization shall have no vote in the General Assembly if the amount of its arrears equals or exceeds the amount of the contributions due from it for the preceding two full years. The General Assembly may, nevertheless, permit such a Member to vote if it is satisfied that the failure to pay is due to conditions beyond the control of the Member.

Procedure

Article 20

The General Assembly shall meet in regular annual sessions and in such special sessions as occasion may require. Special sessions shall be convoked by the Secretary-General at the request of the Security Council or of a majority of the Members of the United Nations.

Article 21

The General Assembly shall adopt its own rules of procedure. It shall elect its President for each session.

Article 22

The General Assembly may establish such subsidiary organs as it deems necessary for the performance of its functions.

The Security Council

Article 23

1. The Security Council shall consist of fifteen Members of the United Nations. The Republic of China, France, the Union of Soviet Socialist Republics, the United Kingdom of Great Britain and Northern Ireland, and the United States of America shall be permanent members of the Security Council. The General Assembly shall elect ten other Members of the United Nations to be non-permanent members of the Security Council, due regard being specially paid, in the first instance to the contribution of Members of the United Nations to

the maintenance of international peace and security and to the other purposes of the Organization, and also to equitable geographical distribution.

The non-permanent members of the Security Council shall be elected for a term of two years. In the first election of the non-permanent members after the increase of the membership of the Security Council from eleven to fifteen, two of the four additional members shall be chosen for a term of one year. A retiring member shall not be eligible for immediate re-election.

Each member of the Security Council shall have one representative.

Functions and Powers

Article 24

1. In order to ensure prompt and effective action by the United Nations, its Members confer on the Security Council primary responsibility for the maintenance of international peace and security, and agree that in carrying out its duties under this responsibility the Security Council acts on their behalf.
2. In discharging these duties the Security Council shall act in accordance with the Purposes and Principles of the United Nations. The specific powers granted to the Security Council for the discharge of these duties are laid down in Chapters VI, VII, VIII, and XII.
3. The Security Council shall submit annual and, when necessary, special reports to the General Assembly for its consideration.

Article 25

The Members of the United Nations agree to accept and carry out the decisions of the Security Council in accordance with the present Charter.

Article 26

In order to promote the establishment and maintenance of international peace and security with the least diversion for armaments of the world's human and economic resources, the Security Council shall be responsible for formulating, with the assistance of the Military Staff Committee referred to in Article 47, plans to be submitted to the Members of the United Nations for the establishment of a system for the regulation of armaments.

Voting

Article 27

1. Each member of the Security Council shall have one vote.
2. Decisions of the Security Council on procedural matters shall be made by an affirmative vote of nine members.
3. Decisions of the Security Council on all other matters shall be made by an affirmative vote of nine members including the concurring votes of the permanent members; provided that, in decisions under Chapter VI, and under paragraph 3 of Article 52, a party to a dispute shall abstain from voting.

Procedure

Article 28

1. The Security Council shall be so organized as to be able to function continuously. Each member of the Security Council shall for this purpose be represented at all times at the seat of the Organization.
2. The Security Council shall hold periodic meetings at which each of its members may, if it so desires, be represented by a member of the government or by some other specially designated representative.
3. The Security Council may hold meetings at such places other than the seat of the Organization as in its judgment will best facilitate its work.

Article 29

The Security Council may establish such subsidiary organs as it deems necessary for the performance of its functions.

Article 30

The Security Council shall adopt its own rules of procedure, including the method of selecting its President.

Article 31

Any Member of the United Nations which is not a member of the Security Council may participate, without vote, in the discussion of any question brought before the Security Council whenever the latter considers that the interests of that Member are specially affected.

Article 32

Any Member of the United Nations which is not a member of the Security Council or any state which is not a Member of the United Nations, if it is a party to a dispute under consideration by the Security Council, shall be invited to participate, without vote, in the discussion relating to the dispute. The Security Council shall lay down such conditions as it deems just for the participation of a state which is not a Member of the United Nations.

Pacific Settlement of Disputes

Article 33

1. The parties to any dispute, the continuance of which is likely to endanger the maintenance of international peace and security, shall, first of all, seek a solution by negotiation, enquiry, mediation, conciliation, arbitration, judicial settlement, resort to regional agencies or arrangements, or other peaceful means of their own choice.
2. The Security Council shall, when it deems necessary, call upon the parties to settle their dispute by such means.

Article 34

The Security Council may investigate any dispute, or any situation which might lead to international friction or give rise to a dispute, in order to determine whether the continuance of the dispute or situation is likely to endanger the maintenance of international peace and security.

Article 35

1. Any Member of the United Nations may bring any dispute, or any situation of the nature referred to in Article 34, to the attention of the Security Council or of the General Assembly.
2. A state which is not a Member of the United Nations may bring to the attention of the Security Council or of the General Assembly any dispute to which it is a party if it accepts in advance, for the purposes of the dispute, the obligations of pacific settlement provided in the present Charter.
3. The proceedings of the General Assembly in respect of matters brought to its attention under this Article will be subject to the provisions of Articles 11 and 12.

Article 36

1. The Security Council may, at any stage of a dispute of the nature referred to in Article 33 or of a situation of like nature, recommend appropriate procedures or methods of adjustment.
2. The Security Council should take into consideration any procedures for the settlement of the dispute which have already been adopted by the parties.
3. In making recommendations under this Article the Security Council should also take into consideration that legal disputes should as a general rule be referred by the parties to the International Court of Justice in accordance with the provisions of the Statute of the Court.

Article 37

1. Should the parties to a dispute of the nature referred to in Article 33 fail to settle it by the means indicated in that Article, they shall refer it to the Security Council.

2. If the Security Council deems that the continuance of the dispute is in fact likely to endanger the maintenance of international peace and security, it shall decide whether to take action under Article 36 or to recommend such terms of settlement as it may consider appropriate.

Article 38

Without prejudice to the provisions of Articles 33 to 37, the Security Council may, if all the parties to any dispute so request, make recommendations to the parties with a view to a pacific settlement of the dispute.

Action with Respect to Threats to the Peace, Breaches of the Peace, and Acts of Aggression

Article 39

The Security Council shall determine the existence of any threat to the peace, breach of the peace, or act of aggression and shall make recommendations, or decide what measures shall be taken in accordance with Articles 41 and 42, to maintain or restore international peace and security.

Article 40

In order to prevent an aggravation of the situation, the Security Council may, before making the recommendations or deciding upon the measures provided for in Article 39, call upon the parties concerned to comply with such provisional measures as it deems necessary or desirable. Such provisional measures shall be without prejudice to the rights, claims, or position of the parties concerned. The Security Council shall duly take account of failure to comply with such provisional measures.

Article 41

The Security Council may decide what measures not involving the use of armed force are to be employed to give effect to its decisions, and it may call upon the Members of the United Nations to apply such measures. These may include complete or partial interruption of economic relations and of rail, sea, air, postal, telegraphic, radio, and other means of communication, and the severance of diplomatic relations.

Article 42

Should the Security Council consider that measures provided for in Article 41 would be inadequate or have proved to be inadequate, it may take such action by air, sea, or land forces as may be necessary to maintain or restore international peace and security. Such action may include demonstrations, blockade, and other operations by air, sea, or land forces of Members of the United Nations.

Article 43

1. All Members of the United Nations, in order to contribute to the maintenance of international peace and security, undertake to make available to the Security Council, on its call and in accordance with a special agreement or agreements, armed forces, assistance, and facilities, including rights of passage, necessary for the purpose of maintaining international peace and security.
2. Such agreement or agreements shall govern the numbers and types of forces. Their degree of readiness and general location, and the nature of the facilities and assistance to be provided.
3. The agreement or agreements shall be negotiated as soon as possible on the initiative of the Security Council. They shall be concluded between the Security Council and Members or between the Security Council and groups of Members and shall be subject to ratification by the signatory states in accordance with their respective constitutional processes.

Article 44

When the Security Council has decided to use force it shall, before calling upon a Member not represented on it to provide armed forces in fulfillment of the obligations assumed under Article 43, invite that Member, if the Member so desires, to participate in the decisions of the Security Council concerning the employment of contingents of that Member's armed forces.

Article 45

In order to enable the United Nations to take urgent military measures Members shall hold immediately available national air-force contingents for combined international enforcement action. The strength and degree of readiness of these contingents and plans for their combined action shall be determined, within the limits laid down in the special agreement or agreements referred to in Article 43, by the Security Council with the assistance of the Military Staff Committee.

Article 46

Plans for the application of armed force shall be made by the Security Council with the assistance of the Military Staff Committee.

Article 47

1. There shall be established a Military Staff Committee to advise and assist the Security Council on all questions relating to the Security Council's military requirements for the maintenance of international peace and security, the employment and command of forces placed at its disposal, the regulation of armaments, and possible disarmament.

2. The Military Staff Committee shall consist of the Chiefs of Staff of the permanent members of the Security Council or their representatives. Any Member of the United Nations not permanently represented on the Committee shall be invited by the Committee to be associated with it when the efficient discharge of the Committee's responsibilities requires the participation of that Member in its work.

3. The Military Staff Committee shall be responsible under the Security Council for the strategic direction of any armed forces placed at the disposal of the Security Council. Questions relating to the command of such forces shall be worked out subsequently.

4. The Military Staff Committee, with the authorization of the Security Council and after consultation with appropriate regional agencies, may establish regional subcommittees.

Article 48

1. The action required to carry out the decisions of the Security Council for the maintenance of international peace and security shall be taken by all the Members of the United Nations or by some of them, as the Security Council may determine.
2. Such decisions shall be carried out by the Members of the United Nations directly and through their action in the appropriate international agencies of which they are members.

Article 49

The Members of the United Nations shall join in affording mutual assistance in carrying out the measures decided upon by the Security Council.

Article 50

If preventive or enforcement measures against any state are taken by the Security Council, any other state, whether a Member of the United Nations or not, which finds itself confronted with special economic problems arising from the carrying out of those measures shall have the right to consult the Security Council with regard to a solution of those problems.

Article 51

Nothing in the present Charter shall impair the inherent right of individual or collective self-defense if an armed attack occurs against a Member of the United Nations, until the Security Council has taken measures necessary to maintain international peace and security. Measures taken by Members in the exercise of this right of self-defense shall be immediately reported to the Security Council and shall not in any way affect the authority and responsibility of the Security Council under the present Charter to take at any time such action as it deems necessary in order to maintain or restore international peace and security.

Regional Arrangements

Article 52

1. Nothing in the present Charter precludes the existence of regional arrangements or agencies for dealing with such matters relating to the maintenance of international peace and security as are appropriate for regional action, provided that such arrangements or agencies and their activities are consistent with the Purposes and Principles of the United Nations.
2. The Members of the United Nations entering into such arrangements or constituting such agencies shall make every effort to achieve pacific settlement of local disputes through such regional arrangements or by such regional agencies before referring them to the Security Council.
3. The Security Council shall encourage the development of pacific settlement of local disputes through such regional arrangements or by such regional agencies either on the initiative of the states concerned or by reference from the Security Council.
4. This Article in no way impairs the application of Articles 34 and 35.

Article 53

1. The Security Council shall, where appropriate, utilize such regional arrangements or agencies for enforcement action under its authority. But no enforcement action shall be taken under regional arrangements or by regional agencies without the authorization of the Security Council, with the exception of measures against any enemy state, as defined in paragraph 2 of this Article, provided for pursuant to Article 107 or in regional arrangements directed against renewal of aggressive policy on the part of any such state, until such time as the Organization may, on request of the Governments concerned, be charged with the

responsibility for preventing further aggression by such a state.

2. The term enemy state as used in paragraph 1 of this Article applies to any state which during the Second World War has been an enemy of any signatory of the present Charter.

Article 54

The Security Council shall at all times be kept fully informed of activities undertaken or in contemplation under regional arrangements or by regional agencies for the maintenance of international peace and security.

International Economic and Social Co-operation

Article 55

With a view to the creation of conditions of stability and well-being which are necessary for peaceful and friendly relations among nations based on respect for the principle of equal rights and self-determination of peoples, the United Nations shall promote:

a. higher standards of living, full employment, and conditions of economic and social progress and development;

b. solutions of international economic, social, health, and related problems; and international cultural and educational co-operation; and

c. universal respect for, and observance of, human rights and fundamental freedoms for all without distinction as to race, sex, language, or religion.

Article 56

All Members pledge themselves to take joint and separate action in cooperation with the Organization for the achievement of the purposes set forth in Article 55.

Article 57

1. The various specialized agencies, established by intergovernmental agreement and having wide

international responsibilities, as defined in their basic instruments, in economic, social, cultural, educational, health, and related fields, shall be brought into relationship with the United Nations in accordance with the provisions of Article 63.

2. Such agencies thus brought into relationship with the United Nations are hereinafter referred to as specialized agencies.

Article 58

The Organization shall make recommendations for the coordination of the policies and activities of the specialized agencies.

Article 59

The Organization shall, where appropriate, initiate negotiations among the states concerned for the creation of any new specialized agencies required for the accomplishment of the purposes set forth in Article 55.

Article 60

Responsibility for the discharge of the functions of the Organization set forth in this Chapter shall be vested in the General Assembly and, under the authority of the General Assembly, in the Economic and Social Council, which shall have for this purpose the powers set forth in Chapter X.

The Economic and Social Council

Composition

Article 61

1. The Economic and Social Council shall consist of fifty-four Members of the United Nations elected by the General Assembly.
2. Subject to the provisions of paragraph 3, eighteen members of the Economic and Social Council shall be elected each year for a term of three years. A retiring member shall be eligible for immediate re-election.

3. At the first election after the increase in the membership of the Economic and Social Council from twenty-seven to fifty-four members, in addition to the members elected in place of the nine members whose term of office expires at the end of that year, twenty-seven additional members shall be elected. Of these twenty-seven additional members, the term of office of nine members so elected shall expire at the end of one year, and of nine other members at the end of two years, in accordance with arrangements made by the General Assembly.
4. Each member of the Economic and Social Council shall have one representative.

Functions and Powers

Article 62

1. The Economic and Social Council may make or initiate studies and reports with respect to international economic, social, cultural, educational, health, and related matters and may make recommendations with respect to any such matters to the General Assembly, to the Members of the United Nations, and to the specialized agencies concerned.
2. It may make recommendations for the purpose of promoting respect for, and observance of, human rights and fundamental freedoms for all.
3. It may prepare draft conventions for submission to the General Assembly, with respect to matters falling within its competence.
4. It may call, in accordance with the rules prescribed by the United Nations, international conferences on matters falling within its competence.

Article 63

1. The Economic and Social Council may enter into agreements with any of the agencies referred to in Article 57, defining the terms on which the agency

concerned shall be brought into relationship with the United Nations. Such agreements shall be subject to approval by the General Assembly.

2. It may coordinate the activities of the specialized agencies through consultation with and recommendations to such agencies and through recommendations to the General Assembly and to the Members of the United Nations.

Article 64

1. The Economic and Social Council may take appropriate steps to obtain regular reports from the specialized agencies. It may make arrangements with the Members of the United Nations and with the specialized agencies to obtain reports on the steps taken to give effect to its own recommendations and to recommendations on matters falling within its competence made by the General Assembly.
2. It may communicate its observations on these reports to the General Assembly.

Article 65

The Economic and Social Council may furnish information to the Security Council and shall assist the Security Council upon its request.

Article 66

1. The Economic and Social Council shall perform such functions as fall within its competence in connection with the carrying out of the recommendations of the General Assembly.
2. It may, with the approval of the General Assembly, perform services at the request of Members of the United Nations and at the request of specialized agencies.
3. It shall perform such other functions as are specified elsewhere in the present Charter or as may be assigned to it by the General Assembly.

Article 67

1. Each member of the Economic and Social Council shall have one vote.
2. Decisions of the Economic and Social Council shall be made by a majority of the members present and voting.

Procedure

Article 68

The Economic and Social Council shall set up commissions in economic and social fields and for the promotion of human rights, and such other commissions as may be required for the performance of its functions.

Article 69

The Economic and Social Council shall invite any Member of the United Nations to participate, without vote, in its deliberations on any matter of particular concern to that Member.

Article 70

The Economic and Social Council may make arrangements for representatives of the specialized agencies to participate, without vote, in its deliberations and in those of the commissions established by it, and for its representatives to participate in the deliberations of the specialized agencies.

Article 71

The Economic and Social Council may make suitable arrangements for consultation with non-governmental organizations which are concerned with matters within its competence. Such arrangements may be made with international organizations and, where appropriate, with national organizations after consultation with the Member of the United Nations concerned.

Article 72

1. The Economic and Social Council shall adopt its own rules of procedure, including the method of selecting its President.

2. The Economic and Social Council shall meet as required in accordance with its rules, which shall include provision for the convening of meetings on the request of a majority of its members.

Declaration Regarding Non-self-governing Territories

Article 73

Members of the United Nations which have or assume responsibilities for the administration of territories whose peoples have not yet attained a full measure of self-government recognize the principle that the interests of the inhabitants of these territories are paramount, and accept as a sacred trust the obligation to promote to the utmost, within the system of international peace and security established by the present Charter, the well-being of the inhabitants of these territories, and, to this end:

a. to ensure, with due respect for the culture of the peoples concerned, their political, economic, social, and educational advancement, their just treatment, and their protection against abuses;

b. to develop self-government, to take due account of the political aspirations of the peoples, and to assist them in the progressive development of their free political institutions, according to the particular circumstances of each territory and its peoples and their varying stages of advancement;

c. to further international peace and security;

d. to promote constructive measures of development, to encourage research, and to cooperate with one another and, when and where appropriate, with specialized international bodies with a view to the practical achievement of the social, economic, and scientific purposes set forth in this Article; and

e. to transmit regularly to the Secretary-General for information purposes, subject to such limitation as security and constitutional considerations may require, statistical and other information of a technical nature relating to economic, social, and educational conditions in the territories for which they are respectively responsible other than those territories to which Chapter XII and XIII apply.

Article 74

Members of the United Nations also agree that their policy in respect of the territories to which this Chapter applies, no less than in respect of their metropolitan areas, must be based on the general principle of good-neighborliness, due account being taken of the interests and well-being of the rest of the world, in social, economic, and commercial matters.

International Trusteeship System

Article 75

The United Nations shall establish under its authority an international trusteeship system for the administration and supervision of such territories as may be placed thereunder by subsequent individual agreements. These territories are hereinafter referred to as trust territories.

Article 76

The basic objectives of the trusteeship system, in accordance with the Purposes of the United Nations laid down in Article 1 of the present Charter, shall be:

a. to further international peace and security;

b. to promote the political, economic, social, and educational advancement of the inhabitants of the trust territories, and their progressive development towards self-government or independence as may be appropriate to the particular circumstances of each territory and its peoples and the freely expressed wishes of the peoples concerned, and as may be provided by the terms of each trusteeship agreement;

c. to encourage respect for human rights and for fundamental freedoms for all without distinction as to race, sex, language, or religion, and to encourage recognition of the interdependence of the peoples of the world; and

d. to ensure equal treatment in social, economic, and commercial matters for all Members of the United Nations and their nationals and also equal treatment for the latter in the administration of justice without prejudice to the attainment of the foregoing objectives and subject to the provisions of Article 80.

Article 77

1. The trusteeship system shall apply to such territories in the following categories as may be placed thereunder by means of trusteeship agreements:
   a. territories now held under mandate;
   b. territories which may be detached from enemy states as a result of the Second World War, and
   c. territories voluntarily placed under the system by states responsible for their administration.
2. It will be a matter for subsequent agreement as to which territories in the foregoing categories will be brought under the trusteeship system and upon what terms.

Article 78

The trusteeship system shall not apply to territories which have become Members of the United Nations, relationship among which shall be based on respect for the principle of sovereign equality.

Article 79

The terms of trusteeship for each territory to be placed under the trusteeship system, including any alteration or amendment, shall be agreed upon by the states directly concerned, including the mandatory power in the case of territories held under mandate by a Member of the United Nations, and shall be approved as provided for in Articles 83 and 85.

Article 80

1. Except as may be agreed upon in individual trusteeship agreements, made under Articles 77, 79, and 81, placing each territory under the trusteeship system, and until such agreements have been concluded, nothing in this Chapter shall be construed in or of itself to alter in any manner the rights whatsoever of any states or any peoples or the terms of existing international instruments to which Members of the United Nations may respectively be parties.
2. Paragraph 1 of this Article shall not be interpreted as giving grounds for delay or postponement of the negotiation and conclusion of agreements for placing mandated and other territories under the trusteeship system as provided for in Article 77.

Article 81

The trusteeship agreement shall in each case include the terms under which the trust territory will be administered and designate the authority which will exercise the administration of the trust territory. Such authority, hereinafter called the administering authority, may be one or more states or the Organization itself.

Article 82

There may be designated, in any trusteeship agreement, a strategic area or areas which may include part or all of the trust territory to which the agreement applies, without prejudice to any special agreement or agreements made under Article 43.

Article 83

1. All functions of the United Nations relating to strategic areas, including the approval of the terms of the trusteeship agreements and of their alteration or amendment, shall be exercised by the Security Council.
2. The basic objectives set forth in Article 76 shall be applicable to the people of each strategic area.

3. The Security Council shall, subject to the provisions of the trusteeship agreements and without prejudice to security considerations, avail itself of the assistance of the Trusteeship Council to perform those functions of the United Nations under the trusteeship system relating to political, economic, social, and educational matters in the strategic areas.

Article 84

It shall be the duty of the administering authority to ensure that the trust territory shall play its part in the maintenance of international peace and security. To this end the administering authority may make use of volunteer forces, facilities, and assistance from the trust territory in carrying out the obligations towards the Security Council undertaken in this regard by the administering authority, as well as for local defense and the maintenance of law and order within the trust territory.

Article 85

1. The functions of the United Nations with regard to trusteeship agreements for all areas not designated as strategic, including the approval of the terms of the trusteeship agreements and of their alteration or amendment, shall be exercised by the General Assembly.
2. The Trusteeship Council, operating under the authority of the General Assembly, shall assist the General Assembly in carrying out these functions.

The Trusteeship Council

Composition

Article 86

1. The Trusteeship Council shall consist of the following Members of the United Nations:
    a. those Members administering trust territories;
    b. such of those Members mentioned by name in Article 23 as are not administering trust territories; and

c. as many other Members elected for three-year terms by the General Assembly as may be necessary to ensure that the total number of members of the Trusteeship Council is equally divided between those Members of the United Nations which administer trust territories and those which do not.

2. Each member of the Trusteeship Council shall designate one specially qualified person to represent it therein.

Functions and Powers

Article 87

The General Assembly and, under its authority, the Trusteeship Council, in carrying out their functions, may:

a. consider reports submitted by the administering authority;

b. accept petitions and examine them in consultation with the administering authority;

c. provide for periodic visits to the respective trust territories at times agreed upon with the administering authority; and

d. take these and other actions in conformity with the terms of the trusteeship agreements.

Article 88

The Trusteeship Council shall formulate a questionnaire on the political, economic, social, and educational advancement of the inhabitants of each trust territory, and the administering authority for each trust territory within the competence of the General Assembly shall make an annual report to the General Assembly upon the basis of such questionnaire.

Voting

Article 89

1. Each member of the Trusteeship Council shall have one vote.
2. Decisions of the Trusteeship Council shall be made by a majority of the members present and voting.

Procedure

Article 90

1. The Trusteeship Council shall adopt its own rules of procedure, including the method of selecting its President.
2. The Trusteeship Council shall meet as required in accordance with its rules, which shall include provision for the convening of meetings on the request of a majority of its members.

Article 91

The Trusteeship Council shall, when appropriate, avail itself of the assistance of the Economic and Social Council and of the specialized agencies in regard to matters with which they are respectively concerned.

The International Court of Justice

Article 92

The International Court of Justice shall be the principal judicial organ of the United Nations. It shall function in accordance with the annexed Statute which is based upon the Statute of the Permanent Court of International Justice and forms an integral part of the present Charter.

Article 93

1. All Members of the United Nations are ipso facto parties to the Statute of the International Court of Justice.
2. A state which is not a Member of the United Nations may become a party to the Statute of the International Court of Justice on conditions to be determined in each case by the General Assembly upon the recommendation of the Security Council.

Article 94

1. Each Member of the United Nations undertakes to comply with the decision of the International Court of Justice in any case to which it is a party.

2. If any party to a case fails to perform the obligations incumbent upon it under a judgment rendered by the Court, the other party may have recourse to the Security Council, which may, if it deems necessary, make recommendations or decide upon measures to be taken to give effect to the judgment.

Article 95

Nothing in the present Charter shall prevent Members of the United Nations from entrusting the solution of their differences to other tribunals by virtue of agreements already in existence or which may be concluded in the future.

Article 96

1. The General Assembly or the Security Council may request the International Court of Justice to give an advisory opinion on any legal question.
2. Other organs of the United Nations and specialized agencies, which may at any time be so authorized by the General Assembly, may also request advisory opinions of the Court on legal questions arising within the scope of their activities.

The Secretariat

Article 97

The Secretariat shall comprise a Secretary-General and such staff as the Organization may require. The Secretary-General shall be appointed by the General Assembly upon the recommendation of the Security Council. He shall be the chief administrative officer of the Organization.

Article 98

The Secretary-General shall act in that capacity in all meetings of the General Assembly, of the Security Council, of the Economic and Social Council, and of the Trusteeship Council, and shall perform such other functions as are entrusted to him by these organs. The Secretary-General shall make an annual report to the General Assembly on the work of the Organization.

Article 99

The Secretary-General may bring to the attention of the Security Council any matter which in his opinion may threaten the maintenance of international peace and security.

Article 100

1. In the performance of their duties the Secretary-General and the staff shall not seek or receive instructions from any government or from any other authority external to the Organization. They shall refrain from any action which might reflect on their position as international officials responsible only to the Organization.
2. Each Member of the United Nations undertakes to respect the exclusively international character of the responsibilities of the Secretary-General and the staff and not to seek to influence them in the discharge of their responsibilities.

Article 101

1. The staff shall be appointed by the Secretary-General under regulations established by the General Assembly.
2. Appropriate staffs shall be permanently assigned to the Economic and Social Council, the Trusteeship Council, and, as required, to other organs of the United Nations. These staffs shall form a part of the Secretariat.
3. The paramount consideration in the employment of the staff and in the determination of the conditions of service shall be the necessity of securing the highest standards of efficiency, competence, and integrity. Due regard shall be paid to the importance of recruiting the staff on as wide a geographical basis as possible.

Miscellaneous Provisions

Article 102

1. Every treaty and every international agreement entered into by any Member of the United Nations after the present Charter comes into force shall as soon as possible be registered with the Secretariat and published by it.

2. No party to any such treaty or international agreement which has not been registered in accordance with the provisions of paragraph I of this Article may invoke that treaty or agreement before any organ of the United Nations.

Article 103

In the event of a conflict between the obligations of the Members of the United Nations under the present Charter and their obligations under any other international agreement, their obligations under the present Charter shall prevail.

Article 104

The Organization shall enjoy in the territory of each of its Members such legal capacity as may be necessary for the exercise of its functions and the fulfillment of its purposes.

Article 105

1. The Organization shall enjoy in the territory of each of its Members such privileges and immunities as are necessary for the fulfillment of its purposes.
2. Representatives of the Members of the United Nations and officials of the Organization shall similarly enjoy such privileges and immunities as are necessary for the independent exercise of their functions in connection with the Organization.
3. The General Assembly may make recommendations with a view to determining the details of the application of paragraphs 1 and 2 of this Article or may propose conventions to the Members of the United Nations for this purpose.

Transitional Security Arrangements

Article 106

Pending the coming into force of such special agreements referred to in Article 43 as in the opinion of the Security Council enable it to begin the exercise of its responsibilities under Article 42, the parties to the Four-Nation Declaration, signed at Moscow October 30, 1943, and France, shall, in accordance with the provisions of paragraph 5 of that Declaration, consult with one another and as occasion requires with other Members of the United Nations with a view to such joint action on behalf of the Organization as may be necessary for the purpose of maintaining international peace and security.

Article 107

Nothing in the present Charter shall invalidate or preclude action, in relation to any state which during the Second World War has been an enemy of any signatory to the present Charter, taken or authorized as a result of that war by the Governments having responsibility for such action.

Amendments

Article 108

Amendments to the present Charter shall come into force for all Members of the United Nations when they have been adopted by a vote of two thirds of the members of the General Assembly and ratified in accordance with their respective constitutional processes by two thirds of the Members of the United Nations, including all the permanent members of the Security Council.

Article 109

1. A General Conference of the Members of the United Nations for the purpose of reviewing the present Charter may be held at a date and place to be fixed by a two-thirds vote of the members of the General Assembly and by a vote of any seven members of the Security Council. Each Member of the United Nations shall have one vote in the conference.
2. Any alteration of the present Charter recommended by a two-thirds vote of the conference shall take effect when ratified in accordance with their respective constitutional processes by two thirds of the Members of the United Nations including all the permanent members of the Security Council.

3. If such a conference has not been held before the tenth annual session of the General Assembly following the coming into force of the present Charter, the proposal to call such a conference shall be placed on the agenda of that session of the General Assembly, and the conference shall be held if so decided by a majority vote of the members of the General Assembly and by a vote of any seven members of the Security Council.

Ratification and Signature

Article 110

1. The present Charter shall be ratified by the signatory states in accordance with their respective constitutional processes.
2. The ratifications shall be deposited with the Government of the United States of America, which shall notify all the signatory states of each deposit as well as the Secretary-General of the Organization when he has been appointed.
3. The present Charter shall come into force upon the deposit of ratifications by the Republic of China, France, the Union of Soviet Socialist Republics, the United Kingdom of Great Britain and Northern Ireland, and the United States of America, and by a majority of the other signatory states. A protocol of the ratifications deposited shall thereupon be drawn up by the Government of the United States of America which shall communicate copies thereof to all the signatory states.
4. The states signatory to the present Charter which ratify it after it has come into force will become original Members of the United Nations on the date of the deposit of their respective ratifications.

Article 111

The present Charter, of which the Chinese, French, Russian, English, and Spanish texts are equally authentic, shall remain deposited in the archives of the Government of the United

States of America. Duly certified copies thereof shall be transmitted by that Government to the Governments of the other signatory states.

IN FAITH WHEREOF the representatives of the Governments of the United Nations have signed the present Charter.

DONE at the city of San Francisco the twenty-sixth day of June, one thousand nine hundred and forty-five.

Universal Declaration of Human Rights 1948

United Nations

Note : Adopted and proclaimed by General Assembly resolution 217 A (III) of 10 December 1948

On December 10, 1948 the General Assembly of the United Nations adopted and proclaimed the Universal Declaration of Human Rights the full text of which appears in the following pages. Following this historic act the Assembly called upon all Member countries to publicize the text of the Declaration and "to cause it to be disseminated, displayed, read and expounded principally in schools and other educational institutions, without distinction based on the political status of countries or territories.

Preamble

Whereas recognition of the inherent dignity and of the equal and inalienable rights of all members of the human family is the foundation of freedom, justice and peace in the world,

Whereas disregard and contempt for human rights have resulted in barbarous acts which have outraged the conscience of mankind, and the advent of a world in which human beings shall enjoy freedom of speech and belief and freedom from fear and want has been proclaimed as the highest aspiration of the common people.

Whereas it is essential, if man is not to be compelled to have recourse, as a last resort, to rebellion against

tyranny and oppression, that human rights should be protected by the rule of law,

Whereas it is essential to promote the development of friendly relations between nations,

Whereas the peoples of the United Nations have in the Charter reaffirmed their faith in fundamental human rights, in the dignity and worth of the human person and in the equal rights of men and women and have determined to promote social progress and better standards of life in larger freedom,

Whereas Member States have pledged themselves to achieve, in co-operation with the United Nations, the promotion of universal respect for and observance of human rights and fundamental freedoms,

Whereas a common understanding of these rights and freedoms is of the greatest importance for the full realization of this pledge,

Now, Therefore THE GENERAL ASSEMBLY proclaims THIS UNIVERSAL DECLARATION OF HUMAN RIGHTS as a common standard of achievement for all peoples and all nations, to the end that every individual and every organ of society, keeping this Declaration constantly in mind, shall strive by teaching and education to promote respect for these rights and freedoms and by progressive measures, national and international, to secure their universal and effective recognition and observance, both among the peoples of Member States themselves and among the peoples of territories under their jurisdiction.

Article 1

All human beings are born free and equal in dignity and rights. They are endowed with reason and conscience and should act towards one another in a spirit of brotherhood.

Article 2

Everyone is entitled to all the rights and freedoms set forth in this Declaration, without distinction of any kind, such as race, colour, sex, language, religion, political or other opinion, national or social origin, property, birth or other status. Furthermore, no distinction shall be made on the basis of the political, jurisdictional or international status of the country or territory to which a person belongs, whether it be independent, trust, non-self-governing or under any other limitation of sovereignty.

Article 3

Everyone has the right to life, liberty and security of person.

Article 4

No one shall be held in slavery or servitude; slavery and the slave trade shall be prohibited in all their forms.

Article 5

No one shall be subjected to torture or to cruel, inhuman or degrading treatment or punishment.

Article 6

Everyone has the right to recognition everywhere as a person before the law.

Article 7

All are equal before the law and are entitled without any discrimination to equal protection of the law. All are entitled to equal protection against any discrimination in violation of this Declaration and against any incitement to such discrimination.

Article 8

Everyone has the right to an effective remedy by the competent national tribunals for acts violating the fundamental rights granted him by the constitution or by law.

Article 9

No one shall be subjected to arbitrary arrest, detention or exile.

Article 10

Everyone is entitled in full equality to a fair and public

hearing by an independent and impartial tribunal, in the determination of his rights and obligations and of any criminal charge against him.

Article 11

1. Everyone charged with a penal offence has the right to be presumed innocent until proved guilty according to law in a public trial at which he has had all the guarantees necessary for his defence.
2. No one shall be held guilty of any penal offence on account of any act or omission which did not constitute a penal offence, under national or international law, at the time when it was committed. Nor shall a heavier penalty be imposed than the one that was applicable at the time the penal offence was committed.

Article 12

No one shall be subjected to arbitrary interference with his privacy, family, home or correspondence, nor to attacks upon his honour and reputation. Everyone has the right to the protection of the law against such interference or attacks.

Article 13

1. Everyone has the right to freedom of movement and residence within the borders of each state.
2. Everyone has the right to leave any country, including his own, and to return to his country.

Article 14

1. Everyone has the right to seek and to enjoy in other countries asylum from persecution.
2. This right may not be invoked in the case of prosecutions genuinely arising from non-political crimes or from acts contrary to the purposes and principles of the United Nations.

Article 15

1. Everyone has the right to a nationality.

2. No one shall be arbitrarily deprived of his nationality nor denied the right to change his nationality.

Article 16

1. Men and women of full age, without any limitation due to race, nationality or religion, have the right to marry and to found a family. They are entitled to equal rights as to marriage, during marriage and at its dissolution.
2. Marriage shall be entered into only with the free and full consent of the intending spouses.
3. The family is the natural and fundamental group unit of society and is entitled to protection by society and the State.

Article 17

1. Everyone has the right to own property alone as well as in association with others.
2. No one shall be arbitrarily deprived of his property.

Article 18

Everyone has the right to freedom of thought, conscience and religion; this right includes freedom to change his religion or belief, and freedom, either alone or in community with others and in public or private, to manifest his religion or belief in teaching, practice, worship and observance.

Article 19

Everyone has the right to freedom of opinion and expression; this right includes freedom to hold opinions without interference and to seek, receive and impart information and ideas through any media and regardless of frontiers.

Article 20

1. Everyone has the right to freedom of peaceful assembly and association.
2. No one may be compelled to belong to an association.

Article 21

1. Everyone has the right to take part in the government

of his country, directly or through freely chosen representatives.

2. Everyone has the right of equal access to public service in his country.
3. The will of the people shall be the basis of the authority of government; this will shall be expressed in periodic and genuine elections which shall be by universal and equal suffrage and shall be held by secret vote or by equivalent free voting procedures.

Article 22

Everyone, as a member of society, has the right to social security and is entitled to realization, through national effort and international co-operation and in accordance with the organization and resources of each State, of the economic, social and cultural rights indispensable for his dignity and the free development of his personality.

Article 23

1. Everyone has the right to work, to free choice of employment, to just and favourable conditions of work and to protection against unemployment.
2. Everyone, without any discrimination, has the right to equal pay for equal work.
3. Everyone who works has the right to just and favourable remuneration ensuring for himself and his family an existence worthy of human dignity, and supplemented, if necessary, by other means of social protection.
4. Everyone has the right to form and to join trade unions for the protection of his interests.

Article 24

Everyone has the right to rest and leisure, including reasonable limitation of working hours and periodic holidays with pay.

Article 25

1. Everyone has the right to a standard of living adequate

for the health and well-being of himself and of his family, including food, clothing, housing and medical care and necessary social services, and the right to security in the event of unemployment, sickness, disability, widowhood, old age or other lack of livelihood in circumstances beyond his control.

2. Motherhood and childhood are entitled to special care and assistance. All children, whether born in or out of wedlock, shall enjoy the same social protection.

Article 26

1. Everyone has the right to education. Education shall be free, at least in the elementary and fundamental stages. Elementary education shall be compulsory. Technical and professional education shall be made generally available and higher education shall be equally accessible to all on the basis of merit.
2. Education shall be directed to the full development of the human personality and to the strengthening of respect for human rights and fundamental freedoms. It shall promote understanding, tolerance and friendship among all nations, racial or religious groups, and shall further the activities of the United Nations for the maintenance of peace.
3. Parents have a prior right to choose the kind of education that shall be given to their children.

Article 27

1. Everyone has the right freely to participate in the cultural life of the community, to enjoy the arts and to share in scientific advancement and its benefits.
2. Everyone has the right to the protection of the moral and material interests resulting from any scientific, literary or artistic production of which he is the author.

Article 28

Everyone is entitled to a social and international order in which the rights and freedoms set forth in this Declaration can be fully realized.

Article 29

1. Everyone has duties to the community in which alone the free and full development of his personality is possible.
2. In the exercise of his rights and freedoms, everyone shall be subject only to such limitations as are determined by law solely for the purpose of securing due recognition and respect for the rights and freedoms of others and of meeting the just requirements of morality, public order and the general welfare in a democratic society.
3. These rights and freedoms may in no case be exercised contrary to the purposes and principles of the United Nations.

Article 30

Nothing in this Declaration may be interpreted as implying for any State, group or person any right to engage in any activity or to perform any act aimed at the destruction of any of the rights and freedoms set forth herein.

International Covenant on Economic, Social and Cultural Rights 1966

Adopted and opened for signature, ratification and accession by General Assembly resolution 2200A (XXI) of 16 December 1966 entry into force *3 January 1976, in accordance with article 27* status of ratifications declarations and reservations.

Preamble

The States Parties to the present Covenant, Considering that, in accordance with the principles proclaimed in the Charter of the United Nations, recognition of the inherent dignity and of the equal and inalienable rights of all members of the human family is the foundation of freedom, justice and peace in the world:

Recognizing that these rights derive from the inherent dignity of the human person,

Recognizing that, in accordance with the Universal Declaration of Human Rights, the ideal of free human beings enjoying freedom from fear and want can only be achieved if conditions are created whereby everyone may enjoy his economic, social and cultural rights, as well as his civil and political rights,

Considering the obligation of States under the Charter of the United Nations to promote universal respect for, and observance of, human rights and freedoms,

Realizing that the individual, having duties to other individuals and to the community to which he belongs, is under a responsibility to strive for the promotion and observance of the rights recognized in the present Covenant,

Agree upon the following articles:

PART-I

Article 1

1. All peoples have the right of self-determination. By virtue of that right they freely determine their political status and freely pursue their economic, social and cultural development.
2. All peoples may, for their own ends, freely dispose of their natural wealth and resources without prejudice to any obligations arising out of international economic co-operation, based upon the principle of mutual benefit, and international law. In no case may a people be deprived of its own means of subsistence.
3. The States Parties to the present Covenant, including those having responsibility for the administration of Non-Self-Governing and Trust Territories, shall promote the realization of the right of self-determination, and shall respect that right, in conformity with the provisions of the Charter of the United Nations.

PART-II

Article 2

1. Each State Party to the present Covenant undertakes to take steps, individually and through international

assistance and co-operation, especially economic and technical, to the maximum of its available resources, with a view to achieving progressively the full realization of the rights recognized in the present Covenant by all appropriate means, including particularly the adoption of legislative measures.

General Comment on its Implementation

2. The States Parties to the present Covenant undertake to guarantee that the rights enunciated in the present Covenant will be exercised without discrimination of any kind as to race, colour, sex, language, religion, political or other opinion, national or social origin, property, birth or other status.
3. Developing countries, with due regard to human rights and their national economy, may determine to what extent they would guarantee the economic rights recognized in the present Covenant to non-nationals.

Article 3

The States Parties to the present Covenant undertake to ensure the equal right of men and women to the enjoyment of all economic, social and cultural rights set forth in the present Covenant.

Article 4

The States Parties to the present Covenant recognize that, in the enjoyment of those rights provided by the State in conformity with the present Covenant, the State may subject such rights only to such limitations as are determined by law only in so far as this may be compatible with the nature of these rights and solely for the purpose of promoting the general welfare in a democratic society.

Article 5

1. Nothing in the present Covenant may be interpreted as implying for any State, group or person any right to engage in any activity or to perform any act aimed

at the destruction of any of the rights or freedoms recognized herein, or at their limitation to a greater extent than is provided for in the present Covenant.

2. No restriction upon or derogation from any of the fundamental human rights recognized or existing in any country in virtue of law, conventions, regulations or custom shall be admitted on the pretext that the present Covenant does not recognize such rights or that it recognizes them to a lesser extent.

PART-III

Article 6

1. The States Parties to the present Covenant recognize the right to work, which includes the right of everyone to the opportunity to gain his living by work which he freely chooses or accepts, and will take appropriate steps to safeguard this right.
2. The steps to be taken by a State Party to the present Covenant to achieve the full realization of this right shall include technical and vocational guidance and training programmes, policies and techniques to achieve steady economic, social and cultural development and full and productive employment under conditions safeguarding fundamental political and economic freedoms to the individual.

Article 7

The States Parties to the present Covenant recognize the right of everyone to the enjoyment of just and favourable conditions of work which ensure, in particular:

(a) Remuneration which provides all workers, as a minimum, with:

(i) Fair wages and equal remuneration for work of equal value without distinction of any kind, in particular women being guaranteed conditions of work not inferior to those enjoyed by men, with equal pay for equal work;

(ii) A decent living for themselves and their families in accordance with the provisions of the present Covenant;

(b) Safe and healthy working conditions;

(c) Equal opportunity for everyone to be promoted in his employment to an appropriate higher level, subject to no considerations other than those of seniority and competence;

(d) Rest, leisure and reasonable limitation of working hours and periodic holidays with pay, as well as remuneration for public holidays

Article 8

1. The States Parties to the present Covenant undertake to ensure:

    (a) The right of everyone to form trade unions and join the trade union of his choice, subject only to the rules of the organization concerned, for the promotion and protection of his economic and social interests. No restrictions may be placed on the exercise of this right other than those prescribed by law and which are necessary in a democratic society in the interests of national security or public order or for the protection of the rights and freedoms of others;

    (b) The right of trade unions to establish national federations or confederations and the right of the latter to form or join international trade-union organizations;

    (c) The right of trade unions to function freely subject to no limitations other than those prescribed by law and which are necessary in a democratic society in the interests of national security or public order or for the protection of the rights and freedoms of others;

    (d) The right to strike, provided that it is exercised in conformity with the laws of the particular country.

2. This article shall not prevent the imposition of lawful restrictions on the exercise of these rights by members of the armed forces or of the police or of the administration of the State.
3. Nothing in this article shall authorize States Parties to the International Labour Organisation Convention of 1948 concerning Freedom of Association and Protection of the Right to Organize to take legislative measures which would prejudice, or apply the law in such a manner as would prejudice, the guarantees provided for in that Convention.

Article 9

The States Parties to the present Covenant recognize the right of everyone to social security, including social insurance.

Article 10

The States Parties to the present Covenant recognize that:

1. The widest possible protection and assistance should be accorded to the family, which is the natural and fundamental group unit of society, particularly for its establishment and while it is responsible for the care and education of dependent children. Marriage must be entered into with the free consent of the intending spouses.
2. Special protection should be accorded to mothers during a reasonable period before and after childbirth. During such period working mothers should be accorded paid leave or leave with adequate social security benefits.
3. Special measures of protection and assistance should be taken on behalf of all children and young persons without any discrimination for reasons of parentage or other conditions. Children and young persons should be protected from economic and social exploitation. Their employment in work harmful to their morals or health or dangerous to life or likely to hamper their normal development should be punishable by law. States should

also set age limits below which the paid employment of child labour should be prohibited and punishable by law.

Article 11 General Comment on its Implementation

1. The States Parties to the present Covenant recognize the right of everyone to an adequate standard of living for himself and his family, including adequate food, clothing and housing, and to the continuous improvement of living conditions. The States Parties will take appropriate steps to ensure the realization of this right, recognizing to this effect the essential importance of international co-operation based on free consent.

General Comment on its Implementation

2. The States Parties to the present Covenant, recognizing the fundamental right of everyone to be free from hunger, shall take, individually and through international co-operation, the measures, including specific programmes, which are needed:
   (a) To improve methods of production, conservation and distribution of food by making full use of technical and scientific knowledge, by disseminating knowledge of the principles of nutrition and by developing or reforming agrarian systems in such a way as to achieve the most efficient development and utilization of natural resources;
   (b) Taking into account the problems of both food-importing and food-exporting countries, to ensure an equitable distribution of world food supplies in relation to need.

Article 12

General Comment on its Implementation

1. The States Parties to the present Covenant recognize the right of everyone to the enjoyment of the highest attainable standard of physical and mental health.

2. The steps to be taken by the States Parties to the present Covenant to achieve the full realization of this right shall include those necessary for:
   (a) The provision for the reduction of the stillbirth-rate and of infant mortality and for the healthy development of the child;
   (b) The improvement of all aspects of environmental and industrial hygiene;
   (c) The prevention, treatment and control of epidemic, endemic, occupational and other diseases;
   (d) The creation of conditions which would assure to all medical service and medical attention in the event of sickness.

Article 13

General Comment on its Implementation

1. The States Parties to the present Covenant recognize the right of everyone to education. They agree that education shall be directed to the full development of the human personality and the sense of its dignity, and shall strengthen the respect for human rights and fundamental freedoms. They further agree that education shall enable all persons to participate effectively in a free society, promote understanding, tolerance and friendship among all nations and all racial, ethnic or religious groups, and further the activities of the United Nations for the maintenance of peace.
2. The States Parties to the present Covenant recognize that, with a view to achieving the full realization of this right:
   (a) Primary education shall be compulsory and available free to all;
   (b) Secondary education in its different forms, including technical and vocational secondary education, shall be made generally available and accessible to all by every appropriate means, and in particular by the progressive introduction of free education;

(c) Higher education shall be made equally accessible to all, on the basis of capacity, by every appropriate means, and in particular by the progressive introduction of free education;

(d) Fundamental education shall be encouraged or intensified as far as possible for those persons who have not received or completed the whole period of their primary education;

(e) The development of a system of schools at all levels shall be actively pursued, an adequate fellowship system shall be established, and the material conditions of teaching staff shall be continuously improved.

3. The States Parties to the present Covenant undertake to have respect for the liberty of parents and, when applicable, legal guardians to choose for their children schools, other than those established by the public authorities, which conform to such minimum educational standards as may be laid down or approved by the State and to ensure the religious and moral education of their children in conformity with their own convictions.

4. No part of this article shall be construed so as to interfere with the liberty of individuals and bodies to establish and direct educational institutions, subject always to the observance of the principles set forth in paragraph I of this article and to the requirement that the education given in such institutions shall conform to such minimum standards as may be laid down by the State.

Article 14

General Comment on its Implementation

Each State Party to the present Covenant which, at the time of becoming a Party, has not been able to secure in its metropolitan territory or other territories under its jurisdiction compulsory primary education, free of charge, undertakes, within two years, to work out and adopt a detailed plan of action for the progressive implementation, within a reasonable number of years, to be fixed in the plan, of the principle of compulsory education free of charge for all.

Article 15

1. The States Parties to the present Covenant recognize the right of everyone:
   (a) To take part in cultural life;
   (b) To enjoy the benefits of scientific progress and its applications;
   (c) To benefit from the protection of the moral and material interests resulting from any scientific, literary or artistic production of which he is the author.
2. The steps to be taken by the States Parties to the present Covenant to achieve the full realization of this right shall include those necessary for the conservation, the development and the diffusion of science and culture.
3. The States Parties to the present Covenant undertake to respect the freedom indispensable for scientific research and creative activity.
4. The States Parties to the present Covenant recognize the benefits to be derived from the encouragement and development of international contacts and co-operation in the scientific and cultural fields.

PART-IV

Article 16

1. The States Parties to the present Covenant undertake to submit in conformity with this part of the Covenant reports on the measures which they have adopted and the progress made in achieving the observance of the rights recognized herein.

2. (a) All reports shall be submitted to the Secretary-General of the United Nations, who shall transmit copies to the Economic and Social Council for consideration in accordance with the provisions of the present Covenant;

(b) The Secretary-General of the United Nations shall also transmit to the specialized agencies copies of the reports, or any relevant parts therefrom, from States Parties to the present Covenant which are also members of these specialized agencies in so far as these reports, or parts therefrom, relate to any matters which fall within the responsibilities of the said agencies in accordance with their constitutional instruments.

Article 17

General Comment on its Implementation

1. The States Parties to the present Covenant shall furnish their reports in stages, in accordance with a programme to be established by the Economic and Social Council within one year of the entry into force of the present Covenant after consultation with the States Parties and the specialized agencies concerned.
2. Reports may indicate factors and difficulties affecting the degree of fulfilment of obligations under the present Covenant.
3. Where relevant information has previously been furnished to the United Nations or to any specialized agency by any State Party to the present Covenant, it will not be necessary to reproduce that information, but a precise reference to the information so furnished will suffice.

Article 18

Pursuant to its responsibilities under the Charter of the United Nations in the field of human rights and fundamental freedoms, the Economic and Social Council may make arrangements with the specialized agencies in respect of their reporting to it on the progress made in achieving the observance of the provisions of the present Covenant falling within the scope of their activities. These reports may include particulars of decisions and recommendations on such implementation adopted by their competent organs.

Article 19

The Economic and Social Council may transmit to the Commission on Human Rights for study and general recommendation or, as appropriate, for information the reports concerning human rights submitted by States in accordance with articles 16 and 17, and those concerning human rights submitted by the specialized agencies in accordance with article 18.

Article 20

The States Parties to the present Covenant and the specialized agencies concerned may submit comments to the Economic and Social Council on any general recommendation under article 19 or reference to such general recommendation in any report of the Commission on Human Rights or any documentation referred to therein.

Article 21

The Economic and Social Council may submit from time to time to the General Assembly reports with recommendations of a general nature and a summary of the information received from the States Parties to the present Covenant and the specialized agencies on the measures taken and the progress made in achieving general observance of the rights recognized in the present Covenant.

Article 22

General Comment on its Implementation

The Economic and Social Council may bring to the attention of other organs of the United Nations, their subsidiary organs and specialized agencies concerned with furnishing technical assistance any matters arising out of the reports referred to in this part of the present Covenant which may assist such bodies in deciding, each within its field of competence, on the advisability of international measures likely to contribute to the effective progressive implementation of the present Covenant.

Article 23

The States Parties to the present Covenant agree that international action for the achievement of the rights recognized in the present Covenant includes such methods as the conclusion of conventions, the adoption of recommendations, the furnishing of technical assistance and the holding of regional meetings and technical meetings for the purpose of consultation and study organized in conjunction with the Governments concerned.

Article 24

Nothing in the present Covenant shall be interpreted as impairing the provisions of the Charter of the United Nations and of the constitutions of the specialized agencies which define the respective responsibilities of the various organs of the United Nations and of the specialized agencies in regard to the matters dealt with in the present Covenant.

Article 25

Nothing in the present Covenant shall be interpreted as impairing the inherent right of all peoples to enjoy and utilize fully and freely their natural wealth and resources.

PART-V

Article 26

1. The present Covenant is open for signature by any State Member of the United Nations or member of any of its specialized agencies, by any State Party to the Statute of the International Court of Justice, and by any other State which has been invited by the General Assembly of the United Nations to become a party to the present Covenant.
2. The present Covenant is subject to ratification. Instruments of ratification shall be deposited with the Secretary-General of the United Nations.
3. The present Covenant shall be open to accession by any State referred to in paragraph 1 of this article.
4. Accession shall be effected by the deposit of an

instrument of accession with the Secretary-General of the United Nations.

5. The Secretary-General of the United Nations shall inform all States which have signed the present Covenant or acceded to it of the deposit of each instrument of ratification or accession.

Article 27

1. The present Covenant shall enter into force three months after the date of the deposit with the Secretary-General of the United Nations of the thirty-fifth instrument of ratification or instrument of accession.
2. For each State ratifying the present Covenant or acceding to it after the deposit of the thirty-fifth instrument of ratification or instrument of accession, the present Covenant shall enter into force three months after the date of the deposit of its own instrument of ratification or instrument of accession.

Article 28

The provisions of the present Covenant shall extend to all parts of federal States without any limitations or exceptions.

Article 29

1. Any State Party to the present Covenant may propose an amendment and file it with the Secretary-General of the United Nations. The Secretary-General shall thereupon communicate any proposed amendments to the States Parties to the present Covenant with a request that they notify him whether they favour a conference of States Parties for the purpose of considering and voting upon the proposals. In the event that at least one third of the States Parties favours such a conference, the Secretary-General shall convene the conference under the auspices of the United Nations. Any amendment adopted by a majority of the States Parties present and voting at the conference shall be submitted to the General Assembly of the United Nations for approval.

2. Amendments shall come into force when they have been approved by the General Assembly of the United Nations and accepted by a two-thirds majority of the States Parties to the present Covenant in accordance with their respective constitutional processes.
3. When amendments come into force they shall be binding on those States Parties which have accepted them, other States Parties still being bound by the provisions of the present Covenant and any earlier amendment which they have accepted.

Article 30

Irrespective of the notifications made under article 26, paragraph 5, the Secretary-General of the United Nations shall inform all States referred to in paragraph I of the same article of the following particulars:

(a) Signatures, ratifications and accessions under article 26;

(b) The date of the entry into force of the present Covenant under article 27 and the date of the entry into force of any amendments under article 29.

Article 31

1. The present Covenant, of which the Chinese, English, French, Russian and Spanish texts are equally authentic, shall be deposited in the archives of the United Nations.
2. The Secretary-General of the United Nations shall transmit certified copies of the present Covenant to all States referred to in article 26.

International Covenant on Civil and Political Rights

Adopted and opened for signature, ratification and accession by General Assembly resolution 2200A (XXI) of 16 December 1966 entry into force 23 March 1976, in accordance with Article 49.

Preamble

The States Parties to the present Covenant, Considering that, in accordance with the principles proclaimed in the Charter of the United Nations, recognition of the inherent dignity and of the equal and inalienable rights of all members of the human family is the foundation of freedom, justice and peace in the world,

Recognizing that these rights derive from the inherent dignity of the human person,

Recognizing that, in accordance with the Universal Declaration of Human Rights, the ideal of free human beings enjoying civil and political freedom and freedom from fear and want can only be achieved if conditions are created whereby everyone may enjoy his civil and political rights, as well as his economic, social and cultural rights,

Considering the obligation of States under the Charter of the United Nations to promote universal respect for, and observance of, human rights and freedoms,

Realizing that the individual, having duties to other individuals and to the community to which he belongs, is under a responsibility to strive for the promotion and observance of the rights recognized in the present Covenant,

Agree upon the following articles:

PART-I

Article 1

1. All peoples have the right of self-determination. By virtue of that right they freely determine their political status and freely pursue their economic, social and cultural development.
2. All peoples may, for their own ends, freely dispose of their natural wealth and resources without prejudice to any obligations arising out of international economic co-operation, based upon the principle of mutual benefit, and international law. In no case may a people be deprived of its own means of subsistence.
3. The States Parties to the present Covenant, including those having responsibility for the administration of Non-Self-Governing and Trust Territories, shall promote

the realization of the right of self-determination, and shall respect that right, in conformity with the provisions of the Charter of the United Nations.

PART-II

Article 2

1. Each State Party to the present Covenant undertakes to respect and to ensure to all individuals within its territory and subject to its jurisdiction the rights recognized in the present Covenant, without distinction of any kind, such as race, colour, sex, language, religion, political or other opinion, national or social origin, property, birth or other status.
2. Where not already provided for by existing legislative or other measures, each State Party to the present Covenant undertakes to take the necessary steps, in accordance with its constitutional processes and with the provisions of the present Covenant, to adopt such laws or other measures as may be necessary to give effect to the rights recognized in the present Covenant.
3. Each State Party to the present Covenant undertakes:
   (a) To ensure that any person whose rights or freedoms as herein recognized are violated shall have an effective remedy, notwithstanding that the violation has been committed by persons acting in an official capacity;
   (b) To ensure that any person claiming such a remedy shall have his right thereto determined by competent judicial, administrative or legislative authorities, or by any other competent authority provided for by the legal system of the State, and to develop the possibilities of judicial remedy;
   (c) To ensure that the competent authorities shall enforce such remedies when granted.

Article 3

The States Parties to the present Covenant undertake to

ensure the equal right of men and women to the enjoyment of all civil and political rights set forth in the present Covenant.

Article 4

1. In time of public emergency which threatens the life of the nation and the existence of which is officially proclaimed, the States Parties to the present Covenant may take measures derogating from their obligations under the present Covenant to the extent strictly required by the exigencies of the situation, provided that such measures are not inconsistent with their other obligations under international law and do not involve discrimination solely on the ground of race, colour, sex, language, religion or social origin.
2. No derogation from articles 6, 7, 8 (paragraphs I and 2), 11, 15, 16 and 18 may be made under this provision.
3. Any State Party to the present Covenant availing itself of the right of derogation shall immediately inform the other States Parties to the present Covenant, through the intermediary of the Secretary-General of the United Nations, of the provisions from which it has derogated and of the reasons by which it was actuated. A further communication shall be made, through the same intermediary, on the date on which it terminates such derogation.

Article 5

1. Nothing in the present Covenant may be interpreted as implying for any State, group or person any right to engage in any activity or perform any act aimed at the destruction of any of the rights and freedoms recognized herein or at their limitation to a greater extent than is provided for in the present Covenant.
2. There shall be no restriction upon or derogation from any of the fundamental human rights recognized or existing in any State Party to the present Covenant pursuant to law, conventions, regulations or custom on the pretext that the present Covenant does not recognize such rights or that it recognizes them to a lesser extent.

PART-III

Article 6

1. Every human being has the inherent right to life. This right shall be protected by law. No one shall be arbitrarily deprived of his life.
2. In countries which have not abolished the death penalty, sentence of death may be imposed only for the most serious crimes in accordance with the law in force at the time of the commission of the crime and not contrary to the provisions of the present Covenant and to the Convention on the Prevention and Punishment of the Crime of Genocide. This penalty can only be carried out pursuant to a final judgement rendered by a competent court.
3. When deprivation of life constitutes the crime of genocide, it is understood that nothing in this article shall authorize any State Party to the present Covenant to derogate in any way from any obligation assumed under the provisions of the Convention on the Prevention and Punishment of the Crime of Genocide.
4. Anyone sentenced to death shall have the right to seek pardon or commutation of the sentence. Amnesty, pardon or commutation of the sentence of death may be granted in all cases.
5. Sentence of death shall not be imposed for crimes committed by persons below eighteen years of age and shall not be carried out on pregnant women.
6. Nothing in this article shall be invoked to delay or to prevent the abolition of capital punishment by any State Party to the present Covenant.

Article 7

No one shall be subjected to torture or to cruel, inhuman or degrading treatment or punishment. In particular, no one shall be subjected without his free consent to medical or scientific experimentation.

Article 8

1. No one shall be held in slavery; slavery and the slave-trade in all their forms shall be prohibited.
2. No one shall be held in servitude.
3. (a) No one shall be required to perform forced or compulsory labour;
   (b) Paragraph 3 (a) shall not be held to preclude, in countries where imprisonment with hard labour may be imposed as a punishment for a crime, the performance of hard labour in pursuance of a sentence to such punishment by a competent court;
   (c) For the purpose of this paragraph the term "forced or compulsory labour" shall not include:
      (i) Any work or service, not referred to in subparagraph (b), normally required of a person who is under detention in consequence of a lawful order of a court, or of a person during conditional release from such detention;
      (ii) Any service of a military character and, in countries where conscientious objection is recognized, any national service required by law of conscientious objectors;
      (iii) Any service exacted in cases of emergency or calamity threatening the life or well-being of the community;
      (iv) Any work or service which forms part of normal civil obligations.

Article 9

1. Everyone has the right to liberty and security of person. No one shall be subjected to arbitrary arrest or detention. No one shall be deprived of his liberty except on such grounds and in accordance with such procedure as are established by law.
2. Anyone who is arrested shall be informed, at the time of arrest, of the reasons for his arrest and shall be promptly informed of any charges against him.

3. Anyone arrested or detained on a criminal charge shall be brought promptly before a judge or other officer authorized by law to exercise judicial power and shall be entitled to trial within a reasonable time or to release. It shall not be the general rule that persons awaiting trial shall be detained in custody, but release may be subject to guarantees to appear for trial, at any other stage of the judicial proceedings, and, should occasion arise, for execution of the judgement.
4. Anyone who is deprived of his liberty by arrest or detention shall be entitled to take proceedings before a court, in order that that court may decide without delay on the lawfulness of his detention and order his release if the detention is not lawful.
5. Anyone who has been the victim of unlawful arrest or detention shall have an enforceable right to compensation.

Article 10

1. All persons deprived of their liberty shall be treated with humanity and with respect for the inherent dignity of the human person.
2. (a) Accused persons shall, save in exceptional circumstances, be segregated from convicted persons and shall be subject to separate treatment appropriate to their status as unconvicted persons;
   (b) Accused juvenile persons shall be separated from adults and brought as speedily as possible for adjudication.
3. The penitentiary system shall comprise treatment of prisoners the essential aim of which shall be their reformation and social rehabilitation. Juvenile offenders shall be segregated from adults and be accorded treatment appropriate to their age and legal status.

Article 11

No one shall be imprisoned merely on the ground of inability to fulfil a contractual obligation.

Article 12

1. Everyone lawfully within the territory of a State shall, within that territory, have the right to liberty of movement and freedom to choose his residence.
2. Everyone shall be free to leave any country, including his own.
3. The above-mentioned rights shall not be subject to any restrictions except those which are provided by law, are necessary to protect national security, public order (ordre public), public health or morals or the rights and freedoms of others, and are consistent with the other rights recognized in the present Covenant.
4. No one shall be arbitrarily deprived of the right to enter his own country.

Article 13

An alien lawfully in the territory of a State Party to the present Covenant may be expelled therefrom only in pursuance of a decision reached in accordance with law and shall, except where compelling reasons of national security otherwise require, be allowed to submit the reasons against his expulsion and to have his case reviewed by, and be represented for the purpose before, the competent authority or a person or persons especially designated by the competent authority.

Article 14

1. All persons shall be equal before the courts and tribunals. In the determination of any criminal charge against him, or of his rights and obligations in a suit at law, everyone shall be entitled to a fair and public hearing by a competent, independent and impartial tribunal established by law. The press and the public may be excluded from all or part of a trial for reasons of morals, public order (ordre public) or national security in a democratic society, or when the interest of the private lives of the parties so requires, or to the extent strictly necessary in the opinion of the court in special circumstances where publicity would prejudice the interests of justice; but any judgement rendered in a

criminal case or in a suit at law shall be made public except where the interest of juvenile persons otherwise requires or the proceedings concern matrimonial disputes or the guardianship of children.

2. Everyone charged with a criminal offence shall have the right to be presumed innocent until proved guilty according to law.
3. In the determination of any criminal charge against him, everyone shall be entitled to the following minimum guarantees, in full equality:
   (a) To be informed promptly and in detail in a language which he understands of the nature and cause of the charge against him;
   (b) To have adequate time and facilities for the preparation of his defence and to communicate with counsel of his own choosing;
   (c) To be tried without undue delay;
   (d) To be tried in his presence, and to defend himself in person or through legal assistance of his own choosing; to be informed, if he does not have legal assistance, of this right; and to have legal assistance assigned to him, in any case where the interests of justice so require, and without payment by him in any such case if he does not have sufficient means to pay for it;
   (e) To examine, or have examined, the witnesses against him and to obtain the attendance and examination of witnesses on his behalf under the same conditions as witnesses against him;
   (f) To have the free assistance of an interpreter if he cannot understand or speak the language used in court;
   (g) Not to be compelled to testify against himself or to confess guilt.
4. In the case of juvenile persons, the procedure shall be such as will take account of their age and the desirability of promoting their rehabilitation.

5. Everyone convicted of a crime shall have the right to his conviction and sentence being reviewed by a higher tribunal according to law.
6. When a person has by a final decision been convicted of a criminal offence and when subsequently his conviction has been reversed or he has been pardoned on the ground that a new or newly discovered fact shows conclusively that there has been a miscarriage of justice, the person who has suffered punishment as a result of such conviction shall be compensated according to law, unless it is proved that the non-disclosure of the unknown fact in time is wholly or partly attributable to him.
7. No one shall be liable to be tried or punished again for an offence for which he has already been finally convicted or acquitted in accordance with the law and penal procedure of each country.

Article 15

1. No one shall be held guilty of any criminal offence on account of any act or omission which did not constitute a criminal offence, under national or international law, at the time when it was committed. Nor shall a heavier penalty be imposed than the one that was applicable at the time when the criminal offence was committed. If, subsequent to the commission of the offence, provision is made by law for the imposition of the lighter penalty, the offender shall benefit thereby.
2. Nothing in this article shall prejudice the trial and punishment of any person for any act or omission which, at the time when it was committed, was criminal according to the general principles of law recognized by the community of nations.

Article 16

Everyone shall have the right to recognition everywhere as a person before the law.

Article 17

1. No one shall be subjected to arbitrary or unlawful interference with his privacy, family, or correspondence, nor to unlawful attacks on his honour and reputation.
2. Everyone has the right to the protection of the law against such interference or attacks.

Article 18

1. Everyone shall have the right to freedom of thought, conscience and religion. This right shall include freedom to have or to adopt a religion or belief of his choice, and freedom, either individually or in community with others and in public or private, to manifest his religion or belief in worship, observance, practice and teaching.
2. No one shall be subject to coercion which would impair his freedom to have or to adopt a religion or belief of his choice.
3. Freedom to manifest one's religion or beliefs may be subject only to such limitations as are prescribed by law and are necessary to protect public safety, order, health, or morals or the fundamental rights and freedoms of others.
4. The States Parties to the present Covenant undertake to have respect for the liberty of parents and, when applicable, legal guardians to ensure the religious and moral education of their children in conformity with their own convictions.

Article 19

1. Everyone shall have the right to hold opinions without interference.
2. Everyone shall have the right to freedom of expression; this right shall include freedom to seek, receive and impart information and ideas of all kinds, regardless of frontiers, either orally, in writing or in print, in the form of art, or through any other media of his choice.

3. The exercise of the rights provided for in paragraph 2 of this article carries with it special duties and responsibilities. It may therefore be subject to certain restrictions, but these shall only be such as are provided by law and are necessary:
   (a) For respect of the rights or reputations of others;
   (b) For the protection of national security or of public order (ordre public), or of public health or morals.

Article 20

1. Any propaganda for war shall be prohibited by law.
2. Any advocacy of national, racial or religious hatred that constitutes incitement to discrimination, hostility or violence shall be prohibited by law.

Article 21

The right of peaceful assembly shall be recognized. No restrictions may be placed on the exercise of this right other than those imposed in conformity with the law and which are necessary in a democratic society in the interests of national security or public safety, public order (ordre public), the protection of public health or morals or the protection of the rights and freedoms of others.

Article 22

1. Everyone shall have the right to freedom of association with others, including the right to form and join trade unions for the protection of his interests.
2. No restrictions may be placed on the exercise of this right other than those which are prescribed by law and which are necessary in a democratic society in the interests of national security or public safety, public order (ordre public), the protection of public health or morals or the protection of the rights and freedoms of others. This article shall not prevent the imposition of lawful restrictions on members of the armed forces and of the police in their exercise of this right.

3. Nothing in this article shall authorize States Parties to the International Labour Organisation Convention of 1948 concerning Freedom of Association and Protection of the Right to Organize to take legislative measures which would prejudice, or to apply the law in such a manner as to prejudice, the guarantees provided for in that Convention.

Article 23

1. The family is the natural and fundamental group unit of society and is entitled to protection by society and the State.
2. The right of men and women of marriageable age to marry and to found a family shall be recognized.
3. No marriage shall be entered into without the free and full consent of the intending spouses.
4. States Parties to the present Covenant shall take appropriate steps to ensure equality of rights and responsibilities of spouses as to marriage, during marriage and at its dissolution. In the case of dissolution, provision shall be made for the necessary protection of any children.

Article 24

1. Every child shall have, without any discrimination as to race, colour, sex, language, religion, national or social origin, property or birth, the right to such measures of protection as are required by his status as a minor, on the part of his family, society and the State.
2. Every child shall be registered immediately after birth and shall have a name.
3. Every child has the right to acquire a nationality.

Article 25

Every citizen shall have the right and the opportunity, without any of the distinctions mentioned in article 2 and without unreasonable restrictions:

(a) To take part in the conduct of public affairs, directly or through freely chosen representatives;

(b) To vote and to be elected at genuine periodic elections which shall be by universal and equal suffrage and shall be held by secret ballot, guaranteeing the free expression of the will of the electors;

(c) To have access, on general terms of equality, to public service in his country.

Article 26

All persons are equal before the law and are entitled without any discrimination to the equal protection of the law. In this respect, the law shall prohibit any discrimination and guarantee to all persons equal and effective protection against discrimination on any ground such as race, colour, sex, language, religion, political or other opinion, national or social origin, property, birth or other status.

Article 27

In those States in which ethnic, religious or linguistic minorities exist, persons belonging to such minorities shall not be denied the right, in community with the other members of their group, to enjoy their own culture, to profess and practise their own religion, or to use their own language.

PART-IV

Article 28

1. There shall be established a Human Rights Committee (hereafter referred to in the present Covenant as the Committee). It shall consist of eighteen members and shall carry out the functions hereinafter provided.
2. The Committee shall be composed of nationals of the States Parties to the present Covenant who shall be persons of high moral character and recognized competence in the field of human rights, consideration being given to the usefulness of the participation of some persons having legal experience.

3. The members of the Committee shall be elected and shall serve in their personal capacity.

Article 29

1. The members of the Committee shall be elected by secret ballot from a list of persons possessing the qualifications prescribed in article 28 and nominated for the purpose by the States Parties to the present Covenant.
2. Each State Party to the present Covenant may nominate not more than two persons. These persons shall be nationals of the nominating State.
3. A person shall be eligible for renomination.

Article 30

1. The initial election shall be held no later than six months after the date of the entry into force of the present Covenant.
2. At least four months before the date of each election to the Committee, other than an election to fill a vacancy declared in accordance with article 34, the Secretary-General of the United Nations shall address a written invitation to the States Parties to the present Covenant to submit their nominations for membership of the Committee within three months.
3. The Secretary-General of the United Nations shall prepare a list in alphabetical order of all the persons thus nominated, with an indication of the States Parties which have nominated them, and shall submit it to the States Parties to the present Covenant no later than one month before the date of each election.
4. Elections of the members of the Committee shall be held at a meeting of the States Parties to the present Covenant convened by the Secretary General of the United Nations at the Headquarters of the United Nations. At that meeting, for which two thirds of the States Parties to the present Covenant shall constitute a quorum, the persons elected to the Committee shall

be those nominees who obtain the largest number of votes and an absolute majority of the votes of the representatives of States Parties present and voting.

Article 31

1. The Committee may not include more than one national of the same State.
2. In the election of the Committee, consideration shall be given to equitable geographical distribution of membership and to the representation of the different forms of civilization and of the principal legal systems.

Article 32

1. The members of the Committee shall be elected for a term of four years. They shall be eligible for re-election if renominated. However, the terms of nine of the members elected at the first election shall expire at the end of two years; immediately after the first election, the names of these nine members shall be chosen by lot by the Chairman of the meeting referred to in article 30, paragraph 4.
2. Elections at the expiry of office shall be held in accordance with the preceding articles of this part of the present Covenant.

Article 33

1. If, in the unanimous opinion of the other members, a member of the Committee has ceased to carry out his functions for any cause other than absence of a temporary character, the Chairman of the Committee shall notify the Secretary-General of the United Nations, who shall then declare the seat of that member to be vacant.
2. In the event of the death or the resignation of a member of the Committee, the Chairman shall immediately notify the Secretary-General of the United Nations, who shall declare the seat vacant from the date of death or the date on which the resignation takes effect.

Article 34

1. When a vacancy is declared in accordance with article 33 and if the term of office of the member to be replaced does not expire within six months of the declaration of the vacancy, the Secretary-General of the United Nations shall notify each of the States Parties to the present Covenant, which may within two months submit nominations in accordance with article 29 for the purpose of filling the vacancy.
2. The Secretary-General of the United Nations shall prepare a list in alphabetical order of the persons thus nominated and shall submit it to the States Parties to the present Covenant. The election to fill the vacancy shall then take place in accordance with the relevant provisions of this part of the present Covenant.
3. A member of the Committee elected to fill a vacancy declared in accordance with article 33 shall hold office for the remainder of the term of the member who vacated the seat on the Committee under the provisions of that article.

Article 35

The members of the Committee shall, with the approval of the General Assembly of the United Nations, receive emoluments from United Nations resources on such terms and conditions as the General Assembly may decide, having regard to the importance of the Committee's responsibilities.

Article 36

The Secretary-General of the United Nations shall provide the necessary staff and facilities for the effective performance of the functions of the Committee under the present Covenant.

Article 37

1. The Secretary-General of the United Nations shall convene the initial meeting of the Committee at the Headquarters of the United Nations.

2. After its initial meeting, the Committee shall meet at such times as shall be provided in its rules of procedure.
3. The Committee shall normally meet at the Headquarters of the United Nations or at the United Nations Office at Geneva.

Article 38

Every member of the Committee shall, before taking up his duties, make a solemn declaration in open committee that he will perform his functions impartially and conscientiously.

Article 39

1. The Committee shall elect its officers for a term of two years. They may be re-elected.
2. The Committee shall establish its own rules of procedure, but these rules shall provide, inter alia, that:
   (a) Twelve members shall constitute a quorum;
   (b) Decisions of the Committee shall be made by a majority vote of the members present.

Article 40

1. The States Parties to the present Covenant undertake to submit reports on the measures they have adopted which give effect to the rights recognized herein and on the progress made in the enjoyment of those rights:
   (a) Within one year of the entry into force of the present Covenant for the States Parties concerned;
   (b) Thereafter whenever the Committee so requests.
2. All reports shall be submitted to the Secretary-General of the United Nations, who shall transmit them to the Committee for consideration. Reports shall indicate the factors and difficulties, if any, affecting the implementation of the present Covenant.
3. The Secretary-General of the United Nations may, after consultation with the Committee, transmit to the specialized agencies concerned copies of such parts of the reports as may fall within their field of competence.

4. The Committee shall study the reports submitted by the States Parties to the present Covenant. It shall transmit its reports, and such general comments as it may consider appropriate, to the States Parties. The Committee may also transmit to the Economic and Social Council these comments along with the copies of the reports it has received from States Parties to the present Covenant.
5. The States Parties to the present Covenant may submit to the Committee observations on any comments that may be made in accordance with paragraph 4 of this article.

Article 41

1. A State Party to the present Covenant may at any time declare under this article that it recognizes the competence of the Committee to receive and consider communications to the effect that a State Party claims that another State Party is not fulfilling its obligations under the present Covenant. Communications under this article may be received and considered only if submitted by a State Party which has made a declaration recognizing in regard to itself the competence of the Committee. No communication shall be received by the Committee if it concerns a State Party which has not made such a declaration. Communications received under this article shall be dealt with in accordance with the following procedure:
   (a) If a State Party to the present Covenant considers that another State Party is not giving effect to the provisions of the present Covenant, it may, by written communication, bring the matter to the attention of that State Party. Within three months after the receipt of the communication the receiving State shall afford the State which sent the communication an explanation, or any other statement in writing clarifying the matter which should include, to the extent possible and pertinent,

reference to domestic procedures and remedies taken, pending, or available in the matter;

(b) If the matter is not adjusted to the satisfaction of both States Parties concerned within six months after the receipt by the receiving State of the initial communication, either State shall have the right to refer the matter to the Committee, by notice given to the Committee and to the other State;

(c) The Committee shall deal with a matter referred to it only after it has ascertained that all available domestic remedies have been invoked and exhausted in the matter, in conformity with the generally recognized principles of international law. This shall not be the rule where the application of the remedies is unreasonably prolonged;

(d) The Committee shall hold closed meetings when examining communications under this article;

(e) Subject to the provisions of subparagraph (c), the Committee shall make available its good offices to the States Parties concerned with a view to a friendly solution of the matter on the basis of respect for human rights and fundamental freedoms as recognized in the present Covenant;

(f) In any matter referred to it, the Committee may call upon the States Parties concerned, referred to in subparagraph (b), to supply any relevant information;

(g) The States Parties concerned, referred to in subparagraph (b), shall have the right to be represented when the matter is being considered in the Committee and to make submissions orally and/or in writing;

(h) The Committee shall, within twelve months after the date of receipt of notice under subparagraph (b), submit a report:

(i) If a solution within the terms of subparagraph (e) is reached, the Committee shall confine its report to a brief statement of the facts and of the solution reached;

(ii) If a solution within the terms of subparagraph (e) is not reached, the Committee shall confine its report to a brief statement of the facts; the written submissions and record of the oral submissions made by the States Parties concerned shall be attached to the report. In every matter, the report shall be communicated to the States Parties concerned.

2. The provisions of this article shall come into force when ten States Parties to the present Covenant have made declarations under paragraph I of this article. Such declarations shall be deposited by the States Parties with the Secretary-General of the United Nations, who shall transmit copies thereof to the other States Parties. A declaration may be withdrawn at any time by notification to the Secretary-General. Such a withdrawal shall not prejudice the consideration of any matter which is the subject of a communication already transmitted under this article; no further communication by any State Party shall be received after the notification of withdrawal of the declaration has been received by the Secretary-General, unless the State Party concerned has made a new declaration.

Article 42

1. (a) If a matter referred to the Committee in accordance with article 41 is not resolved to the satisfaction of the States Parties concerned, the Committee may, with the prior consent of the States Parties concerned, appoint an ad hoc Conciliation Commission (hereinafter referred to as the Commission). The good offices of the Commission shall be made available to the States Parties concerned with a view to an amicable solution of the matter on the basis of respect for the present Covenant;

(b) The Commission shall consist of five persons acceptable to the States Parties concerned. If the

States Parties concerned fail to reach agreement within three months on all or part of the composition of the Commission, the members of the Commission concerning whom no agreement has been reached shall be elected by secret ballot by a two-thirds majority vote of the Committee from among its members.

2. The members of the Commission shall serve in their personal capacity. They shall not be nationals of the States Parties concerned, or of a State not Party to the present Covenant, or of a State Party which has not made a declaration under article 41.

3. The Commission shall elect its own Chairman and adopt its own rules of procedure.

4. The meetings of the Commission shall normally be held at the Headquarters of the United Nations or at the United Nations Office at Geneva. However, they may be held at such other convenient places as the Commission may determine in consultation with the Secretary-General of the United Nations and the States Parties concerned.

5. The secretariat provided in accordance with article 36 shall also service the commissions appointed under this article.

6. The information received and collated by the Committee shall be made available to the Commission and the Commission may call upon the States Parties concerned to supply any other relevant information.

7. When the Commission has fully considered the matter, but in any event not later than twelve months after having been seized of the matter, it shall submit to the Chairman of the Committee a report for communication to the States Parties concerned:

   (a) If the Commission is unable to complete its consideration of the matter within twelve months, it shall confine its report to a brief statement of the status of its consideration of the matter;

(b) If an amicable solution to the matter on tie basis of respect for human rights as recognized in the present Covenant is reached, the Commission shall confine its report to a brief statement of the facts and of the solution reached;

(c) If a solution within the terms of subparagraph (b) is not reached, the Commission's report shall embody its findings on all questions of fact relevant to the issues between the States Parties concerned, and its views on the possibilities of an amicable solution of the matter. This report shall also contain the written submissions and a record of the oral submissions made by the States Parties concerned;

(d) If the Commission's report is submitted under subparagraph (c), the States Parties concerned shall, within three months of the receipt of the report, notify the Chairman of the Committee whether or not they accept the contents of the report of the Commission.

8. The provisions of this article are without prejudice to the responsibilities of the Committee under article 41.

9. The States Parties concerned shall share equally all the expenses of the members of the Commission in accordance with estimates to be provided by the Secretary-General of the United Nations.

10. The Secretary-General of the United Nations shall be empowered to pay the expenses of the members of the Commission, if necessary, before reimbursement by the States Parties concerned, in accordance with paragraph 9 of this article.

Article 43

The members of the Committee, and of the ad hoc conciliation commissions which may be appointed under article 42, shall be entitled to the facilities, privileges and immunities of experts on mission for the United Nations as laid down in the relevant sections of the Convention on the Privileges and Immunities of the United Nations.

Article 44

The provisions for the implementation of the present Covenant shall apply without prejudice to the procedures prescribed in the field of human rights by or under the constituent instruments and the conventions of the United Nations and of the specialized agencies and shall not prevent the States Parties to the present Covenant from having recourse to other procedures for settling a dispute in accordance with general or special international agreements in force between them.

Article 45

The Committee shall submit to the General Assembly of the United Nations, through the Economic and Social Council, an annual report on its activities.

PART-V

Article 46

Nothing in the present Covenant shall be interpreted as impairing the provisions of the Charter of the United Nations and of the constitutions of the specialized agencies which define the respective responsibilities of the various organs of the United Nations and of the specialized agencies in regard to the matters dealt with in the present Covenant.

Article 47

Nothing in the present Covenant shall be interpreted as impairing the inherent right of all peoples to enjoy and utilize fully and freely their natural wealth and resources.

PART-VI

Article 48

1. The present Covenant is open for signature by any State Member of the United Nations or member of any of its specialized agencies, by any State Party to the Statute of the International Court of Justice, and by any other State which has been invited by the General

Assembly of the United Nations to become a Party to the present Covenant.

2. The present Covenant is subject to ratification. Instruments of ratification shall be deposited with the Secretary-General of the United Nations.
3. The present Covenant shall be open to accession by any State referred to in paragraph 1 of this article.
4. Accession shall be effected by the deposit of an instrument of accession with the Secretary-General of the United Nations.
5. The Secretary-General of the United Nations shall inform all States which have signed this Covenant or acceded to it of the deposit of each instrument of ratification or accession.

Article 49

1. The present Covenant shall enter into force three months after the date of the deposit with the Secretary-General of the United Nations of the thirty-fifth instrument of ratification or instrument of accession.
2. For each State ratifying the present Covenant or acceding to it after the deposit of the thirty-fifth instrument of ratification or instrument of accession, the present Covenant shall enter into force three months after the date of the deposit of its own instrument of ratification or instrument of accession.

Article 50

The provisions of the present Covenant shall extend to all parts of federal States without any limitations or exceptions.

Article 51

1. Any State Party to the present Covenant may propose an amendment and file it with the Secretary-General of the United Nations. The Secretary-General of the United Nations shall thereupon communicate any proposed amendments to the States Parties to the present Covenant with a request that they notify him whether they favour a conference of States Parties for

the purpose of considering and voting upon the proposals. In the event that at least one third of the States Parties favours such a conference, the Secretary-General shall convene the conference under the auspices of the United Nations. Any amendment adopted by a majority of the States Parties present and voting at the conference shall be submitted to the General Assembly of the United Nations for approval.

2. Amendments shall come into force when they have been approved by the General Assembly of the United Nations and accepted by a two-thirds majority of the States Parties to the present Covenant in accordance with their respective constitutional processes. 3. When amendments come into force, they shall be binding on those States Parties which have accepted them, other States Parties still being bound by the provisions of the present Covenant and any earlier amendment which they have accepted.

Article 52

1. Irrespective of the notifications made under article 48, paragraph 5, the Secretary-General of the United Nations shall inform all States referred to in paragraph I of the same article of the following particulars:

(a) Signatures, ratifications and accessions under article 48;

(b) The date of the entry into force of the present Covenant under article 49 and the date of the entry into force of any amendments under article 51.

Article 53

1. The present Covenant, of which the Chinese, English, French, Russian and Spanish texts are equally authentic, shall be deposited in the archives of the United Nations.

2. The Secretary-General of the United Nations shall transmit certified copies of the present Covenant to all States referred to in article 48.

Unit III

Human Rights : Indian Context

Constitutional Provisions of Human Rights—Fundamental Rights and Directive Principles of State Policy

Rights which are considered essential or fundamental for the well-being of a person are called Fundamental Rights. The **Fundamental Rights in India** enshrined in the Part III of the Constitution of India guarantee civil liberties such that all Indians can lead their lives in peace and harmony as citizens of India. These include individual rights common to most liberal democracies, such as equality before law, freedom of speech and expression, freedom of association and peaceful assembly, freedom to practice religion, and the right to constitutional remedies for the protection of civil rights by means of writs such as habeas corpus. Violations of these rights result in punishments as prescribed in the Indian Penal Code, subject to discretion of the judiciary. The Fundamental Rights are defined as basic human freedoms which every Indian citizen has the right to enjoy for a proper and harmonious development of personality. These rights universally apply to all citizens, irrespective of race, place of birth, religion, caste, creed, colour or sex. They are enforceable by the courts, subject to certain restrictions. The Rights have their origins in many sources, including England's Bill of Rights, the United States Bill of Rights and France's Declaration of the Rights of Man.

The six fundamental rights are:

1. Right to equality
2. Right to freedom
3. Right against exploitation
4. Right to freedom of religion
5. Cultural and educational rights
6. Right to constitutional remedies

Rights literally mean those freedoms which are essential for personal good as well as the good of the community. The rights guaranteed under the Constitution of India are fundamental as they have been incorporated into the *Fundamental Law of the Land* and are enforceable in a court of law. However, this does not mean that they are absolute or that they are immune from Constitutional amendment.

Fundamental rights for Indians have also been aimed at overturning the inequalities of pre-independence social practices. Specifically, they have also been used to abolish untouchability and hence prohibit discrimination on the grounds of religion, race, caste, sex, or place of birth. They also forbid trafficking of human beings and forced labour. They also protect cultural and educational rights of ethnic and religious minorities by allowing them to preserve their languages and also establish and administer their own education institutions.

Genesis

The development of constitutionally guaranteed fundamental human rights in India was inspired by historical examples such as England's Bill of Rights (1689), the United States Bill of Rights (approved on 17 September 1787, final ratification on 15 December 1791) and France's Declaration of the Rights of Man (created during the revolution of 1789, and ratified on 26 August 1789). Under the educational system of British Raj, students were exposed to ideas of democracy, human rights and European political history. The Indian student community in England was further inspired by the workings of parliamentary democracy and British political parties.

In 1919, the Rowlatt Acts gave extensive powers to the British government and police, and allowed indefinite arrest and detention of individuals, warrant-less searches and seizures, restrictions on public gatherings, and intensive censorship of media and publications. The public opposition to this act eventually led to mass campaigns of non-violent civil disobedience throughout the country demanding guaranteed civil freedoms, and limitations on government power. Indians, who were seeking independence and their own government, were particularly influenced by the independence of Ireland and the development of the Irish constitution. Also, the directive principles of state policy in Irish constitution were looked upon by the people of India as an inspiration for the independent India's government to comprehensively tackle complex social and economic challenges across a vast, diverse nation and population.

In 1928, the Nehru Commission composing of representatives of Indian political parties proposed constitutional reforms for India that apart from calling for dominion status for India and elections under universal suffrage, would guarantee rights deemed fundamental, representation for religious and ethnic minorities, and limit the powers of the government. In 1931, the Indian National Congress (the largest Indian political party of the time) adopted resolutions committing itself to the defense of fundamental civil rights, as well as socio-economic rights such as the minimum wage and the abolition of untouchability and serfdom. Committing themselves to socialism in 1936, the Congress leaders took examples from the constitution of the erstwhile USSR, which inspired the fundamental duties of citizens as a means of collective patriotic responsibility for national interests and challenges.

When India obtained independence on 15 August 1947, the task of developing a constitution for the nation was undertaken by the Constituent Assembly of India, composing of elected representatives under the presidency of Rajendra Prasad. While members of Congress composed of a large majority, Congress leaders appointed persons from diverse political backgrounds to responsibilities of developing the constitution and national laws. Notably, Bhimrao Ramji Ambedkar became the chairperson of the drafting committee, while Jawaharlal Nehru and Sardar Vallabhbhai Patel became chairpersons of committees and sub-committees responsible for different subjects. A notable development during that period having significant effect on the Indian constitution took place on 10 December 1948 when the United Nations General Assembly adopted the Universal Declaration of Human Rights and called upon all member states to adopt these rights in their respective constitutions.

The Fundamental Rights were included in the Ist Draft Constitution (February 1948), the IInd Draft Constitution (17 October 1948) and the IIIrd and final Draft Constitution (26 November 1949), being prepared by the Drafting Committee.

Significance and Characteristics

The Fundamental Rights were included in the constitution because they were considered essential for the development of the personality of every individual and to preserve human dignity. The writers of the constitution regarded democracy of no avail if civil liberties, like freedom of speech and religion were not recognized and protected by the State. According to them, "democracy" is, in essence, a government by opinion and therefore, the means of formulating public opinion should be secured to the people of a democratic nation. For this purpose, the constitution guaranteed to all the citizens of India the freedom of speech and expression and various other freedoms in the form of the Fundamental Rights.

All people, irrespective of race, religion, caste or sex, have been given the right to move the Supreme Court and the High Courts for the enforcement of their Fundamental Rights. It is not necessary that the aggrieved party has to be the one to do so. Poverty stricken people may not have the means to do so and therefore, in the public interest, anyone can commence litigation in the court on their behalf. This is known as "Public interest litigation". In some cases, High Court judges have acted on their own on the basis of newspaper reports.

These Fundamental Rights help not only in protection but also the prevention of gross violations of human rights. They emphasize on the fundamental unity of India by guaranteeing to all citizens the access and use of the same facilities, irrespective of background. Some Fundamental Rights apply for persons of any nationality whereas others are available only to the citizens of India. The right to life and personal liberty is available to all people and so is the right to freedom of religion. On the other hand, freedoms of speech and expression and freedom to reside and settle in any part of the country are reserved to citizens alone, including non-resident Indian citizens. The right to equality in matters of public employment cannot be conferred to overseas citizens of India.

Fundamental rights primarily protect individuals from any arbitrary state actions, but some rights are enforceable against individuals. For instance, the Constitution abolishes untouchability and also prohibits *begar*. These provisions act as a check both on state action as well as the action of private individuals.

However, these rights are not absolute or uncontrolled and are subject to reasonable restrictions as necessary for the protection of general welfare. They can also be selectively curtailed. The Supreme Court has ruled that all provisions of the Constitution, including Fundamental Rights can be amended. However, the Parliament cannot alter the basic structure of the constitution. Features such as secularism and democracy fall under this category. Since the Fundamental Rights can only be altered by a constitutional amendment, their inclusion is a check not only on the executive branch, but also on the Parliament and state legislatures.

A state of national emergency has an adverse effect on these rights. Under such a state, the rights conferred by Article 19 (freedoms of speech, assembly and movement, etc.) remain suspended. Hence, in such a situation, the legislature may make laws which go against the rights given in Article 19. Also, the President may by order suspend the right to move court for the enforcement of other rights as well.

Right to Equality

Right to equality is an important right provided for in Articles 14, 15, 16, 17 and 18 of the constitution. It is the principal foundation of all other rights and liberties, and guarantees the following:

- *Equality before law:* Article 14 of the constitution guarantees that all citizens shall be equally protected by the laws of the country. It means that the State cannot discriminate against a citizen on the basis of caste, creed, colour, sex, religion or place of birth. According to the *Electricity Act* of 26 January 2003 the Parliament has the power to create special courts for the speedy trial of offences committed by persons holding high offices. Creation of special courts is not a violation of this right.
- *Social equality and equal access to public areas:* Article 15 of the constitution states that no person shall be discriminated on the basis of caste, colour, language etc. Every person shall have equal access to public places like public parks, museums, wells, bathing ghats and temples etc. However, the State may make any special provision for women and children. Special provisions may be made for the advancements of any socially or educationally backward class or scheduled castes or scheduled tribes.
- *Equality in matters of public employment:* Article 16 of the constitution lays down that the State cannot discriminate against anyone in the matters of employment. All citizens can apply for government jobs. There are some exceptions. The Parliament may enact a law stating that certain jobs can only be filled by applicants who are domiciled in the area. This may be meant for posts that require knowledge of the locality and language of the area. The State may also reserve posts for members of backward classes, scheduled castes or scheduled tribes which are not adequately represented in the services under the State to bring up the weaker sections of the society. Also, there a law

may be passed which requires that the holder of an office of any religious institution shall also be a person professing that particular religion. According to the *Citizenship (Amendment) Bill*, 2003, this right shall not be conferred to Overseas citizens of India.

- *Abolition of untouchability:* Article 17 of the constitution abolishes the practice of untouchability. Practice of untouchability is an offense and anyone doing so is punishable by law. The *Untouchability Offences Act* of 1955 (renamed to *Protection of Civil Rights Act* in 1976) provided penalties for preventing a person from entering a place of worship or from taking water from a tank or well.
- *Abolition of Titles:* Article 18 of the constitution prohibits the State from conferring any titles. Citizens of India cannot accept titles from a foreign State. The British government had created an aristocratic class known as *Rai Bahadurs* and *Khan Bahadurs* in India — these titles were also abolished. However, Military and academic distinctions can be conferred on the citizens of India. The awards of *Bharat Ratna* and *Padma Vibhushan* cannot be used by the recipient as a title and do not, accordingly, come within the constitutional prohibition". The Supreme Court, on 15 December 1995, upheld the validity of such awards.

Right to Freedom

The Constitution of India contains the right to freedom, given in articles 19, 20, 21 and 22, with the view of guaranteeing individual rights that were considered vital by the framers of the constitution. The right to freedom in Article 19 guarantees the following six freedoms:

- Freedom of speech and expression, which enable an individual to participate in public activities. The phrase, "freedom of press" has not been used in Article 19, but freedom of expression includes freedom of press. Reasonable restrictions can be imposed in the interest of public order, security of State, decency or morality.

- Freedom to assemble peacefully without arms, on which the State can impose reasonable restrictions in the interest of public order and the sovereignty and integrity of India.
- Freedom to form associations or unions on which the State can impose reasonable restrictions on this freedom in the interest of public order, morality and the sovereignty and integrity of India.
- Freedom to move freely throughout the territory of India though reasonable restrictions can be imposed on this right in the interest of the general public, for example, restrictions may be imposed on movement and travelling, so as to control epidemics.
- Freedom to reside and settle in any part of the territory of India which is also subject to reasonable restrictions by the State in the interest of the general public or for the protection of the scheduled tribes because certain safeguards as are envisaged here seem to be justified to protect indigenous and tribal peoples from exploitation and coercion.
- Freedom to practice any profession or to carry on any occupation, trade or business on which the State may impose reasonable restrictions in the interest of the general public. Thus, there is no right to carry on a business which is dangerous or immoral. Also, professional or technical qualifications may be prescribed for practicing any profession or carrying on any trade.

The constitution also guarantees the right to life and personal liberty, which in turn cites specific provisions in which these rights are applied and enforced:

- Protection with respect to conviction for offences is guaranteed in the right to life and personal liberty. According to Article 20, no one can be awarded punishment which is more than what the law of the land prescribes at that time. This legal axiom is based on the principle that no criminal law can be made retrospective, that is, for an act to become an offence, the essential condition is that it should have been an offence legally at the time of committing it. Moreover, no person accused of any offence shall be compelled to be a witness against himself. "Compulsion" in this article refers to what in law is called "Duress" (injury, beating or unlawful imprisonment to make a person do something that he does not want to do). This article is known as a safeguard against self incrimination. The other principle enshrined in this article is known as the principle of double jeopardy, that is, no person can be convicted twice for the same offence, which has been derived from Anglo Saxon law. This principle was first established in the Magna Carta.

- Protection of life and personal liberty is also stated under right to life and personal liberty. Article 21 declares that no citizen can be denied his life and liberty except by law. This means that a person's life and personal liberty can only be disputed if that person has committed a crime. However, the right to life does not include the right to die, and hence, suicide or an attempt thereof, is an offence. (Attempted suicide being interpreted as a crime has seen many debates. The Supreme Court of India gave a landmark ruling in the year 1994. The court repealed section 309 of the Indian penal code, under which people attempting suicide could face prosecution and prison terms of up to one year. In the year 1996 however another Supreme Court ruling nullified the earlier one.) "Personal liberty" includes all the freedoms which are not included in Article 19 (that is, the six freedoms). The right to travel abroad is also covered under "personal liberty" in Article 21.
- In 2002, through the 86th Amendment Act, Article 21(A) was incorporated. It made the right to primary education part of the right to freedom, stating that the State would provide free and compulsory education to children from six to fourteen years of age. Six years after an amendment was made in the Indian

Constitution, the union cabinet cleared the Right to Education Bill in 2008. It is now soon to be tabled in Parliament for approval before it makes a fundamental right of every child to get free and compulsory education.

- Rights of a person arrested under ordinary circumstances is laid down in the right to life and personal liberty. No one can be arrested without being told the grounds for his arrest. If arrested the person has the right to defend himself by a lawyer of his choice. Also an arrested citizen has to be brought before the nearest magistrate within 24 hours. The rights of a person arrested under ordinary circumstances are not available to an enemy alien. They are also not available to persons detained under the *Preventive Detention Act*. Under preventive detention, the government can imprison a person for a maximum of three months. It means that if the government feels that a person being at liberty can be a threat to the law and order or to the unity and integrity of the nation, it can detain or arrest that person to prevent him from doing this possible harm. After three months such a case is brought before an advisory board for review.

The constitution also imposes restrictions on these rights. The government restricts these freedoms in the interest of the independence, sovereignty and integrity of India. In the interest of morality and public order, the government can also impose restrictions. However, the right to life and personal liberty cannot be suspended. The six freedoms are also automatically suspended or have restrictions imposed on them during a state of emergency.

Right against Exploitation

Child labour and Begar is prohibited under Right against exploitation.

The right against exploitation, given in Articles 23 and 24, provides for two provisions, namely the abolition of trafficking in human beings and *Begar* (forced labor), and abolition of employment of children below the age of 14 years in dangerous jobs like factories and mines. Child labour is considered a gross violation of the spirit and provisions of the constitution. *Begar*, practised in the past by landlords, has been declared a crime and is punishable by law. Trafficking in humans for the purpose of slave trade or prostitution is also prohibited by law. An exception is made in employment without payment for compulsory services for public purposes. Compulsory military conscription is covered by this provision.

Right to Freedom of Religion

Right to freedom of religion, covered in Articles 25, 26, 27 and 28, provides religious freedom to all citizens of India. The objective of this right is to sustain the principle of secularism in India. According to the Constitution, all religions are equal before the State and no religion shall be given preference over the other. Citizens are free to preach, practice and propagate any religion of their choice. However, certain practices like wearing and carrying of *Kirpans* in the profession of the Sikh religion, can be restricted in the interest of public order, morality and health.

Religious communities can set up charitable institutions of their own. However, activities in such institutions which are not religious are performed according to the laws laid down by the government. Establishing a charitable institution can also be restricted in the interest of public order, morality and health. No person shall be compelled to pay taxes for the promotion of a particular religion. A State run institution cannot impart education that is pro-religion. Also, nothing in this article shall affect the operation of any existing law or prevent the State from making any further law regulating or restricting any economic, financial, political or other secular activity which may be associated with religious practice, or providing for social welfare and reform.

Cultural and Educational Rights

The Flag of India: As India is a country of many languages, religions, and cultures, the Constitution provides special measures, in Articles 29 and 30, to protect the rights of the minorities. Any community which has a language and a script of its own has the right to conserve and develop them. No citizen can be discriminated against for admission in State or State aided institutions.

All minorities, religious or linguistic, can set up their own educational institutions in order to preserve and develop their own culture. In granting aid to institutions, the State cannot discriminate against any institution on the basis of the fact that it is administered by a minority institution. But the right to administer does not mean that the State can not interfere in case of maladministration. In a precedent-setting judgment in 1980, the Supreme Court held that "the State can certainly take regulatory measures to promote the efficiency and excellence of educational standards. It can also issue guidelines for ensuring the security of the services of the teachers or other employees of the institution. In another landmark judgement delivered on 31 October 2002, the Supreme Court ruled that in case of aided minority institutions offering professional courses, admission could only be through a common entrance test conducted by State or a university. Even an unaided minority institution ought not to ignore the merit of the students for admission.

Right to Constitutional Remedies

Right to constitutional remedies empowers the citizens to move a court of law in case of any denial of the fundamental rights. For instance, in case of imprisonment, the citizen can ask the court to see if it is according to the provisions of the law of the country. If the court finds that it is not, the person will have to be freed. This procedure of asking the courts to preserve or safeguard the citizens' fundamental rights can be done in various ways. The courts can issue various kinds of *writs*. These writs are *habeas corpus*, *mandamus*, *prohibition*, *quo warranto* and *certiorari*. When a national or state emergency is declared, this right is suspended by the central government.

Right to Property—A Former Fundamental Right

The Constitution originally provided for the right to property under Articles 19 and 31. Article 19 guaranteed to all citizens the right to acquire, hold and dispose off property. Article 31 provided that "no person shall be deprived of his property save by authority of law." It also provided that compensation would be paid to a person whose property has been taken for public purposes.

The provisions relating to the right to property were changed a number of times. The 44th amendment act of 1978 deleted the right to property from the list of Fundamental Rights. A new article, Article 300-A, was added to the constitution which provided that "no person shall be deprived of his property save by authority of law". Thus if a legislature makes a law depriving a person of his property, there would be no obligation on the part of the State to pay anything as compensation. The aggrieved person shall have no right to move the court under Article 32. Thus, the right to property is no longer a fundamental right, though it is still a constitutional right. If the government appears to have acted unfairly, the action can be challenged in a court of law by citizens.

- *Revival :* With the Liberalization of the economy and govt's initiative to setup special economic zones has led to many protest by farmers and have thrown the fundamental right to private property reinstatement. The supreme Court has sent a notice to the govt questioning why the right shouldn't be brought back as in 2007 The supreme court unanimously said that the fundamental rights are a basic structure of the constitution and cannot be removed or diluted.

Critical Analysis

The Fundamental Rights have been criticised for many reasons. Political groups have demanded that the right to work, the right to economic assistance in case of unemployment, old age, and similar rights be enshrined as constitutional guarantees to address issues of poverty and economic insecurity, though these provisions have been enshrined in the Directive Principles of state policy. The right to freedom and personal liberty has a number of limiting clauses, and thus have been criticized for failing to check the sanctioning of powers often deemed "excessive". There is also the provision of preventive detention and suspension of Fundamental Rights in times of Emergency. The provisions of acts like the Maintenance of Internal Security Act (MISA) and the National Security Act (NSA) are a means of countering the fundamental rights, because they sanction excessive powers with the aim of fighting internal and cross-border terrorism and political violence, without safeguards for civil rights. The phrases "security of State", "public order" and "morality" are of wide implication. People of alternate sexuality is criminalized in India with prison term up to 10 years. The meaning of phrases like "reasonable restrictions" and "the interest of public order" have not been explicitly stated in the constitution, and this ambiguity leads to unnecessary litigation. The freedom to assemble peacably and without arms is exercised, but in some cases, these meetings are broken up by the police through the use of non-fatal methods.

"Freedom of press" has not been included in the right to freedom, which is necessary for formulating public opinion and to make freedom of expression more legitimate. Employment of child labour in hazardous job environments has been reduced, but their employment even in non-hazardous jobs, including their prevalent employment as domestic help violates the spirit and ideals of the constitution. More than 16.5 million children are employed and working in India. India was ranked 88 out of 159 in 2005, according to the degree to which corruption is perceived to exist among public officials and politicians worldwide. The right to equality in matters regarding public employment shall not be conferred to Overseas citizens of India, according to the *Citizenship (Amendment) Bill*, 2003.

Amendments

Changes in Fundamental Rights require a Constitutional amendment which has to be passed by a special majority of both houses of the Parliament. This means that an amendment requires the approval of two-thirds of the members present and voting. However, the number of members voting should not be less than the simple majority of the house — whether the Lok Sabha or Rajya Sabha.

- The right to property was originally included as a fundamental right. However, the 44th Amendment passed in 1978, revised the status of property rights by stating that "No person shall be deprived of his property save by authority of law" to further the goals of socialism.
- The right to education at elementary level has been made one of the Fundamental Rights under right to life and personal liberty by the 86th constitutional amendment of 2002.

Directive Principles in India

The **Directive Principles of State Policy** are guidelines to the central and state governments of India, to be kept in mind while framing laws and policies. These provisions, contained in Part IV of the Constitution of India, are not enforceable by any court, but the principles laid down therein are considered fundamental in the governance of the country, making it the duty of the State to apply these principles in making laws to establish a just society in the country. The principles have been inspired by the Directive Principles given in the Constitution of Ireland and also by the principles of Gandhism; and relate to social justice, economic welfare, foreign policy, and legal and administrative matters.

Directive Principles are classified under the following categories: Gandhian, economic and socialistic, political and administrative, justice and legal, environmental, protection of monuments and peace and security.

History

The concept of Directive Principles of State Policy was borrowed from the Irish Constitution. The makers of the Constitution of India were influenced by the Irish nationalist movement. Hence, the Directive Principles of the Indian constitution have been greatly influenced by the Directive Principles of State Policy. The idea of such policies "can be traced to the Declaration of the Rights of Man proclaimed Revolutionary France and the Declaration of Independence by the American Colonies." The Indian constitution was also influenced by the United Nations Universal Declaration of Human Rights.

In 1919, the Rowlatt Acts gave extensive powers to the British government and police, and allowed indefinite arrest and detention of individuals, warrant-less searches and seizures, restrictions on public gatherings, and intensive censorship of media and publications. The public opposition to this act eventually led to mass campaigns of non-violent civil disobedience throughout the country demanding guaranteed civil freedoms, and limitations on government power. Indians, who were seeking independence and their own government, were particularly influenced by the independence of Ireland and the development of the Irish constitution. Also, the directive principles of state policy in Irish constitution were looked upon by the people of India as an inspiration for the independent India's government to comprehensively tackle complex social and economic challenges across a vast, diverse nation and population.

In 1928, the Nehru Commission composing of representatives of Indian political parties proposed constitutional reforms for India that apart from calling for dominion status for India and elections under universal suffrage, would guarantee rights deemed fundamental, representation for religious and ethnic minorities, and limit the powers of the government. In 1931, the Indian National Congress (the largest Indian political party of the time) adopted resolutions committing itself to the defense of fundamental civil rights, as well as socio-economic rights such as the minimum wage and the abolition of untouchability and serfdom. Committing themselves to socialism in 1936, the Congress leaders took examples from the constitution of the erstwhile USSR, which inspired the fundamental duties of citizens as a means of collective patriotic responsibility for national interests and challenges.

When India obtained independence on 15 August 1947, the task of developing a constitution for the nation was undertaken by the Constituent Assembly of India, composing of elected representatives under the presidency of Dr. Rajendra Prasad.

While members of Congress composed of a large majority, Congress leaders appointed persons from diverse political backgrounds to responsibilities of developing the constitution and national laws. Notably, Bhimrao Ramji Ambedkar became the chairperson of the drafting committee, while Jawaharlal Nehru and Sardar Vallabhbhai Patel became chairpersons of committees and sub-committees responsible for different subjects. A notable development during that period having significant effect on the Indian constitution took place on 10 December 1948 when the United Nations General Assembly adopted the Universal Declaration of Human Rights and called upon all member states to adopt these rights in their respective constitutions.

Both the Fundamental Rights and the Directive Principles of State Policy were included in the I Draft Constitution (February 1948), the II Draft Constitution (17 October 1948) and the III and final Draft Constitution (26 November 1949), being prepared by the Drafting Committee.

Characteristics

DPSPs aim to create social and economic conditions under which the citizens can lead a good life. They also aim to establish social and economic democracy through a welfare state. They act as a check on the government, theorized as a yardstick in the hands of the people to measure the performance of the government and vote it out of power if it does not fulfill the promises made during the elections. The Directive Principles are non-justiciable rights of the people. Article 31-C, inserted by the 25th Amendment Act of 1971 seeks to upgrade the Directive Principles. If laws are made to give effect to the Directive Principles over Fundamental Rights, they shall not be invalid on the grounds that they take away the Fundamental Rights. In case of a conflict between Fundamental Rights and DPSP's, if the DPSP aims at promoting larger interest of the society, the courts shall have to uphold the case in favour of the DPSP. The Directive Principles, though not justiciable, are fundamental in the governance of the country. It shall be the duty of the State to apply these principles in making laws. Besides, all executive agencies should also be guided by these principles. Even the judiciary has to keep them in mind in deciding cases.

Directives

The directive principles ensure that the State shall strive to promote the welfare of the people by promoting a social order in which social, economic and political justice is informed in all institutions of life. Also, the State shall work towards reducing economic inequality as well as inequalities in status and opportunities, not only among individuals, but also among groups of people residing in different areas or engaged in different vocations. The State shall aim for securing right to an adequate means of livelihood for all citizens, both men and women as well as equal pay for equal work for both men and women.

The State should work to prevent concentration of wealth and means of production in a few hands, and try to ensure that ownership and control of the material resources is distributed to best serve the common good. Child abuse and exploitation of workers should be prevented. Children should be allowed to develop in a healthy manner and should be protected against exploitation and against moral and material abandonment. The State shall provide free legal aid to ensure that equal opportunities for securing justice is ensured to all, and is not denied by reason of economic or other disabilities. The State shall also work for organisation of village panchayats and help enable them to function as units of self-government. The State shall endeavour to provide the right to work, to education and to public assistance in cases of unemployment, old age, sickness and disablement, within the limits of economic capacity, as well as provide for just and humane conditions of work and maternity relief.

The State should also ensure living wage and proper working conditions for workers, with full enjoyment of leisure and social and cultural activities. Also, the promotion of cottage industries in rural areas is one of the obligations of the State. The State shall take steps to promote their participation in management of industrial undertakings.

Also, the State shall endeavour to secure a uniform civil code for all citizens, and provide free and compulsory education to all children till they attain the age of 14 years. This directive regarding education of children was added by the 86th Amendment Act, 2002. It should and work for the economic and educational upliftment of scheduled castes, scheduled tribes and other weaker sections of the society.

The directive principles commit the State to raise the level of nutrition and the standard of living and to improve public health, particularly by prohibiting intoxicating drinks and drugs injurious to health except for medicinal purposes. It should also organise agriculture and animal husbandry on modern and scientific lines by improving breeds and prohibiting slaughter of cows, calves, other milch and draught cattle It should protect and improve the environment and safeguard the forests and wild life of the country. This directive, regarding protection of forests and wildlife was added by the 42nd Amendment Act, 1976.

Protection of monuments, places and objects of historic and artistic interest and national importance against destruction and damage, and separation of judiciary from executive in public services are also the obligations of the State as laid down in the directive principles. Finally, the directive principles, in Article 51 ensure that the State shall strive for the promotion and maintenance of international peace and security, just and honourable relations between nations, respect for international law and treaty obligations, as well as settlement of international disputes by arbitration.

Implementation

The State has made many efforts to implement the **Directive Principles**. The Programme of Universalisation of Elementary Education and the five year plans has been accorded the highest priority in order to provide free education to all children up to the age of 14 years. The 86th constitutional amendment of 2002 inserted a new article, Article 21-A, into the Constitution, that seeks to provide free and compulsory education to all children aged 6 to 14 years. Welfare schemes for the weaker sections are being implemented both by the Central and state governments. These include programmes such as boys' and girls' hostels for scheduled castes' or scheduled tribes' students. The year 1990-1991 was declared as the "Year of Social Justice" in the memory of B.R. Ambedkar. The government provides free textbooks to students belonging to scheduled castes or scheduled tribes pursuing medicine and engineering courses. During 2002-2003, a sum of Rs. 4.77 crore was released for this purpose. In order that scheduled castes and scheduled tribes are protected from atrocities, the Government enacted the *Prevention of Atrocities Act* in 1995, which provided severe punishments for such atrocities.

Several Land Reform Acts were enacted to provide ownership rights to poor farmers. Up to September 2001, more than 20,000,000 acres (80,000 km^2) of land had been distributed to scheduled castes, scheduled tribes and the landless poor. The thrust of banking policy in India has been to improve banking facilities in the rural areas. The *Minimum Wages Act* of 1948 empowers government to fix minimum wages for employees engaged in various employments. The *Consumer Protection Act* of 1986 provides for the better protection of consumers. The act is intended to provide simple, speedy and inexpensive redressal to the consumers' grievances, award relief and compensation wherever appropriate to the consumer. The *Equal Remuneration Act* of 1976, provides for equal pay for equal work for both men and women. The *Sampoorna Grameen Rozgar Yojana* was launched in 2001 to attain the objective of gainful employment for the rural poor. The programme was implemented through the Panchayati Raj institutions.

Panchayati Raj now covers almost all states and Union territories. One-third of the total number of seats have been reserved for women in Panchayats at every level; in the case of Bihar, half the seats have been reserved for women. Legal aid at the expense of the State has been made compulsory in all cases pertaining to criminal law, if the accused is too poor to engage a lawyer. Judiciary has been separated from the executive in all the states and Union territories except Jammu and Kashmir and Nagaland.

India's Foreign Policy has also to some degree been influenced by the DPSPs. India has in the past condemned all acts of aggression and has also supported the United Nations' peace-keeping activities. By 2004, the Indian Army had participated in 37 UN peace-keeping operations. India played a key role in the passing of a UN resolution in 2003, which envisaged better cooperation between the Security Council and the troop-contributing countries. India has also been in favour of nuclear disarmament.

Amendments

Changes in Directive Principles require a Constitutional amendment which has to be passed by a special majority of both houses of the Parliament. This means that an amendment requires the approval of two-thirds of the members present and voting. However, the number of members voting should not be less than the simple majority of the house — whether the Lok Sabha or Rajya Sabha.

- **Article 31-C**, inserted into the Directive Principles of State Policy by the 25th Amendment Act of 1971 seeks to upgrade the DPSPs. If laws are made to give effect to the Directive Principles over Fundamental Rights, they shall not be invalid on the grounds that they take away the Fundamental Rights.
- **Article 45**, which ensures *Provision for free and compulsory education for children*, was added by the 86th Amendment Act, 2002.
- **Article 48-A**, which ensures *Protection and improvement of environment and safeguarding of forests and wild life*, was added by the 42nd Amendment Act, 1976.

Unit-IV

Human Rights : International Machanism

International Councils and Commission on Human Rights—International Court of Justice

The **International Court of Justice** (French: *Cour internationale de justice*; commonly referred to as the **World Court** or **ICJ**) is the primary judicial organ of the United Nations. It is based in the Peace Palace in The Hague, Netherlands. Its main functions are to settle legal disputes submitted to it by states and to give advisory opinions on legal questions submitted to it by duly authorized international organs, agencies, and the UN General Assembly. The ICJ should not be confused with the International Criminal Court, which also potentially has "global" jurisdiction.

Activities

Established in 1945 by the UN Charter, the Court began work in 1946 as the successor to the Permanent Court of International Justice. The Statute of the International Court of Justice, similar to that of its predecessor, is the main constitutional document constituting and regulating the Court.

The Court's workload is characterised by a wide range of judicial activity. The ICJ has dealt with relatively few cases in its history, but there has clearly been an increased willingness to use the Court since the 1980s, especially among developing countries. The United States withdrew from compulsory jurisdiction in 1986, and so accepts the court's jurisdiction only on a case-to-case basis. Chapter XIV of the United Nations Charter authorizes the UN Security Council to enforce World Court rulings, but such enforcement is subject to the veto power of the five permanent members of the Council. Presently there are twelve cases on the World Court's docket.

Composition

The ICJ is composed of fifteen judges elected to nine year terms by the UN General Assembly and the UN Security Council from a list of persons nominated by the national groups in the Permanent Court of Arbitration. The election process is set out in Articles 4–12 of the ICJ statute. Judges serve for nine year terms and may be re-elected for up to two further terms. Elections take place every three years, with one-third of the judges retiring (and possibly standing for re-election) each time, in order to ensure continuity within the court.

Should a judge die in office, the practice has generally been to elect a judge of the same nationality to complete the term. No two may be nationals of the same country. According to Article 9, the membership of the Court is supposed to represent the "main forms of civilization and of the principal legal systems of the world". Essentially, this has meant common law, civil law and socialist law (now post-communist law). Since the 1960s four of the five permanent members of the Security Council (France, Russia, the United Kingdom, and the United States) have always had a judge on the Court. The exception was China (the Republic of China until 1971, the People's Republic of China from 1971 onwards), which did not have a judge on the Court from 1967–1985, because it did not put forward a candidate. The rule on a geopolitical composition of the bench exists despite the fact that there is no provision for it in the Statute of the ICJ.

Article 2 of the Statute provides that all judges should be "elected regardless of their nationality among persons of high moral character", who are either qualified for the highest judicial office in their home states or known as lawyers with sufficient competence in international law. Judicial independence is dealt specifically with in Articles 16-18. Judges of the ICJ are not able to hold any other post, nor act as counsel. In practice the Members of the Court have their own interpretation of these rules. This allows them to be involved in outside arbitration and hold professional posts as long as there is no conflict of interest.

A judge can be dismissed only by a unanimous vote of other members of the Court. Despite these provisions, the independence of ICJ judges has been questioned. For example, during the *Nicaragua Case*, the USA issued a communique suggesting that it could not present sensitive material to the Court because of the presence of judges from Eastern bloc states. Judges may deliver joint judgments or give their own separate opinions. Decisions and Advisory Opinions are by majority and, in the event of an equal division, the President's vote becomes decisive. Judges may also deliver separate dissenting opinions.

Ad hoc Judges

Article 31 of the statute sets out a procedure whereby *ad hoc* judges sit on contentious cases before the Court. This system allows any party to a contentious case to nominate a judge of their choice (usually of their nationality), if a judge of their nationality is not already on the bench. *Ad hoc* judges participate fully in the case and the deliberations, along with the permanent bench. Thus, it is possible that as many as seventeen judges may sit on one case.

This system may seem strange when compared with domestic court processes, but its purpose is to encourage states to submit cases to the Court. For example, if a state knows it will have a judicial officer who can participate in deliberation and offer other judges local knowledge and an understanding of the state's perspective, that state may be more willing to submit to the Court's jurisdiction. Although this system does not sit well with the judicial nature of the body, it is usually of little practical consequence. *Ad hoc* judges usually (but not always) vote in favour of the state that appointed them and thus cancel each other out.

Chambers

Generally, the Court sits as full bench, but in the last fifteen years it has on occasion sat as a chamber. Articles 26-29 of the statute allow the Court to form smaller chambers, usually 3 or 5 judges, to hear cases. Two types of chambers are contemplated by Article 26: firstly, chambers for special categories of cases, and second, the formation of *ad hoc* chambers to hear particular disputes. In 1993 a special chamber was established, under Article 26(1) of the ICJ statute, to deal specifically with environmental matters (although this chamber has never been used).

Ad hoc chambers are more frequently convened. For example, chambers were used to hear the *Gulf of Maine Case* (USA v Canada). In that case, the parties made clear they would withdraw the case unless the Court appointed judges to the chamber who were acceptable to the parties. Judgments of chambers may have less authority than full Court judgments, or may diminish the proper interpretation of universal international law informed by a variety of cultural and legal perspectives. On the other hand, the use of chambers might encourage greater recourse to the Court and thus enhance international dispute resolution.

Current Composition

As of 6 February 2009, the composition of the Court is as follows:

Name	Country	Position	Elected	Term End
Hisashi Owada	Japan	President	2003	2012
Peter Tomka	Slovakia	Vice-President	2003	2012
Shi Jiuyong	China	Member	1994, 2003	2012
Abdul G. Koroma	Sierra Leone	Member	1994, 2003	2012
Awn Shawkat Al-Khasawneh	Jordan	Member	2000, 2009	2018
Thomas Buergenthal	United States	Member	2000, 2006	2015
Bruno Simma	Germany	Member	2003	2012
Ronny Abraham	France	Member	2005, 2009	2018
Sir Kenneth Keith	New Zealand	Member	2006	2015
Bernardo Sepúlveda Amor	Mexico	Member	2006	2015
Mohamed Bennouna	Morocco	Member	2006	2015
Leonid Skotnikov	Russia	Member	2006	2015
Antônio Augusto Cançado Trindade	Brazil	Member	2009	2018
Abdulqawi Yusuf	Somalia	Member	2009	2018
Christopher John Greenwood	United Kingdom	Member	2009	2018

Results of the last election of 6 November 2008:

- Re-elected were France's Ronny Abraham and Awn Shawkat Al-Khasawneh (terms expire on 5 February 2009), while UK's Christopher Greenwood, Brazil's Antonio Augusto Cancado Trindade and Somalia's Abdulqawi Yusuf (terms begin on 6 February 2009) were newly elected.
- The declared candidates Sayeman Bula-Bula (Democratic Republic of the Congo), Miriam Defensor-Santiago (Philippines) and Maurice Kamto (Cameroon) lost in the final voting. The 3 new judges replaced UK's Rosalyn Higgins (as ICJ President), Gonzalo Parra Aranguren of Venezuela and Madagascar's Raymond Ranjeva (terms all expire on 5 February 2009).

Jurisdiction

As stated in Article 93 of the UN Charter, all 192 UN members are automatically parties to the Court's statute. Non-UN members may also become parties to the Court's statute under the Article 93(2) procedure. For example, before becoming a UN member state, Switzerland used this procedure in 1948 to become a party. And Nauru became a party in 1988. Once a state is a party to the Court's statute, it is entitled to participate in cases before the Court. However, being a party to the statute does not automatically give the Court jurisdiction over disputes involving those parties. The issue of jurisdiction is considered in the two types of ICJ cases: contentious issues and advisory opinions.

Contentious Issues

In contentious cases (adversarial proceedings seeking to settle a dispute), the ICJ produces a binding ruling between states that agree to submit to the ruling of the court. Only states may be parties in contentious cases. Individuals, corporations, parts of a federal state, NGOs, UN organs and self-determination groups are excluded from direct participation in cases, although the Court may receive information from public international organisations. This does not preclude non-state interests from being the subject of proceedings if one state brings the case against another. For example, a state may, in case of "diplomatic protection", bring a case on behalf of one of its nationals or corporations.

Jurisdiction is often a crucial question for the Court in contentious cases. (See Procedure below.) The key principle is that the ICJ has jurisdiction only on the basis of consent. Article 36 outlines four bases on which the Court's jurisdiction may be founded.

- First, 36(1) provides that parties may refer cases to the Court (jurisdiction founded on "special agreement" or "*compromis*"). This method is based on explicit consent rather than true compulsory jurisdiction. It is, perhaps, the most effective basis for the Court's jurisdiction because the parties concerned have a desire for the dispute to be resolved by the Court and are thus more likely to comply with the Court's judgment.
- Second, 36(1) also gives the Court jurisdiction over "matters specifically provided for ... in treaties and conventions in force". Most modern treaties will contain a compromissory clause, providing for dispute resolution by the ICJ. Cases founded on compromissory clauses have not been as effective as cases founded on special agreement, since a state may have no interest in having the matter examined by the Court and may refuse to comply with a judgment. For example, during the Iran hostage crisis, Iran refused to participate in a case brought by the US based on a compromissory clause contained in the Vienna Convention on Diplomatic Relations, nor did it comply with the judgment. Since the 1970s, the use of such clauses has declined. Many modern treaties set out their own dispute resolution regime, often based on forms of arbitration.
- Third, Article 36(2) allows states to make optional clause declarations accepting the Court's jurisdiction. The label "compulsory" which is sometimes placed on Article 36(2) jurisdiction is misleading since declarations by states

are voluntary. Furthermore, many declarations contain reservations, such as exclusion from jurisdiction certain types of disputes ("*ratione materia*"). The principle of reciprocity may further limit jurisdiction. As of October 2006, sixty-seven states had a declaration in force. Of the permanent Security Council members, only the United Kingdom has a declaration. In the Court's early years, most declarations were made by industrialised countries. Since the *Nicaragua Case*, declarations made by developing countries have increased, reflecting a growing confidence in the Court since the 1980s. Industrialised countries however have sometimes increased exclusions or removed their declarations in recent years. Examples include the USA, as mentioned previously and Australia who modified their declaration in 2002 to exclude disputes on maritime boundaries (most likely to prevent an impending challenge from East Timor who gained their independence two months later).

- Finally, 36(5) provides for jurisdiction on the basis of declarations made under the Permanent Court of International Justice's statute. Article 37 of the Statute similarly transfers jurisdiction under any compromissory clause in a treaty that gave jurisdiction to the PCIJ.
- In addition, the Court may have jurisdiction on the basis of tacit consent (*forum prorogatum*). In the absence of clear jurisdiction under Article 36, jurisdiction will be established if the respondent accepts ICJ jurisdiction explicitly or simply pleads on the merits. The notion arose in the *Corfu Channel Case* (UK v Albania) (1949) in which the Court held that a letter from Albania stating that it submitted to the jurisdiction of the ICJ was sufficient to grant the court jurisdiction.

Advisory Opinion

An advisory opinion is a function of the Court open only to specified United Nations bodies and agencies. On receiving a request, the Court decides which States and organizations might provide useful information and gives them an opportunity to present written or oral statements. Advisory Opinions were intended as a means by which UN agencies could seek the Court's help in deciding complex legal issues that might fall under their respective mandates. In principle, the Court's advisory opinions are only consultative in character, though they are influential and widely respected. Whilst certain instruments or regulations can provide in advance that the advisory opinion shall be specifically binding on particular agencies or states, they are inherently non-binding under the Statute of the Court.

This non-binding character does not mean that advisory opinions are without legal effect, because the legal reasoning embodied in them reflects the Court's authoritative views on important issues of international law and, in arriving at them, the Court follows essentially the same rules and procedures that govern its binding judgments delivered in contentious cases submitted to it by sovereign states. An advisory opinion derives its status and authority from the fact that it is the official pronouncement of the principal judicial organ of the United Nations.

Advisory Opinions have often been controversial, either because the questions asked are controversial, or because the case was pursued as an indirect "backdoor" way of bringing what is really a contentious case before the Court. Examples of advisory opinions can be found in the section advisory opinions in the List of International Court of Justice cases article. One such well-known advisory opinion is the *Nuclear Weapons Case*.

The ICJ and the Security Council

Article 94 establishes the duty of all UN members to comply with decisions of the Court involving them. If parties do not comply, the issue may be taken before the Security Council for enforcement action. There are obvious problems with such a method of enforcement. If the judgment is against one of the permanent five members of the Security Council or its allies, any resolution on enforcement would then be vetoed. This occurred, for example, after the *Nicaragua* case, when Nicaragua brought the issue of the U.S.'s non-compliance with the Court's decision before the Security Council. Furthermore, if the Security Council refuses to enforce a judgment against any other state, there is no method of forcing the state to comply.

The relationship between the ICJ and the Security Council, and the separation of their powers, was considered by the Court in 1992 in the *Pan Am* case. The Court had to consider an application from Libya for the order of provisional measures to protect its rights, which, it alleged, were being infringed by the threat of economic sanctions by the United Kingdom and United States. The problem was that these sanctions had been authorised by the Security Council, which resulted with a potential conflict between the Chapter VII functions of the Security Council and the judicial function of the Court.

The Court decided, by eleven votes to five, that it could not order the requested provisional measures because the rights claimed by Libya, even if legitimate under the Montreal Convention, prima facie could not be regarded as appropriate since the action was ordered by the Security Council. In accordance with Article 103 of the UN Charter, obligations under the Charter took precedence over other treaty obligations. Nevertheless the Court declared the application admissible in 1998. A decision on the merits has not been given since the parties (United Kingdom, United States and Libya) settled the case out of court in 2003.

There was a marked reluctance on the part of a majority of the Court to become involved in a dispute in such a way as to bring it potentially into conflict with the Council. The Court stated in the *Nicaragua* case that there is no necessary inconsistency between action by the Security Council and adjudication by the ICJ. However, where there is room for conflict, the balance appears to be in favour of the Security Council.

Should either party fail "to perform the obligations incumbent upon it under a judgment rendered by the Court", the Security Council may be called upon to "make recommendations or decide upon measures" if the Security Council deems such actions necessary. In practice, the Court's powers have been limited by the unwillingness of the losing party to abide by the Court's ruling, and by the Security Council's unwillingness to impose consequences. However, in theory, "so far as the parties to the case are concerned, a judgment of the Court is binding, final and without appeal," and "by signing the Charter, a State Member of the United Nations undertakes to comply with any decision of the International Court of Justice in a case to which it is a party."

For example, the United States had previously accepted the Court's compulsory jurisdiction upon its creation in 1946, but in *Nicaragua v. United States* withdrew its acceptance following the Court's judgment in 1984 that called on the U.S. to "cease and to refrain" from the "unlawful use of force" against the government of Nicaragua. The Court ruled (with only the American judge dissenting) that the United States was "in breach of its obligation under the Treaty of Friendship with Nicaragua not to use force against Nicaragua" and ordered the United States to pay war reparations (see note 2).

Examples of contentious cases include:

- A complaint by the United States in 1980 that Iran was detaining American diplomats in Tehran in violation of international law.
- A dispute between Tunisia and Libya over the delimitation of the continental shelf between them.
- A dispute over the course of the maritime boundary dividing the U.S. and Canada in the Gulf of Maine area.
- A complaint by the Federal Republic of Yugoslavia against the member states of the North Atlantic Treaty Organisation regarding their actions in the Kosovo War. This was denied on 15 December 2004 due to lack of jurisdiction, because the FRY was not a party to the ICJ statute at the time it made the application.

Generally, the Court has been most successful resolving border delineation and the use of oceans and waterways. While the Court has, in some instances, resolved claims by one State espoused on behalf of its nationals, the Court has generally refrained from hearing contentious cases that are political in nature, due in part to its lack of enforcement mechanism and its lack of compulsory jurisdiction. The Court has generally found it did not have jurisdiction to hear cases involving the use of force.

Law Applied

When deciding cases, the Court applies international law as summarised in Article 38. Article 38 of the ICJ Statute provides that in arriving at its decisions the Court shall apply international conventions, international custom, and the "general principles of law recognized by civilized nations". It may also refer to academic writing ("the teachings of the most highly qualified publicists of the various nations") and previous judicial decisions to help interpret the law, although the Court is not formally bound by its previous decisions under the doctrine of stare decisis. Article 59 makes clear that the common law notion of precedent or *stare decisis* does not apply to the decisions of the ICJ. The Court's decision binds only the parties to that particular controversy. Under 38(1)(d), however, the Court may consider its own previous decisions. In reality, the ICJ rarely departs from its own previous decisions and treats them as precedent in a way similar to superior courts in common law systems. Additionally, international lawyers commonly operate as though ICJ judgments had precedential value.

If the parties agree, they may also grant the Court the liberty to decide *ex aequo et bono* ("in justice and fairness"), granting the ICJ the freedom to make an equitable decision based on what is fair under the circumstances. This provision has not been used in the Court's history. So far the International Court of Justice has dealt with about 130 cases.

International Criminal Tribunals and Criminal Courts

The United Nations established special international criminal tribunals in Rwanda and Yugoslavia to prosecute those responsible for atrocities during times of war and genocide.

Successful convictions of these political and military leaders are meant to bring justice to victims and to deter others from committing such crimes in the future.

These special tribunals gave impetus to the formation of the International Criminal Court (ICC), finally established in 2003. Unlike the ICC, the special tribunals have limited jurisdictions and do not threaten the possible prosecution of leaders or nationals of powerful countries like the United States.

This section follows important cases in the Yugoslavia and Rwanda tribunals, as well as developments at the Special Courts in Sierra Leone, Lebanon, Cambodia and East Timor. In addition, the page covers discussions about the trials of Saddam Hussein and other top Baath Party officials, as well as the implications for international justice and criminal law.

International Criminal Court

The **International Criminal Court (ICC or ICCt)** is a permanent tribunal to prosecute individuals for genocide, crimes against humanity, war crimes, and the crime of aggression (although it cannot currently exercise jurisdiction over the crime of aggression).

The court came into being on 1 July 2002 — the date its founding treaty, the Rome Statute of the International Criminal Court, entered into force—and it can only prosecute crimes committed on or after that date. The official seat of the court is in The Hague, Netherlands, but its proceedings may take place anywhere.

As of March 2009, 108 states are members of the Court; A further 40 countries have signed but not ratified the Rome Statute. However, a number of states, including China, Russia, India and the United States, are critical of the court and have not joined.

The ICC can generally exercise jurisdiction only in cases where the accused is a national of a state party, the alleged crime took place on the territory of a state party, or a situation is referred to the court by the United Nations Security Council. The court is designed to complement existing national judicial systems: it can exercise its jurisdiction only when national courts are unwilling or unable to investigate or prosecute such crimes. Primary responsibility to investigate and punish crimes is therefore left to individual states.

To date, the court has opened investigations into four situations: Northern Uganda, the Democratic Republic of the Congo, the Central African Republic and Darfur. The court has issued public arrest warrants for thirteen people; seven of them remain free, two have died, and four are in custody. The ICC's first trial, of Congolese militia leader Thomas Lubanga, began on 26 January 2009.

History

In 1948, following the Nuremberg and Tokyo Tribunals, the United Nations General Assembly recognised the need for a permanent international court to deal with atrocities of the kind committed during World War II. At the request of the General Assembly, the International Law Commission drafted two draft statutes by the early 1950s but these were shelved as the Cold War made the establishment of an international criminal court politically unrealistic.

Benjamin B. Ferencz, an investigator of Nazi war crimes after World War II and the Chief Prosecutor for the United States Army at the Einsatzgruppen Trial, one of the twelve military trials held by the U.S. authorities at Nuremberg, later became a vocal advocate of the establishment of an international rule of law and of an International Criminal Court. In his first book published in 1975, entitled *Defining International Aggression-The Search for World Peace*, he argued for the establishment of such an international court.

The idea was revived in 1989 when A. N. R. Robinson, then Prime Minister of Trinidad and Tobago, proposed the creation of a permanent international court to deal with the illegal drug trade. While work began on a draft statute, the international community established *ad hoc* tribunals to try war crimes in the former Yugoslavia and Rwanda, further highlighting the need for a permanent international criminal court.

Following years of negotiations, the General Assembly convened a conference in Rome in June 1998, with the aim of finalising a treaty. On 17 July 1998, the Rome Statute of the International Criminal Court was adopted by a vote of 120 to 7, with 21 countries abstaining. The seven countries that voted against the treaty were China, Iraq, Israel, Libya, Qatar, the United States, and Yemen.

The Rome Statute became a binding treaty on 11 April 2002, when the number of countries that had ratified it reached 60. The Statute legally came into force on 1 July 2002, and the ICC can only prosecute crimes committed after that date. The first bench of 18 judges was elected by an Assembly of States Parties in February 2003. They were sworn in at the inaugural session of the court on 1 March 2003. The court issued its first arrest warrants on 8 July 2005, and the first pre-trial hearings were held in 2006.

Membership

As of March 2009, 108 countries have joined the court, including nearly all of Europe and South America, and roughly half the countries in Africa. However, these countries only account for a minority of the world's population.

A further 40 states have signed but not ratified the Rome Statute; the law of treaties obliges these states to refrain from "acts which would defeat the object and purpose" of the treaty. In 2002, two of these states, the United States and Israel, "unsigned" the Rome Statute, indicating that they no longer intend to become states parties and, as such, they have no legal obligations arising from their signature of the statute.

Jurisdiction

Crimes within the Jurisdiction of the Court: Article 5 of the Rome Statute grants the court jurisdiction over four groups of crimes, which it refers to as the "most serious crimes of concern to the international community as a whole": the crime of genocide, crimes against humanity, war crimes, and the crime of aggression. The statute defines each of these crimes except for aggression: it provides that the court will not exercise its jurisdiction over the crime of aggression until such time as the states parties agree on a definition of the crime and set out the conditions under which it may be prosecuted.

Many states wanted to add terrorism and drug trafficking to the list of crimes covered by the Rome Statute; however, the states were unable to agree on a definition for terrorism and it was decided not to include drug trafficking as this might overwhelm the court's limited resources. India lobbied to have the use of nuclear weapons and other weapons of mass destruction included as war crimes but this move was also defeated. India has expressed concern that "the Statute of the ICC lays down, by clear implication, that the use of weapons of mass destruction is not a war crime. This is an extraordinary message to send to the international community."

Some commentators have argued that the Rome Statute defines crimes too broadly or too vaguely. For example, China has argued that the definition of 'war crimes' goes beyond that accepted under customary international law.

A Review Conference is due to take place in the first half of 2010. Among other things, the conference will review the list of crimes contained in Article 5. The final resolution on adoption of the Rome Statute specifically recommended that terrorism and drug trafficking be reconsidered at this conference.

Territorial Jurisdiction

During the negotiations that led to the Rome Statute, a large number of states argued that the court should be allowed to exercise universal jurisdiction. However, this proposal was defeated due in large part to opposition from the United States. A compromise was reached, allowing the court to exercise jurisdiction only under the following limited circumstances:

- where the person accused of committing a crime is a national of a state party (or where the person's state has accepted the jurisdiction of the court);
- where the alleged crime was committed on the territory of a state party (or where the state on whose territory

the crime was committed has accepted the jurisdiction of the court); or

- where a situation is referred to the court by the UN Security Council.

Temporal Jurisdiction

The court's jurisdiction does not apply retroactively: it can only prosecute crimes committed on or after 1 July 2002 (the date on which the Rome Statute entered into force). Where a state becomes party to the Rome Statute after that date, the court can exercise jurisdiction automatically with respect to crimes committed after the statute enters into force for that state.

Complementarity

The ICC is intended as a court of last resort, investigating and prosecuting only where national courts have failed. Article 17 of the Statute provides that a case is inadmissible if:

(a) The case is being investigated or prosecuted by a State which has jurisdiction over it, unless the State is unwilling or unable genuinely to carry out the investigation or prosecution;

(b) The case has been investigated by a State which has jurisdiction over it and the State has decided not to prosecute the person concerned, unless the decision resulted from the unwillingness or inability of the State genuinely to prosecute;

(c) The person concerned has already been tried for conduct which is the subject of the complaint, and a trial by the Court is not permitted under article 20, paragraph 3;

(d) The case is not of sufficient gravity to justify further action by the Court.

Article 20, paragraph 3, specifies that, if a person has already been tried by another court, the ICC cannot try them again for the same conduct unless the proceedings in the other court:

(a) Were for the purpose of shielding the person concerned from criminal responsibility for crimes within the jurisdiction of the Court; or

(b) Otherwise were not conducted independently or impartially in accordance with the norms of due process recognized by international law and were conducted in a manner which, in the circumstances, was inconsistent with an intent to bring the person concerned to justice.

Structure

The ICC is governed by an Assembly of States Parties. The court consists of four organs: the Presidency, the Judicial Divisions, the Office of the Prosecutor, and the Registry.

Assembly of States Parties

The court's management oversight and legislative body, the Assembly of States Parties, consists of one representative from each state party. Each state party has one vote and "every effort" has to be made to reach decisions by consensus. If consensus cannot be reached, decisions are made by vote.

The Assembly meets in full session once a year in New York or The Hague, and may also hold special sessions where circumstances require. Sessions are open to observer states and non-governmental organisations.

The Assembly elects the judges and prosecutors, decides the court's budget, adopts important texts (such as the Rules of Procedure and Evidence), and provides management oversight to the other organs of the court. Article 46 of the Rome Statute allows the Assembly to remove from office a judge or prosecutor who "is found to have committed serious misconduct or a serious breach of his or her duties" or "is unable to exercise the functions required by this Statute".

The states parties cannot interfere with the judicial functions of the court. Disputes concerning individual cases are settled by the Judicial Divisions.

At the seventh session of the Assembly of States Parties in November 2008, the Assembly decided that the Review

Conference of the Rome Statute shall be held in Kampala, Uganda, during the first semester of 2010.

Presidency

The Presidency is responsible for the proper administration of the court (apart from the Office of the Prosecutor). It comprises the President and the First and Second Vice-Presidents — three judges of the court who are elected to the Presidency by their fellow judges for a maximum of two three-year terms. The current President is Sang-Hyun Song, who was elected on 11 March 2009.

Judicial Divisions

The Judicial Divisions consist of the 18 judges of the court, organized into three divisions — the Pre-Trial Division, Trial Division and Appeals Division — which carry out the judicial functions of the court. Judges are elected to the court by the Assembly of States Parties. They serve nine-year terms and are not generally eligible for re-election. All judges must be nationals of states parties to the Rome Statute, and no two judges may be nationals of the same state. They must be "persons of high moral character, impartiality and integrity who possess the qualifications required in their respective States for appointment to the highest judicial offices".

The Prosecutor or any person being investigated or prosecuted may request the disqualification of a judge from "any case in which his or her impartiality might reasonably be doubted on any ground". Any request for the disqualification of a judge from a particular case is decided by an absolute majority of the other judges. A judge may be removed from office if he or she "is found to have committed serious misconduct or a serious breach of his or her duties" or is unable to exercise his or her functions. The removal of a judge requires both a two-thirds majority of the other judges and a two-thirds majority of the states parties.

Office of the Prosecutor

The Office of the Prosecutor is responsible for conducting investigations and prosecutions. It is headed by the Prosecutor, who is assisted by two Deputy Prosecutors. The Rome Statute provides that the Office of the Prosecutor shall act independently; as such, no member of the Office may seek or act on instructions from any external source, such as states, international organisations, non-governmental organisations or individuals.

The Prosecutor may open an investigation under three circumstances:

- when a situation is referred to him by a state party;
- when a situation is referred to him by the United Nations Security Council, acting to address a threat to international peace and security; or
- when the Pre-Trial Chamber authorises him to open an investigation on the basis of information received from other sources, such as individuals or non-governmental organisations.

Any person being investigated or prosecuted may request the disqualification of a prosecutor from any case "in which their impartiality might reasonably be doubted on any ground". Requests for the disqualification of prosecutors are decided by the Appeals Division. A prosecutor may be removed from office by an absolute majority of the states parties if he or she "is found to have committed serious misconduct or a serious breach of his or her duties" or is unable to exercise his or her functions. However, critics of the court argue that there are "insufficient checks and balances on the authority of the ICC prosecutor and judges" and "insufficient protection against politicized prosecutions or other abuses". Henry Kissinger says the checks and balances are so weak that the prosecutor "has virtually unlimited discretion in practice".

As of March 2009, the Prosecutor is Luis Moreno-Ocampo of Argentina, who was elected by the Assembly of States Parties on 21 April 2003 for a term of nine years.

Registry

The Registry is responsible for the non-judicial aspects of the administration and servicing of the court. This includes, among other things, "the administration of legal aid matters, court management, victims and witnesses matters, defence counsel, detention unit, and the traditional services provided by administrations in international organisations, such as finance, translation, building management, procurement and personnel". The Registry is headed by the Registrar, who is elected by the judges to a five-year term.. The current Registrar is Silvana Arbia, who was elected on 28 February 2009.

Rights of the Accused

The Rome Statute provides that all persons are presumed innocent until proven guilty beyond reasonable doubt, and establishes certain rights of the accused and persons during investigations. These include the right to be fully informed of the charges against him or her; the right to have a lawyer appointed, free of charge; the right to a speedy trial; and the right to examine the witnesses against him or her and to obtain the attendance and examination of witnesses on his or her behalf.

Some argue that the protections offered by the ICC are insufficient. According to one conservative think-tank, the Heritage Foundation, "Americans who appear before the court would be denied such basic constitutional rights as trial by a jury of one's peers, protection from double jeopardy, and the right to confront one's accusers." The Human Rights Watch argues that the ICC standards are sufficient, saying, "the ICC has one of the most extensive lists of due process guarantees ever written", including "presumption of innocence; right to counsel; right to present evidence and to confront witnesses; right to remain silent; right to be present at trial; right to have charges proved beyond a reasonable doubt; and protection against double jeopardy". According to David Scheffer, who led the US delegation to the Rome Conference (and who voted against adoption of the treaty), "when we were negotiating the Rome treaty, we always kept very close tabs on, 'Does this meet U.S. constitutional tests, the formation of this court and the due process rights that are accorded defendants?' And we were very confident at the end of Rome that those due process rights, in fact, are protected, and that this treaty does meet a constitutional test."

In order to ensure "equality of arms" between defence and prosecution teams, the ICC has established an independent Office of Public Counsel for the Defence (OPCD) to provide logistical support, advice and information to defendants and their counsel. The OPCD also helps to safeguard the rights of the accused during the initial stages of an investigation. However, Thomas Lubanga's defence team say they have been given a smaller budget than the Prosecutor and that evidence and witness statements have been slow to arrive.

Amnesty International

Amnesty International (commonly known as **Amnesty** or **AI**) is an international non-governmental organisation which defines its mission as "to conduct research and generate action to prevent and end grave abuses of human rights and to demand justice for those whose rights have been violated." Founded in London, England in 1961, AI draws its attention to human rights abuses and campaigns for compliance with international standards. It works to mobilise public opinion which exerts pressure on individuals who perpetrate abuses. The organisation was awarded the 1977 Nobel Peace Prize for its "campaign against torture" and the United Nations Prize in the Field of Human Rights in 1978, but has been the subject of criticism for both alleged anti-Western and alleged pro-Western bias.

In the field of international human rights organisations (of which there were 300 in 1996), Amnesty has the longest history and broadest name recognition, and "is believed by many to set standards for the movement as a whole."

History

1960s

Amnesty International was founded in London in July 1961 by English labour lawyer Peter Benenson. According to his own account, he was travelling in the London Underground on 19 November 1960, when he read of two Portuguese students who had been sentenced to seven years of imprisonment for having drunk a toast to liberty. In his famous newspaper article *The Forgotten Prisoners*, Benenson later described his reaction as follows: *"Open your newspaper any day of the week and you will find a story from somewhere of someone being imprisoned, tortured or executed because his opinions or religion are unacceptable to his government [...] The newspaper reader feels a sickening sense of impotence. Yet if these feelings of disgust could be united into common action, something effective could be done."*

Benenson worked with friend Eric Baker. Baker was a member of the Religious Society of Friends who had been involved in funding the Campaign for Nuclear Disarmament as well as becoming head of Quaker Peace and Social Witness, and in his memoirs Benenson described him as "a partner in the launching of the project". In consultation with other writers, academics and lawyers and, in particular, Alec Digges, they wrote via Louis Blom-Cooper to David Astor, editor of *The Observer* newspaper, who, on May 28, 1961, published Benenson's article *The Forgotten Prisoners*. The article brought the reader's attention to those "imprisoned, tortured or executed because his opinions or religion are unacceptable to his government" or, put another way, to violations, by governments, of articles 18 and 19 of the Universal Declaration of Human Rights(UDHR). The article described these violations occurring, on a global scale, in the context of restrictions to press freedom, to political oppositions, to timely public trial before impartial courts, and to asylum.

It marked the launch of "Appeal for Amnesty, 1961", the aim of which was to mobilise public opinion, quickly and widely, in defence of these individuals, who Benenson named "Prisoners of Conscience". The "Appeal for Amnesty" was reprinted by a large number of international newspapers. In the same year Benenson had a book published, *Persecution 1961*, which detailed the cases of several prisoners of conscience investigated and compiled by Benenson and Baker. In July 1961 the leadership had decided that the appeal would form the basis of a permanent organisation, which on 30 September 1962 was officially named 'Amnesty International' (Between the 'Appeal for Amnesty, 1961' and September 1962 the organisation had been known simply as 'Amnesty'.)

What started as a short appeal soon became a permanent international movement working to protect those imprisoned for non-violent expression of their views and to secure worldwide recognition of Articles 18 and 19 of the UDHR. From the very beginning, research and campaigning were present in Amnesty International's work. A library was established for information about prisoners of conscience and a network of local groups, called 'THREES' groups, was started. Each group worked on behalf of three prisoners, one from each of the then three main ideological regions of the world: communist, capitalist and developing.

By the mid-1960s Amnesty International's global presence was growing and an International Secretariat and International Executive Committee was established to manage Amnesty International's national organisations, called 'Sections', which had appeared in several countries. The international movement was starting to agree on its core principles and techniques. For example, the issue of whether or not to adopt prisoners who had advocated violence, like Nelson Mandela, brought unanimous agreement that it could not give the name of 'Prisoner of Conscience' to such prisoners. Aside from the work of the library and groups, Amnesty International's activities were expanding to helping prisoner's families, sending observers to trials, making representations to governments, and finding asylum or overseas employment for prisoners. Its activity and influence was also increasing within intergovernmental organisations; it would be awarded consultative status by the United Nations, the Council of Europe and UNESCO before the decade ended.

1970s

Leading Amnesty International in the 1970s were key figureheads Sean MacBride and Martin Ennals. While continuing to work for prisoners of conscience, Amnesty International's purview widened to include "fair trial" and opposition to long detention without trial (UDHR Article 9), and especially to the torture of prisoners (UDHR Article 5). Amnesty International believed that the reasons underlying torture of prisoners, by governments, were either to obtain information or to quell opposition by the use of terror, or both. Also of concern was the export of more sophisticated torture methods, equipment and teaching by the superpowers to "client states", for example by the United States through some activities of the CIA.

Amnesty International drew together reports from countries where torture allegations seemed most persistent and organised an international conference on torture. It sought to influence public opinion in order to put pressure on national governments by organising a campaign for the 'Abolition of Torture' which ran for several years.

Amnesty International's membership increased from 15,000 in 1969 to 200,000 by 1979. This growth in resources enabled an expansion of its program, 'outside of the prison walls', to include work on "disappearances", the death penalty and the rights of refugees. A new technique, the 'Urgent Action', aimed at mobilising the membership into action rapidly was pioneered. The first was issued on March 19, 1973, on behalf of Luiz Basilio Rossi, a Brazilian academic, arrested for political reasons.

At the intergovernmental level Amnesty International pressed for application of the UN's Standard Minimum Rules for the Treatment of Prisoners and of existing humanitarian conventions; to secure ratifications of the two UN Covenants on Human Rights (which came into force in 1976); and was instrumental in obtaining United Nations General Assembly resolution 3059 which formally denounced torture and called on governments to adhere to existing international instruments and provisions forbidding its practice. Consultative status was granted at the Inter-American Commission on Human Rights in 1972.

In 1976 AI started a series of fundraising events informally known as The Secret Policeman's Balls. Initially they were staged in London primarily as comedy galas featuring popular

British comedic performers such as members of Monty Python, later expanding to include leading musical performers. The series was created and developed by Monty Python alumnus John Cleese and entertainment industry executive Martin Lewis working closely with Amnesty staff members Peter Luff (Assistant Director of Amnesty 1976-1977) and subsequently with Peter Walker (Fund-Raising Officer from 1978). Cleese, Lewis and Luff worked together on the first two shows (1976 and 1977).

The organisation was awarded the 1977 Nobel Peace Prize for its "campaign against torture" and the United Nations Prize in the Field of Human Rights in 1978.

1980s

By 1980 Amnesty International was drawing more criticism from governments. The USSR alleged that Amnesty International conducted espionage, the Moroccan government denounced it as a defender of lawbreakers, and the Argentine government banned Amnesty International's 1983 annual report.

Throughout the 1980s, Amnesty International continued to campaign for prisoners of conscience and torture. New issues emerged, including extrajudicial killings, military, security and police transfers, political killings; and disappearances.

Towards the end of the decade, the growing numbers worldwide of refugees was a very visible area of Amnesty International's concern. While many of the world's refugees of the time had been displaced by war and famine, in adherence to its mandate, Amnesty International concentrated on those forced to flee, because of the human rights violations it was seeking to prevent. It argued that rather than focusing on new restrictions on entry for asylum-seekers, governments were to address the human rights violations which were forcing people into exile.

Apart from a second campaign on torture during the first half of the decade, the major AI event of the 1980s was the 1988 Human Rights Now! tour. Designed to increase awareness of

Amnesty and of human rights on the 40th anniversary of the United Nations' Universal Declaration of Human Rights (UDHR), it featured some of the most famous musicians and bands of the day playing a series of concerts on five continents over six weeks.

1990s

Throughout the 1990s, Amnesty International continued to grow, to a membership of over 2.2 million in over 150 countries and territories, led by Senegalese Secretary General Pierre Sane. AI continued to work on a wide range of issues and world events. For example, South African groups joined in 1992 and hosted a visit by Pierre Sane to meet with the apartheid government to press for an investigation into allegations of police abuse, an end to arms sales to the African Great Lakes region and abolition of the death penalty. In particular, Amnesty International brought attention to violations committed on specific groups including: refugees, racial/ethnic/religious minorities, women and those executed or on Death Row. The death penalty report *When the state kills* and the 'Human Rights are Women's Rights' campaign were key actions for the latter two issues and demonstrate that Amnesty International was still very much a reporting and campaigning organisation.

During the 1990s Amnesty International was forced to react to human rights violations occurring in the context of a proliferation of armed conflict in: Angola, East Timor, the Persian Gulf, Rwanda, Somalia and the former Yugoslavia. Amnesty International took no position on whether to support or oppose external military interventions in these armed conflicts. It did not (and does not) reject the use of force, even lethal force, or ask those engaged to lay down their arms. Instead, it questioned the motives behind external intervention and selectivity of international action in relation to the strategic interests of those sending troops. It argued that action should be taken in time to prevent human rights problems becoming human rights catastrophes and that both intervention and inaction represented a failure of the international community.

Amnesty International was proactive in pushing for recognition of the universality of human rights. The campaign 'Get Up, Sign Up' marked 50 years of the UDHR. Thirteen million pledges were collected in support of the Declaration and a music concert was held in Paris on December 10, 1998 (Human Rights Day). At the intergovernmental level, Amnesty International argued in favour of creating a United Nations High Commissioner for Human Rights (established 1993) and an International Criminal Court (established 2002).

After Senator Augusto Pinochet of Chile was arrested in London in 1998 by the Metropolitan Police, Amnesty International became involved in the legal battle of Senator Pinochet, a former Chilean President, who sought to avoid extradition to Spain to face charges relating to his rule of Chile in the 1970s and 80s. It emerged during this legal process that one of the judges in the English House of Lords, Lord Hoffman, had an indirect connection with Amnesty International and this led to an important test for the appearance of bias in legal proceedings in UK law. Amnesty then sought a judicial review of the decision to release Senator Pinochet, taken by the then British Home Secretary Mr. Jack Straw, before that decision had actually been taken, in an attempt to prevent the release of Senator Pinochet. The English High Court refused the application and Senator Pinochet was released and returned to Chile. This legal challenge was a novel attempt to use legal process to challenge a decision before it was taken and could be seen as hard to reconcile with the rule of law, as it was predicated on a presumption that the Home Secretary had erred in law whatever the reasons were for the decision.

2000

After 2000, Amnesty International's agenda turned to the challenges arising from globalisation and the reaction to the September 11, 2001 attacks in the United States. The issue of globalisation provoked a major shift in Amnesty International policy, as the scope of its work was widened to include economic, social and cultural rights, an area that it had declined to work on in the past. Amnesty International felt this shift was important, not just to give credence to its principle of the indivisibility of rights, but because of the growing power of companies and the undermining of many nation states as a result of globalisation.

In the aftermath of the September 11 attacks, the new Amnesty International Secretary General, Irene Khan, reported that a senior government official had said to Amnesty International delegates: "Your role collapsed with the collapse of the Twin Towers in New York". In the years following the attacks, some of the gains made by human rights organisations over previous decades were eroded. Amnesty International argued that human rights were the basis for the security of all, not a barrier to it. Criticism came directly from the Bush administration and *The Washington Post*, when Khan, in 2005, likened the US government's detention facility at Guantanamo Bay, Cuba, to a Soviet Gulag.

During the first half of the new decade, Amnesty International turned its attention to violence against women, controls on the world arms trade and concerns surrounding the effectiveness of the UN. With its membership close to two million by 2005, AI continued to work for prisoners of conscience.

Amnesty International reported, concerning the Iraq war, on March 17, 2008 that despite claims the security situation in Iraq has improved in recent months, the human rights situation is disastrous, after the start of the war five years ago in 2003.

In 2008 Amnesty International launched a mobile donating campaign in the United States, which allows supporters to make $5 micro-donations by sending a text message to the short code 90999 with the keyword RIGHTS. Amnesty International's mobile fundraising campaign was created in partnership with Mgive and the Mobile Giving Foundation.

Work

"Amnesty International's vision is of a world in which every person enjoys all of the human rights enshrined in the Universal Declaration of Human Rights and other international human rights standards.

In pursuit of this vision, Amnesty International's mission is to undertake research and action focused on preventing and ending grave abuses of the rights to physical and mental integrity, freedom of conscience and expression, and freedom from discrimination, within the context of its work to promote all human rights." —Statute of Amnesty International, 27th International Council meeting, 2005

Amnesty International primarily targets governments, but also reports on non-governmental bodies and private individuals ("non-state actors").

There are five key areas which Amnesty deals with:

- Women's Rights,
- Children's Rights,
- Ending Torture and Execution,
- Rights of Refugees and
- Rights of Prisoners of Conscience.

Some specific aims are to abolish the death penalty, end extra judicial executions and "disappearances", ensure prison conditions meet international human rights standards, ensure prompt and fair trial for all political prisoners, ensure free education to all children worldwide, decriminalise abortion, fight impunity from systems of justice, end the recruitment and use of child soldiers, free all prisoners of conscience, promote economic, social and cultural rights for marginalised communities, protect human rights defenders, promote religious tolerance, stop torture and ill-treatment, stop unlawful killings in armed conflict, and to uphold the rights of refugees, migrants and asylum seekers.

To further these aims, Amnesty International has developed several techniques to publicise information and mobilise public opinion. The organisation considers as one of its strengths the publication of impartial and accurate reports. Reports are researched by interviewing victims and officials, observing trials, working with local human rights activists and by monitoring the media. It aims to issue timely press releases and publishes information in newsletters and on web sites. It also sends official missions to countries to make courteous but insistent inquiries.

Campaigns to mobilise public opinion can take the form of individual, country or thematic campaigns. Many techniques are deployed such as direct appeals (for example, letter writing), media and publicity work and public demonstrations. Often fund-raising is integrated with campaigning.

In situations which require immediate attention, Amnesty International calls on existing urgent action networks or crisis response networks; for all other matters, it calls on its membership. It considers the large size of its human resources to be another one of its key strengths.

Rank	Country	#Press Releases	% Total
1	USA	136	4.24
2	Israel and O.T.	128	3.99
3	Indonesia and E. Timor	119	3.71
3	Turkey	119	3.71
4	China	115	3.58
5	Serbia and Montenegro (FRY)	104	3.24
6	U.K.	103	3.21
7	India	85	2.65
8	U.S.S.R. and Russia	80	2.49
9	Rwanda	64	2.00
10	Sri Lanka	59	1.84

Source: *Ronand et al. (2005:568) Data for 1986-2000.*

International Committee of the Red Cross.

The **International Committee of the Red Cross (ICRC)** is a private humanitarian institution based in Geneva, Switzerland. The community of states has given the ICRC a unique role, based on international humanitarian law of the Geneva Conventions as well as customary international law, to protect the victims of international and internal armed conflicts. Such victims include war wounded, prisoners, refugees, civilians, and other non-combatants.

The ICRC is part of the International Red Cross and Red Crescent Movement along with the International Federation and 186 National Societies. It is the oldest and most honoured organization within the Movement and one of the most widely recognized organizations in the world, having won three Nobel Peace Prizes in 1917, 1944, and 1963.

International Red Cross

History

Solferino, Henry Dunant and the Foundation of the ICRC: Up until the middle of the 19 century, there were no organized and well-established army nursing systems for casualties and no safe and protected institutions to accommodate and treat those who were wounded on the battlefield. In June 1859, the Swiss businessman Henry Dunant travelled to Italy to meet French emperor Napoleon III with the intention of discussing difficulties in conducting business in Algeria, at that time occupied by France. When he arrived in the small town of Solferino on the evening of June 24, he witnessed the Battle of Solferino, an engagement in the Austro-Sardinian War. In a single day, about 40,000 soldiers on both sides died or were left wounded on the field. Henry Dunant was shocked by the terrible aftermath of the battle, the suffering of the wounded soldiers, and the near-total lack of medical attendance and basic care. He completely abandoned the original intent of his trip and for several days he devoted himself to helping with the treatment and care for the wounded. He succeeded in organizing an overwhelming level of relief assistance by motivating the local population to aid without discrimination. Back in his home in Geneva, he decided to write a book entitled *A Memory of Solferino* which he published with his own money in 1862.

He sent copies of the book to leading political and military figures throughout Europe. In addition to penning a vivid description of his experiences in Solferino in 1859, he explicitly advocated the formation of national voluntary relief organizations to help nurse wounded soldiers in the case of war. In addition, he called for the development of international treaties to guarantee the neutrality and protection of those wounded on the battlefield as well as medics and field hospitals.

On February 9, 1863 in Geneva, Henry Dunant founded the "Committee of the Five" (together with four other leading figures from well-known Geneva families) as an investigatory commission of the Geneva Society for Public Welfare. Their aim was to examine the feasibility of Dunant's ideas and to organize an international conference about their possible implementation.

The members of this committee, aside from Dunant himself, were Gustave Moynier, lawyer and chairman of the Geneva Society for Public Welfare; physician Louis Appia, who had significant experience working as a field surgeon; Appia's friend and colleague Theodore Maunoir, from the Geneva Hygiene and Health Commission; and Guillaume-Henri Dufour, a Swiss Army general of great renown. Eight days later, the five men decided to rename the committee to the "International Committee for Relief to the Wounded". In October (26-29) 1863, the international conference organized by the committee was held in Geneva to develop possible measures to improve medical services on the battle field.

The conference was attended by 36 individuals: eighteen official delegates from national governments, six delegates from other non-governmental organizations, seven non-official foreign delegates, and the five members of the International Committee. The states and kingdoms represented by official delegates were Baden, Bavaria, France, Britain, Hanover, Hesse, Italy, the Netherlands, Austria, Prussia, Russia, Saxony, Sweden, and Spain. Among the proposals written in the final resolutions of the conference, adopted on October 29, 1863, were:

- The foundation of national relief societies for wounded soldiers;
- Neutrality and protection for wounded soldiers;
- The utilization of volunteer forces for relief assistance on the battlefield;
- The organization of additional conferences to enact these concepts in legally binding international treaties; and

- The introduction of a common distinctive protection symbol for medical personnel in the field, namely a white armlet bearing a red cross.

Only one year later, the Swiss government invited the governments of all European countries, as well as the United States, Brazil, and Mexico, to attend an official diplomatic conference. Sixteen countries sent a total of twenty-six delegates to Geneva. On August 22, 1864, the conference adopted the first Geneva Convention "for the Amelioration of the Condition of the Wounded in Armies in the Field". Representatives of 12 states and kingdoms signed the convention: Baden, Belgium, Denmark, France, Hesse, Italy, the Netherlands, Portugal, Prussia, Switzerland, Spain, and Wurttemberg. The convention contained ten articles, establishing for the first time legally binding rules guaranteeing neutrality and protection for wounded soldiers, field medical personnel, and specific humanitarian institutions in an armed conflict. Furthermore, the convention defined two specific requirements for recognition of a national relief society by the International Committee:

- The national society must be recognized by its own national government as a relief society according to the convention, and
- The national government of the respective country must be a state party to the Geneva Convention.

Directly following the establishment of the Geneva Convention, the first national societies were founded in Belgium, Denmark, France, Oldenburg, Prussia, Spain, and Wurttemberg. Also in 1864, Louis Appia and Charles van de Velde, a captain of the Dutch Army, became the first independent and neutral delegates to work under the symbol of the Red Cross in an armed conflict. Three years later in 1867, the first International Conference of National Aid Societies for the Nursing of the War Wounded was convened.

Also in 1867, Henry Dunant was forced to declare bankruptcy due to business failures in Algeria, partly because he had neglected his business interests during his tireless activities for the International Committee. Controversy surrounding Dunant's business dealings and the resulting negative public opinion, combined with an ongoing conflict with Gustave Moynier, led to Dunant's expulsion from his position as a member and secretary. He was charged with fraudulent bankruptcy and a warrant for his arrest was issued. Thus, he was forced to leave Geneva and never returned to his home city. In the following years, national societies were founded in nearly every country in Europe. In 1876, the committee adopted the name "International Committee of the Red Cross" (ICRC), which is still its official designation today. Five years later, the American Red Cross was founded through the efforts of Clara Barton. More and more countries signed the Geneva Convention and began to respect it in practice during armed conflicts. In a rather short period of time, the Red Cross gained huge momentum as an internationally respected movement, and the national societies became increasingly popular as a venue for volunteer work.

When the first Nobel Peace Prize was awarded in 1901, the Norwegian Nobel Committee opted to give it jointly to Henry Dunant and Frederic Passy, a leading international pacifist. More significant than the honor of the prize itself, the official congratulation from the International Committee of the Red Cross marked the overdue rehabilitation of Henry Dunant and represented a tribute to his key role in the formation of the Red Cross. Dunant died nine years later in the small Swiss health resort of Heiden. Only two months earlier his long-standing adversary Gustave Moynier had also died, leaving a mark in the history of the Committee as its longest-serving president ever.

In 1906, the 1864 Geneva Convention was revised for the first time. One year later, the Hague Convention X, adopted at the Second International Peace Conference in The Hague, extended the scope of the Geneva Convention to naval warfare. Shortly before the beginning of the First World War in 1914, 50 years after the foundation of the ICRC and the adoption of the first Geneva Convention, there were already 45 national relief societies throughout the world. The movement had extended itself beyond Europe and North America to Central and South America (Argentina, Brazil, Chile, Cuba, Mexico, Peru, El Salvador, Uruguay, Venezuela), Asia (the Republic of China, Japan, Korea, Siam), and Africa (Republic of South Africa).

World War One

With the outbreak of World War I, the ICRC found itself confronted with enormous challenges which it could only handle by working closely with the national Red Cross societies. Red Cross nurses from around the world, including the United States and Japan, came to support the medical services of the armed forces of the European countries involved in the war. On October 15, 1914, immediately after the start of the war, the ICRC set up its International Prisoners-of-War (POW) Agency, which had about 1,200 mostly volunteer staff members by the end of 1914. By the end of the war, the Agency had transferred about 20 million letters and messages, 1.9 million parcels, and about 18 million Swiss francs in monetary donations to POWs of all affected countries. Furthermore, due to the intervention of the Agency, about 200,000 prisoners were exchanged between the warring parties, released from captivity and returned to their home country. The organizational card index of the Agency accumulated about 7 million records from 1914 to 1923, each card representing an individual prisoner or missing person. The card index led to the identification of about 2 million POWs and the ability to contact their families. The complete index is on loan today from the ICRC to the International Red Cross and Red Crescent Museum in Geneva. The right to access the index is still strictly restricted to the ICRC.

During the entire war, the ICRC monitored warring parties' compliance with the Geneva Conventions of the 1907 revision and forwarded complaints about violations to the respective country. When chemical weapons were used in this war for the first time in history, the ICRC vigorously protested against this new type of warfare. Even without having a mandate from the Geneva Conventions, the ICRC tried to ameliorate the suffering of civil populations. In territories that were officially designated as "occupied territories," the ICRC could assist the civilian population on the basis of the Hague Convention's "Laws and Customs of War on Land" of 1907. This convention was also the legal basis for the ICRC's work for prisoners of war. In addition to the work of the International Prisoner-of-War Agency as described above this included inspection visits to POW camps. A total of 524 camps throughout Europe were visited by 41 delegates from the ICRC until the end of the war.

Between 1916 and 1918, the ICRC published a number of postcards with scenes from the POW camps. The pictures showed the prisoners in day-to-day activities such as the distribution of letters from home. The intention of the ICRC was to provide the families of the prisoners with some hope and solace and to alleviate their uncertainties about the fate of their loved ones. After the end of the war, the ICRC organized the return of about 420,000 prisoners to their home countries. In 1920, the task of repatriation was handed over to the newly founded League of Nations, which appointed the Norwegian diplomat and scientist Fridtjof Nansen as its "High Commissioner for Repatriation of the War Prisoners." His legal mandate was later extended to support and care for war refugees and displaced persons when his office became that of the League of Nations "High Commissioner for Refugees." Nansen, who invented the *Nansen passport* for stateless refugees and was awarded the Nobel Peace Prize in 1922, appointed two delegates from the ICRC as his deputies.

A year before the end of the war, the ICRC received the 1917 Nobel Peace Prize for its outstanding wartime work. It was the only Nobel Peace Prize awarded in the period from 1914 to 1918. In 1923, the Committee adopted a change in its policy regarding the selection of new members. Until then, only citizens from the city of Geneva could serve in the Committee. This limitation was expanded to include Swiss citizens. As a direct consequence of World War I, an additional protocol to the Geneva Convention was adopted in 1925 which outlawed the use of suffocating or poisonous gases and biological agents as weapons. Four years later, the original Convention was revised and the second Geneva Convention "relative to the

Treatment of Prisoners of War" was established. The events of World War I and the respective activities of the ICRC significantly increased the reputation and authority of the Committee among the international community and led to an extension of its competencies.

As early as in 1934, a draft proposal for an additional convention for the protection of the civil population during an armed conflict was adopted by the International Red Cross Conference. Unfortunately, most governments had little interest in implementing this convention, and it was thus prevented from entering into force before the beginning of World War II.

World War Two

The legal basis of the work of the ICRC during World War II were the Geneva Conventions in their 1929 revision. The activities of the Committee were similar to those during World War I: visiting and monitoring POW camps, organizing relief assistance for civilian populations, and administering the exchange of messages regarding prisoners and missing persons. By the end of the war, 179 delegates had conducted 12,750 visits to POW camps in 41 countries. The Central Information Agency on Prisoners-of-War (*Zentralauskunftsstelle fur Kriegsgefangene*) had a staff of 3,000, the card index tracking prisoners contained 45 million cards, and 120 million messages were exchanged by the Agency. One major obstacle was that the Nazi-controlled German Red Cross refused to cooperate with the Geneva statutes including blatant violations such as the deportation of Jews from Germany and the mass murders conducted in the concentration camps run by the German government. Moreover, two other main parties to the conflict, the Soviet Union and Japan, were not party to the 1929 Geneva Conventions and were not legally required to follow the rules of the conventions. Thus, other countries were not bound to follow the Conventions regarding their prisoners in return.

During the war, the ICRC failed to obtain an agreement with Nazi Germany about the treatment of detainees in concentration camps, and it eventually abandoned applying pressure in order to avoid disrupting its work with POWs. The

ICRC also failed to develop a response to reliable information about the extermination camps and the mass killing of European Jews. This is still considered the greatest failure of the ICRC in its history. After November 1943, the ICRC achieved permission to send parcels to concentration camp detainees with known names and locations. Because the notices of receipt for these parcels were often signed by other inmates, the ICRC managed to register the identities of about 105,000 detainees in the concentration camps and delivered about 1.1 million parcels, primarily to the camps Dachau, Buchenwald, Ravensbruck, and Sachsenhausen.

On March 12, 1945, ICRC president Jacob Burckhardt received a message from SS General Ernst Kaltenbrunner accepting the ICRC's demand to allow delegates to visit the concentration camps. This agreement was bound by the condition that these delegates would have to stay in the camps until the end of the war. Ten delegates, among them Louis Haefliger (Camp Mauthausen), Paul Dunant (Camp Theresienstadt) and Victor Maurer (Camp Dachau), accepted the assignment and visited the camps. Louis Haefliger prevented the forceful eviction or blasting of Mauthausen-Gusen by alerting American troops, thereby saving the lives of about 60,000 inmates. His actions were condemned by the ICRC because they were deemed as acting unduly on his own authority and risking the ICRC's neutrality. Only in 1990, his reputation was finally rehabilitated by ICRC president Cornelio Sommaruga.

Another example of great humanitarian spirit was Friedrich Born (1903-1963), an ICRC delegate in Budapest who saved the lives of about 11,000 to 15,000 Jews in Hungary. Marcel Junod (1904-1961), a physician from Geneva, was another famous delegate during the Second World War. An account of his experiences, which included being one of the first foreigners to visit Hiroshima after the atomic bomb was dropped, can be found in the book *Warrior without Weapons*.

In 1944, the ICRC received its second Nobel Peace Prize. As in World War I, it received the only Peace Prize awarded during the main period of war, 1939 to 1945. At the end of the war, the ICRC worked with national Red Cross societies to organize relief assistance to those countries most severely affected. In 1948, the Committee published a report reviewing its war-era activities from September 1, 1939 to June 30, 1947. Since January 1996, the ICRC archive for this period has been open to academic and public research.

After the Second World War

On August 12, 1949, further revisions to the existing two Geneva Conventions were adopted. An additional convention "for the Amelioration of the Condition of Wounded, Sick and Shipwrecked Members of Armed Forces at Sea", now called the second Geneva Convention, was brought under the Geneva Convention umbrella as a successor to the 1907 Hague Convention X. The 1929 Geneva convention "relative to the Treatment of Prisoners of War" may have been the second Geneva Convention from a historical point of view (because it was actually formulated in Geneva), but after 1949 it came to be called the third Convention because it came later chronologically than the Hague Convention. Reacting to the experience of World War II, the Fourth Geneva Convention, a new Convention "relative to the Protection of Civilian Persons in Time of War," was established. Also, the additional protocols of June 8, 1977 were intended to make the conventions apply to internal conflicts such as civil wars. Today, the four conventions and their added protocols contain more than 600 articles, a remarkable expansion when compared to the mere 10 articles in the first 1864 convention.

In celebration of its centennial in 1963, the ICRC, together with the League of Red Cross Societies, received its third Nobel Peace Prize. Since 1993, non-Swiss individuals have been allowed to serve as Committee delegates abroad, a task which was previously restricted to Swiss citizens. Indeed, since then, the share of staff without Swiss citizenship has increased to about 35%.

On October 16, 1990, the UN General Assembly decided to grant the ICRC observer status for its assembly sessions and sub-committee meetings, the first observer status given to a private organization. The resolution was jointly proposed by 138 member states and introduced by the Italian ambassador, Vieri Traxler, in memory of the organization's origins in the Battle of Solferino. An agreement with the Swiss government signed on March 19, 1993, affirmed the already long-standing policy of full independence of the Committee from any possible interference by Switzerland. The agreement protects the full sanctity of all ICRC property in Switzerland including its headquarters and archive, grants members and staff legal immunity, exempts the ICRC from all taxes and fees, guarantees the protected and duty-free transfer of goods, services, and money, provides the ICRC with secure communication privileges at the same level as foreign embassies, and simplifies Committee travel in and out of Switzerland.

The ICRC continued its activities throughout the 1990s. It broke its customary media silence when it denounced the Rwandan Genocide in 1994. It struggled to prevent the crimes that happened in and around Srebrenica in 1995 but admitted, "We must acknowledge that despite our efforts to help thousands of civilians forcibly expelled from the town and despite the dedication of our colleagues on the spot, the ICRC's impact on the unfolding of the tragedy was extremely limited." It went public once again in 2007 to decry "major human rights abuses" by Burma's military government including forced labor, starvation, and murder of men, women, and children.

Fatalities

At the end of the Cold War, the ICRC's work actually became more dangerous. In the 1990s, more delegates lost their lives than at any point in its history, especially when working in local and internal armed conflicts. These incidents often demonstrated a lack of respect for the rules of the Geneva Conventions and their protection symbols. Among the slain delegates were:

- Frederic Maurice. He died on May 19, 1992 at the age of 39, one day after a Red Cross transport he was escorting was attacked in the former Yugoslavian city of Sarajevo.

- Fernanda Calado (Spain), Ingeborg Foss (Norway), Nancy Malloy (Canada), Gunnhild Myklebust (Norway), Sheryl Thayer (New Zealand), and Hans Elkerbout (Netherlands). They were murdered at point-blank range while sleeping in the early hours of December 17, 1996 in the ICRC field hospital in the Chechen city of Nowije Atagi near Grozny. Their murderers have never been caught and there was no apparent motive for the killings.
- Rita Fox (Switzerland), Veronique Saro (Democratic Republic of Congo, formerly Zaire), Julio Delgado (Colombia), Unen Ufoirworth (DR Congo), Aduwe Boboli (DR Congo), and Jean Molokabonge (DR Congo). On April 26, 2001, they were en route with two cars on a relief mission in the northeast of the Democratic Republic of Congo when they came under fatal fire from unknown attackers.
- Ricardo Munguia (El Salvador). He was working as a water engineer in Afghanistan and travelling with local colleagues when their car was stopped by unknown armed men. He was killed execution-style at point-blank range while his colleagues were allowed to escape. He died at the age of 39.
- Vatche Arslanian (Canada). Since 2001, he worked as a logistics coordinator for the ICRC mission in Iraq. He died when he was travelling through Baghdad together with members of the Iraqi Red Crescent. Their car accidentally came into the crossfire of fighting in the city.
- Nadisha Yasassri Ranmuthu (Sri Lanka). He was killed by unknown attackers on July 22, 2003, when his car was fired upon near the city of Hilla in the south of Baghdad.

The Holocaust

By taking part in the 1995 ceremony to commemorate the liberation of the Auschwitz concentration camp, the President of the ICRC, Cornelio Sommaruga, sought to show that the organization was fully aware of the gravity of The Holocaust and the need to keep the memory of it alive, so as to prevent any repetition of it. He paid tribute to all those who had suffered or lost their lives during the war and publicly regretted the past mistakes and shortcomings of the Red Cross with regard to the victims of the concentration camps.

In 2002, an ICRC official outlined some of the lessons the organization has learned from the failure:

- from a legal point of view, the work that led to the adoption of the Geneva Convention relative to the protection of civilian persons in time of war;
- from an ethical point of view, the adoption of the declaration of the Fundamental Principles of the Red Cross and Red Crescent, building on the distinguished work of Max Huber and the late Jean Pictet, in order to prevent any more abuses such as those that occurred within the Movement after Hitler rose to power in 1933;
- on a political level, the ICRC's relationship with Switzerland was redesigned to ensure its independence;
- with a view to keeping memories alive, the ICRC accepted, in 1955, to take over the direction of the International Tracing Service where records from concentration camps are maintained;
- finally, to establish the historical facts of the case, the ICRC invited Jean-Claude Favez to carry out an independent investigation of its activities on behalf of the victims of Nazi persecution, and gave him unfettered access to its archives relating to this period; out of concern for transparency, the ICRC also decided to give all other historians access to its archives dating back more than 50 years; having gone over the conclusions of Favez's work, the ICRC acknowledged its past failings and expressed its regrets in this regard.

In an official statement made on 27 January 2005, the anniversary of the liberation of Auswitz, the ICRC stated:

Auschwitz also represents the greatest failure in the history of the ICRC, aggravated by its lack of decisiveness in taking steps to aid the victims of Nazi persecution. This failure will remain part of the ICRC's memory, as will the courageous acts of individual ICRC delegates at the time.

Unit-V

Human Rights : Indian Institutions

National Human Rights Commission

The **National Human Rights Commission** (NHRC) of India is an autonomous statutory body established on October 12, after the rights to be held. 1993, under the provisions of *The Protection of Human Rights Act, 1993* (TPHRA). The Commission is in conformity with the Paris Principles-a broad set of principles agreed upon by a number of nations for the promotion and protection of human rights, in Paris in October 1991.

Functions

TPHRA mandates the NHRC to perform the following functions:

- proactively or reactively inquire into violations of human rights or negligence in the prevention of such violation by a public servant
- intervene in any proceeding involving any allegation of violation of human rights pending before a court
- visit any jail or other institution under the control of the State Government, where persons are detained or lodged for purposes of treatment, reformation or protection, for the study of the living conditions of the inmates and make recommendations

- review the safeguards provided by or under the Constitution or any law for the time being in force for the protection of human rights and recommend measures for their effective implementation
- review the factors, including acts of terrorism that inhibit the enjoyment of human rights and recommend appropriate remedial measures
- study treaties and other international instruments on human rights and make recommendations for their effective implementation
- undertake and promote research in the field of human rights
- spread literacy among various sections of society and promote awareness of the safeguards available for the protection of these rights through publications, the media, seminars and other available means
- encourage the efforts of NGOs and institutions working in the field of human rights

Composition and Appointment

Sections 3 and 4 of TPHRA lay down the rules for appointment to The NHRC. The Chairperson and members of the NHRC are appointed by the President of India, on the recommendation of a committee comprising of

- The Prime Minister: Chairperson
- The Speaker of the House of the People: Member
- The Minister-in-charge of the Ministry of Home Affairs in the Government of India: Member
- The Leader of the Opposition in the House of the People: Member
- The Leader of the Opposition in the Council of States: Member
- The Deputy Chairman of the Council of States: Member

The NHRC consists of:

- A Chairperson who has been a Chief Justice of the Supreme Court of India

- One Member who is, or has been, a Judge of the Supreme Court of India
- One Member who is, or has been, the Chief Justice of a High Court
- Two Members to be appointed from among persons having knowledge of, or practical experience in, matters relating to human rights

The Current Composition of Members:

- Hon'ble Justice Shri S. Rajendra Babu: Chairperson
- Hon'ble Justice Shri Govind Prasad Mathur: Member
- Hon'ble Sri Justice Y. Bhaskar Rao: Member
- Shri R.S. Kalha: Member
- Shri P.C.Sharma: Member
- Shri Mohammad Shafi Qureshi (National Commission for Minorities): Chairperson, Ex-officio Member
- Dr. Girija Vyas (National Commission for Women) : Chairperson, Ex-officio Member

State Human Rights Commissions

Protection and promotion of human rights constitute the principal concern of the Commission. Pursuant to this objective, the Commission is committed to discharge its functions assigned to it under the Act with transparency and autonomy. The autonomy of the Commission emanates, inter alia, from the procedures relating to the appointment of the Members, the security of their tenure, their stature, the safeguards provided under Section 23 and 24 of the Act and the status accorded to the Commission under overall scheme of the Act. The financial autonomy of the Commission is implied under provisions of Section 33 of the Act. The procedures adopted by the Commission to conduct its proceedings, the suo motu action taken on complaints regardless of the sources received, the openness of its proceedings and the placement of its reports before the State Legislature are key to the strength and transparency of the Commission's functioning.

The functions of the SHRC include considerable scope and range of the functions envisaged for the Commission under sec 12 of the Act, "all or any" of which except what is stated under clause (f) of the section relating to treaties and other International instruments on Human Rights which can be dealt with by the National Human Rights Commission only, are to be performed by this Commission. These functions are to:

(a) inquire suo motu or on a petition presented to it, by a victim, or any person on his be into complaint of

  (i) Violation of human rights or abetment thereof;

  (or)

  (ii) negligence in the prevention of such violation by a public servant.

(b) Intervene in any proceeding involving any allegation of violation of human rights, per before a Court with the approval of such Court.

(c) visit under intimation to the State Government, any jail or any other institution under the control of the State Government where persons are detained or lodged for purposes of treatment, reformation or protection to study the living conditions of the inmates and make recommendations thereon:

(d) review the safeguards provided by or under the constitution of any law for the time being in force for the protection of human rights and recommend measures for their effective implementation.

(e) Review the factors, including acts of terrorism that inhibit the enjoyment of human rights and recommend appropriate remedial measures.

(f) Not applicable to State Human Rights Commission.

(g) undertake and promote research in the field of human rights.

(h) spread human rights literacy among various sections of society and promote awareness of the safeguards available for the protection of these rights through publications, the n seminars and other available means.

(i) encourage the efforts of Non-Governmental organisations and institutions working in the field of human rights.

(j) such other functions as it may consider necessary for the promotion of human rights.

Constitution of State Human Rights Commissions

(1) A State Government may constitute a body to be known as the .... (name of the State) Human Rights Commission to exercise the powers conferred upon, and to perform the functions assigned to, a State Commission under this chapter.

(2) The State Commission shall consist of

(a) a Chairperson who has been a Chief Justice of a High Court;

(b) one Member who is, or has been, a Judge of a High Court;

(c) one Member who is, or has been, a district judge in that State;

(d) two Members to be appointed from amongst persons having knowledge of, or practical experience in, matters relating to human rights.

(3) There shall be a Secretary who shall be the Chief Executive Officer of the State Commission and shall exercise such powers and discharge such functions of the State Commission as it may delegate to him.

(4) The headquarters of the State Commission shall be at such place as the State Government may, by notification, specify.

(5) A State Commission may inquire into violation of human rights only in respect of matters relatable to any of the entries enumerated in List II and List III in the Seventh Schedule to the Constitution:

Provided that if any such matter is already being inquired into by the Commission or any other Commission duly constituted under any law for the time being in force, the State Commission shall not inquire into the said matter:

Provided further that in relation to the Jammu and Kashmir Human Rights Commission, this sub-section shall have effect as if for the words and figures "List II and List III in the Seventh Schedule to the Constitution", the words and figures "List III in the Seventh Schedule to the Constitution as applicable to the State of Jammu and Kashmir and in respect of matters in relation to which the Legislature of that State has power to make laws" had been substituted.

Appointment of Chairperson and Other Members of State Commission

(1) The Chairperson and other Members shall be appointed by the Governor by warrant under his hand and seal:

Provided that every appointment under this sub-section shall be made after obtaining the recommendation of a Committee consisting of

(a) the Chief Minister — Chairperson

(b) Speaker of the Legislative Assembly — Member

(c) Minister in-charge of the Department of Home, in that tate — Member

(d) Leader of the Opposition in the Legislative Assembly — Member

Provided further that where there is a Legislative Council in a State, the Chairman of that Council and the Leader of the Opposition in that Council shall also be members of the Committee.

Provided also that no sitting Judge of a High Court or a sitting District Judge shall be appointed except after consultation with the Chief Justice of the High Court of the concerned State.

(2) No appointment of a Chairperson or a Member of the State Commission shall be invalid merely by reason of any vacancy in the Committee.

Removal of a Member of the State Commission

(1) Subject to the provisions of sub-section (2), the Chairperson or any other member of the State Commission shall only be removed from his office by order of the President on the ground of proved misbehaviour or incapacity after the Supreme Court, on a reference being made to it by the President, has, on inquiry held in accordance with the procedure prescribed in that behalf by the Supreme Court, reported that the Chairperson or such other Member, as the case may be, ought on any such ground to be removed.

(2) Notwithstanding anything in sub-section (1), the President may by order remove from office the Chairperson or any other Member if the Chairperson or such other Member, as the case may be –

(a) is adjudged an insolvent; OR

(b) engages during his term of office in any paid employment outside the duties of his office; OR

(c) is unfit to continue in office by reason of infirmity of mind or body; OR

(d) is of unsound mind and stands so declared by a competent court; OR

(e) is convicted and sentenced to imprisonment for an offence which in the opinion of the President involves moral turpitude.

Term of Office of Members of the State Commission

(1) A person appointed as Chairperson shall hold office for a term of five years from the date on which he enters upon his office or until he attains the age of seventy years, whichever is earlier;

(2) A person appointed as a Member shall hold office for a term of five years from the date on which he enters upon his office and shall be eligible for re-appointment for another term of five years;

Provided that no Member shall hold office after he has attained the age of seventy years.

(3) On ceasing to hold office, a Chairperson or a Member shall be ineligible for further employment under the Government of a State or under the Government of India.

Member to Act as Chairperson or to Discharge his Functions in Certain Circumstances

(1) In the event of the occurrence of any vacancy in the office of the Chairperson by reason of his death, resignation or otherwise, the Governor may, by notification, authorise one of the Members to act as the Chairperson until the appointment of a new Chairperson to fill such vacancy.

(2) When the Chairperson is unable to discharge his functions owing to absence on leave or otherwise, such one of the Members as the Governor may, by notification, authorise in this behalf, shall discharge the functions of the Chairperson until the date on which the Chairperson resumes his duties.

Terms and Conditions of Service of Members of the State Commission

The salaries and allowances payable to, and other terms and conditions of service of, the Members shall be such as may be prescribed by the State Government.

Provided that neither the salary and allowances nor the other terms and conditions of service of a Member shall be varied to his disadvantage after his appointment.

Officers and Other Staff of the State Commission

(1) The State Government shall make available to the Commission

(a) an officer not below the rank of a Secretary to the State Government who shall be the Secretary of the State Commission; and

(b) such police and investigative staff under an officer not below the rank of an Inspector General of Police and such other officers and staff as may be necessary for the efficient performance of the functions of the State Commission.

(2) subject to such rules as may be made by the State Government in this behalf, the State Commission may appoint such other addministrative, technical and scientific staff as it may consider necessary.

(3) The salaries, allowances and conditions of service of the officers and other staff appointed under sub-section (2) shall be such as may be prescribed by the State Government.

Annual and Special Reports of State Commission

(1) The State Commission shall submit an annual report to the State Government and may at any time submit special reports on any matter which, in its opinion, is of such urgency or importance that it should not be deferred till submission of the annual report.

(2) The State Government shall cause the annual and special reports of the State Commission to be laid before each House of State Legislature where it consists of two Houses, or where such Legislature consists of one House, before that House along with a memorandum of action taken or proposed to be taken on the recommendations of the State Commission and the reasons for non-acceptance of the rections, if any.

Application of Certain Provisions Relating to National Human Rights Commission to State Commissions

The provisions of sections 9, 10, 12, 13, 14, 15, 16, 17 and 18 shall apply to a State Commission and shall have effect, subject to the following modifications, namely :-

(a) references to "Commission" shall be construed as refer ences to "State Commission";

(b) in section 10, in sub-section (3), for the word "Secretary General", the word "Secretary" shall be substituted;

(c) in section 12, clause (f) shall be omitted;

(d) in section 17, in clause (i), the words "Central Government or any" shall be omitted;

Human Rights Courts

For the Purpose of Providing Speedy Trial of Offences Arising Out of Violation of Human Rights, the State

Government may, with the concurrence of the Chief Justice of the High Court, by notification, specify for each district a Court of Session to be a Human Rights Court to try the said offences.

Provided that nothing in this section shall apply if:

(a) a Court of Session is already specified as a special court; or

(b) a special court is already constituted, for such offences under any other law for the time being in force.

Special Public Prosecutor

For every Human Rights Court, the State Government shall, by notification, specify a Public Prosecutor or appoint an advocate who has been in practice as an advocate for not less than seven years, as a Special Public Prosecutor for the purpose of conducting cases in that Court.

Finance, Accounts and Audit

Grants by the Central Government:

(1) The Central Government shall after due appropriation made by Parliament by law in this behalf, pay to the Commission by way of grants such sums of money as the Central Government may think fit for being utilised for the purposes of this Act.

(2) The Commission may spend such sums as it thinks fit for performing the functions under this Act, and such sums shall be treated as expenditure payable out of the grants referred to in sub-section (1).

Grants by the State Government

(1) The State Government shall, after due appropriation made by Legislature by law in this behalf, pay to the State Commission by way of grants such sums of money

as the State Government may think fit for being utilised for the purposes of this Act.

(2) The State Commission may spend such sums as it thinks fit for performing the functions under Chapter V, and such sums shall be treated as expenditure payable out of the grants referred to in sub-section (1).

Accounts and Audit

(1) The Commission shall maintain proper accounts and other relevant records and prepare an annual statement of accounts in such form as may be prescribed by the Central Government in consultation with the Comptroller and Auditor-General of India.

(2) The Accounts of the Commission shall be audited by the Comptroller and Auditor-General at such intervals as may be specified by him and any expenditure incurred in connection with such audit shall be payable by the Commission to the Comptroller and Auditor-General.

(3) The Comptroller and Auditor-General or any person appointed by him in connection with the audit of the accounts of the Commision under this Act shall have the same rights and privileges and the authority in connection with such audit as the Comptroller and Auditor-General generally has in connection with the audit of Government ac counts and, in particular, shall have the right to demand the production of books, accounts, connected vouchers and other documents and papers and to inspect any of the offices of the Commission.

(4) The accounts of the Commission as certified by the Comptroller and Auditor-General or any other person appointed by him in this behalf, together with the audit report thereon shall be forwarded only to the Central Government by the Commission and the Central Government shall cause the audit report to be laid as soon as may be after it is received before each House of Parliament.

Accounts and Audit of State Commission

(1) The State Commission shall maintain proper accounts and other relevant records and prepare an annual statement of accounts in such form as may be prescribed by the State Government in consultation with the Comptroller and Auditor-General of India.

(2) The accounts of the State Commission shall be audited by the Comptroller and Auditor-General at such intervals as may be specified by him and any expenditure incurred in connection with such audit shall be payable by the State Commission to the Comptroller and Auditor-General.

(3) The Comptroller and Auditor-General or any person appointed by him in connection with the audit of the accounts of the State Commission under this Act shall have the same rights and privileges and the authority in connection with such audit as the Comptroller and Auditor-General generally has in connection with the audit of Government accounts and, in particular, shall have the right to demand the production of books, accounts, connected vouchers and other documents and papers and to inspect any of the offices of the State Commission.

(4) The accounts of the State Commission, as certified by the Comptroller and Auditor-General or any other person appointed by him in this behalf, together with the audit report thereon, shall be forwarded annually to the State Government by the State Commission and the State Government shall cause the audit report to be laid, as soon as may be after it is received, before the State Legislature.

Courts in India

One of the objects of the Protection of Human Rights Act, 1993 as stated in the preamble of the Act, is the establishment of human rights courts at district level. The creation of Human Rights Courts at the district level has a great potential to protect and realize human rights at the grassroots.

The Protection of Human Rights Act, 1993 provides for establishment Human Rights Courts for the purpose of providing speedy trial of offences arising out of violation of human rights. It provides that the state Government may, with the concurrence of the Chief Justice of the High Court, by notification, specify for each district a Court of Sessions to be a Human Rights Court to try the said offences. The object of establishment of such Courts at district level is to ensure speedy disposal of cases relating to offences arising out of violation of human rights.

The Act refers to the offences arising out of violations of human rights. But it does not define or explain the meaning of "offences arising out of violations of human rights". It is vague. The Act dose not give any clear indication or clarification as to what type of offences actually are to be tried by the Human Rights Courts. No efforts are made by the Central Government in this direction. Unless the offence is not defined the courts cannot take cognizance of the offences and try them. Till then the Human Rights Courts will remain only for namesake.

Even if "offences arising out of violations of human rights" are defined and clarified or classified, another problem arises in the working of the Human Rights courts in India. The problem is who can take cognizance of the offences. What the Act says is in each district, one Sessions Court has to be specified for trying "offences arising out of human rights violation". It is silent about taking of cognizance of the offence. The Prevention of Corruption Act, 1988 is another law, which provides for appointment of a Sessions Judge in each district as Special Judge to try the offence under the said Act. Provision has been made in section 5 of the Prevention of Corruption Act, 1988 empowering the Special Judge to take cognizance of the offences under the said Act. In the Protection of Human Rights Act, 1993 it is not so.

Sessions Court of the district concerned is considered as the Human Rights Court. Under the Criminal Procedure Code, 1973 a Sessions Judge cannot take cognizance of the offence.

He can only try the cases committed to him by the magistrate under Section 193 of the Cr. P.C.

Similar problem had arisen in working of the Scheduled Castes and Scheduled Tribes (Prevention of Atrocities) Act, 1989 in the beginning. The Special Judges used to take cognizance of the offences. In Potluri Purna Chandra Prabhakara Rao V. State of A.P., 2002(1) Criminal Court cases 150, Ujjagar Singh & Others V. State of Haryana & another, 2003(1) Criminal Court Cases 406 and some other cases it was held that the Special Court (Court of Session) does not get jurisdiction to try the offence under the Act without committal by the Magistrate.

The Supreme Court also held same view in Moly & another V. State of Kerala, 2004(2) Criminal Court Cases 514. Consequently the trial of all the cases under the Prevention of Atrocities Act were stopped and all the cases were sent to the Courts of jurisdictional Magistrates. Thereafter the respective Magistrates took cognizance of the cases and committed them to the Special Courts. The Special Courts started trying the cases after they were committed to them. The Act was later amended giving the Special Courts the power to take cognizance of the offences under Act.

The situation in respect of the Human Rights courts under the Protection of Human Rights Act, 1993 is not different.

Apart from the above, the Special Courts will face yet another question whether provisions of Section 197 of Cr.P.C. are applicable for taking cognizance of the offences under the Protection of Human Rights Act, 1993. In most of the cases of violation of human rights it is the police and other public officers who will be accused.

The offence relate to commission or omission of the public servants in discharge of their duties. Definitely the accused facing the trial under the Act raise the objection. There are plethora of precedents in favour of dispensing with the applicability of Section 197 of Cr.P.C. on the ground that such acts (like the ones which result in violation of human rights) do not come within the purview of the duties of public servants.

But there is scope for speculation as long as there is no specific provision in the Act dispensing with the applicability of Section 197 of Cr.P.C.

The object of establishment of such Courts at district level is to ensure speedy disposal of cases relating to offences arising out of violation of human rights. Unless the lawmakers take note of the above anomalies and remove them by proper amendments the aim for which provisions are made for establishment of special courts will not be achieved.

The National Commission for Women

The National Commission for Women was set up as statutory body in January 1992 under the National Commission for Women Act, 1990 (Act No. 20 of 1990 of Govt. of India) to:

- review the Constitutional and Legal safeguards for women ;
- recommend remedial legislative measures ;
- facilitate redressal of grievances and
- advise the Government on all policy matters affecting women.

In keeping with its mandate, the Commission initiated various steps to improve the status of women and worked for their economic empowerment during the year under report. The Commission completed its visits to all the States/UTs except Lakshdweep and prepared Gender Profiles to assess the status of women and their empowerment. It received a large number of complaints and acted suo-moto in several cases to provide speedy justice.

It took up the issue of child marriage, sponsored legal awareness programmes, Parivarik Mahila Lok Adalats and reviewed laws such as Dowry Prohibition Act, 1961, PNDT Act 1994, Indian Penal Code 1860 and the National Commission for Women Act, 1990 to make them more stringent and effective. It organized workshops/consultations, constituted expert committees on economic empowerment of women, conducted workshops/seminars for gender awareness and took up publicity campaign against female foeticide, violence against women, etc. in order to generate awareness in the society against these social evils.

- The Committee on the Status of Women in India (CSWI) recommended nearly two decades ago, the setting up of a National Commission for women to fulfill the surveillance functions to facilitate redressal of grievances and to accelerate the socio-economic development of women.
- Successive Committees / Commissions / Plans including the National Perspective Plan for Women (1988-2000) recommended the constitution of an apex body for women.
- During 1990, the central government held consultations with NGOs, social workers and experts, regarding the structure, functions, powers etc. of the Commission proposed to be set up.
- In May 1990, the Bill was introduced in the Lok Sabha.
- In July 1990, the HRD Ministry organized a National Level Conference to elicit suggestions regarding the Bill. In August 1990 the government moved several amendments and introduced new provisions to vest the commission with the power of a civil court.
- The Bill was passed and received accent of the President on 30th August 1990.
- The First Commission was constituted on 31st January 1992 with Mrs. Jayanti Patnaik as the Chairperson. The Second Commission was constituted on July 1995 with Dr. (Mrs.) Mohini Giri as the Chairperson. The Third Commission was constituted on January 1999 with Mrs. Vibha Parthasarathy as the Chairperson. The Fourth Commission was constituted on January 2002 and the government had nominated Dr. Poornima Advani as the Chairperson. The Fifth Commission has been constituted on February 2005 and the government has nominated Dr. Girija Vyas as the Chairperson.

SECTION 3
National Commission for Women Act, 1990
(Act No. 20 of 1990 of Govt. of India)

1. The Central Government shall constitute a body to be known as the National Commission for Women to exercise the powers conferred on and to perform the functions assigned to, it under this Act.
2. The Commission shall consist of :-
   a. A Chairperson, committed to the cause of women, to be nominated by the Central Government.
   b. five Members to be nominated by the Central Government from amongst persons of ability, integrity and standing who have had experience in law or legislation, trade unionism, management of an industry potential of women, women's voluntary organisations (including women activist), administration, economic development, health, education or social welfare;

      Provided that at least one Member each shall be from amongst persons belonging to the Scheduled Castes and Scheduled Tribes respectively;
   c. a Member-Secretary to be nominated by the Central Government who shall be :-
      i. an expert in the field of management, organisational structure or sociological movement, or
      ii. an officer who is a member of a civil service of the Union or of an all-India service or holds a civil post under the Union with appropriate experience.

The Mandate of The Commission

SECTION 10
National Commission for Women Act, 1990
(Act No. 20 of 1990 of Govt. of India)

1. The commission shall perform all or any of the following functions, namely:

a. Investigate and examine all matters relating to the safeguards provided for women under the Constitution and other laws;
b. present to the Central Government, annually and at such other times as the Commission may deem fit, reports upon the working of those safeguard;
c. make in such reports recommendations for the effective implementation of those safeguards for the improving the conditions of women by the Union or any state;
d. review, from time to time, the exiting provisions of the Constitution and other laws affecting women and recommend amendments thereto so as to suggest remedial legislative measures to meet any lacunae, inadequacies or shortcomings in such legislations;
e. take up cases of violation of the provisions of the Constitution and of other laws relating to women with the appropriate authorities;
f. look into complaints and take suo moto notice of matters relating to:-
    i. deprivation of women's rights;
    ii. non-implementation of laws enacted to provide protection to women and also to achieve the objective of equality and development;
    iii. non-compliance of policy decisions, guidelines or instructions aimed at mitigating hardships and ensuring welfare and providing relief to women, and take up the issues arising out of such matters with appropriate authorities;
g. call for special studies or investigations into specific problems or situations arising out of discrimination and atrocities against women and identify the constraints so as to recommend strategies for their removal;
h. undertake promotional and educational research so as to suggest ways of ensuring due representation

of women in all spheres and identify factors responsible for impeding their advancement, such as, lack of access to housing and basic services, inadequate support services and technologies for reducing drudgery and occupational health hazards and for increasing their productivity;

i. participate and advice on the planning process of socio-economic development of women;

j. evaluate the progress of the development of women under the Union and any State;

k. inspect or cause to inspected a jail, remand home, women's institution or other place of custody where women are kept as prisoners or otherwise and take up with the concerned authorities for remedial action, if found necessary;

l. fund litigation involving issues affecting a large body of women;

m. make periodical reports to the Government on any matter pertaining to women and in particular various difficulties under which women toil;

n. any other matter which may be referred to it by Central Government.

State Commission for Women

THE KARNATAKA STATE COMMISSION FOR WOMEN ACT, 1995

ARRANGAMENT OF SECTIONS

Statement of Object and Reasons

Sections:

Preliminary

1. Short title and commencement.
2. Definitions.

State Commission for Women

3. Constitution of the Commission.

4. Term of office and conditions of service of chairperson and members.
5. Secretary.
6. Staff of the Commission.
7. Meetings of the Commission.
8. Vacancies etc., not to invalidate proceedings of the Commission.

Functions and Powers of the Commission

9. Functions of the Commission.
10. Powers of the Commission.
11. Committees of the Commission.

Finance, Account and Audit

12. Budget of the Commission and grants by the Government.
13. Account s and Audit.
14. Annual report.
15. Annual report and audit report to be laid before the State Legislature.

National Commission of SC/ST

The framers of the Constitution took note of the fact that certain communities in the country were suffering from extreme social, educational and economic backwardness arising out of age-old practice of untouchability and certain others on account of this primitive agricultural practices, lack of infrastructure facilities and geographical isolation, and who need special consideration for safeguarding their interests and for their accelerated socio-economic development. These communities were notified as Scheduled Castes and Scheduled Tribes as per provisions contained in Clause 1 of Articles 341 and 342 of the Constitution respectively.

With a view to provide safeguards against the exploitation of SCs & STs and to promote and protect their social, educational, economic and cultural interests, special provisions were made in the Constitution. Due to their social disability and economic backwardness, they were grossly handicapped in getting reasonable share in elected offices, Government jobs and educational institutions and, therefore, it was considered necessary to follow a policy of reservations in their favour to ensure their equitable participation in governance. For effective implementation of various safeguards provided in the Constitution for the SCs & STs and various other protective legislations, the Constitution provided for appointment of a Special Officer under Article 338 of the Constitution. The Special Officer who was designated as Commissioner for SCs & STs was assigned the duty to investigate all matters relating to the safeguards for SCs and STs in various statutes and to report to the President upon the working of these safeguards. In order to facilitate effective functioning of the office of the Commissioner for SCs & STs 17 regional offices of the Commissioner were set up in different parts of the country.

On persistent demand of the Members of Parliament that the Office of the Commissioner for SCs & STs alone was not enough to monitor the implementation of Constitutional safeguards, a proposal was moved for amendment of Article 338 of the Constitution (46 Amendment) for replacing the arrangement of one Member system with a Multi-Member system while the amendment to Article 338 was still under consideration, the Government decided to set up a Multi-Member Commission through an administrative decision vide Ministry of Home Affairs' Resolution No.13013/9/77-SCT(1) dated 21.7.1978. The first Commission for SCs & STs was, therefore, set up in August, 1978 with Shri Bhola Paswan Shastri as Chairman and other four Members. The field offices of the erstwhile Commissioner for Scheduled Castes and Scheduled Tribes, which were transferred under the control of DG backward classes welfare in 1965, were brought back under the control of this Commission. The functions of the Commission for SCs & STs broadly corresponded with those of the Commissioner for SCs & STs.

The functions of the Multi-Member Commission set-up in 1978 were modified vide Ministry of Welfare's Resolution No.

BC-13015/12/86-SCD VI dated 1-9-1987 and the Commission for SCs & STs was renamed as the National Commission for Scheduled Castes and Scheduled Tribes. It was set up as a National Level Advisory Body to advise the Government on broad policy issues and levels of development of Scheduled Castes and Scheduled Tribes.

The statutory National Commission for Scheduled Castes and Scheduled Tribes (hereinafter referred to as the Commission) came into being consequent upon passing of the Constitution (Sixty fifth Amendment) Bill, 1990 which was notified on 8-6-1990 **(Annexure I of the handbook)** and the Rules there under were notified on 3-11-1990. The first Commission under the Constitution (65tAmendment) Act was constituted on 12-3-1992 replacing the Commissioner for Scheduled Castes and Scheduled Tribes and the Commission set up under the Ministry of Welfare's Resolution of 1987. The first Commission consisted of Shri Ram Dhan as the Chairman, Shri Bandi Oraon as the Vice-Chairman and Shri B. Sammaiah, Dr. Sarojini Mahishi, Choudhary Hari Singh, Shri N. Brahma and Shri Jina Bhai Darjee as Members.

The second Commission was constituted on 5-10-1995 with Shri H. Hanumanthappa as Chairman and Smt. Omem Moyong Deori as Vice-Chairperson. The Members of the Commission were Shri N.C. Chaturvedi, Shri Anand Mohan Biswas, Ven. Lama Lobzang, Shri Nar Singh Baitha and Shri B. Yadaiah.

The third Commission was constituted in December, 1998 vide Ministry of Social Justice and Empowerment's Notification No.5035(E) dated 27 January,1999 consisting of Shri Dileep Singh Bhuria as the Chairman, Shri Kameshwar Paswan as the Vice-Chairman and Shri Harinder Singh Khalsa, Ven. Lama Lobzang, Shri Chhotray Majhi and Shri M. Kannan as Members, Smt. Veena Nayyar, Member was also appointed as Member vide Ministry of Social Justice & Empowerment" Notification No. S.O. 529 (E) dated 30 June 1999. On the resignation of Shri M. Kannan, Shri C. Chellappan was appointed, as Member vides Ministry of Social Justice & Empowerment's Notification No. S.O. 722 (E) dated 3-7-2000.

The fourth Commission was constituted in March, 2002 vide Ministry of Social Justice and Empowerment's Notification No. S.O. 351 (E) dated 21-3-2002 consisting of Dr. Bizay Sonkar Shastri as the Chairperson, Ven. Lama Chosphel Zotpa, Vice-Chairperson and Shri Vijay Kumar Choudhary, Shri Narayan Singh Kesari and Shri Tapir Gao as Members, Smt. Veena Premkumar Sharma assumed office on 23-8-2002 as Member and Shri C. Chellappan as Member completed his tenure on 2 July, 2003. Shri Sampath Kumar assumed office on 30-9-2003 in place of Sh. C. Chellappan.

Consequent upon the Constitution (Eighty-Ninth Amendment) Act, 2003 (Annexure II **of the handbook)** coming into force on 19-2-2004 vide Notification of that date (Annexure III **of the handbook)** the erstwhile National Commission for Scheduled Castes & Scheduled Tribes has been replaced by (1) National Commission for Scheduled Castes, and (2) National Commission for Scheduled Tribes. The Rules of the National Commission for Scheduled Castes were notified on 20 February, 2004 by the Ministry of Social Justice & Empowerment (Annexure IV **of the handbook)** . National Commission for Scheduled Castes was constituted with S/Shri Suraj Bhan, Chairperson, Fakirbhai Vaghela, Vice-Chairperson, Phool Chand Verma, V. Devendra and Smt. Surekha Lambture as Members. Due to sudden and unexpected demise of Dr. Suraj Bhan, Chairperson on 6.8.2006, the duties and function of the chairperson were discharged by Shri Fakirbhai Vaghela, Vice-Chairperson of the Commission.

The Second National Commission for Scheduled Castes in series was constituted on 25.05.2007 vide Ministry of Social Justice & Empowerment's letter No.17016/21/2006-SCD-VI with Dr. Buta Singh as the Chairperson, Prof. Narendra M.Kamble, the Vice-Chairperson and Smt. Satya Bahin, Shri Murtyunjay Nayak and Shri Mahendra Boddh respectively as Members.

The Chairman and Vice-Chairman of the Commission has been conferred the status of Union Cabinet Minister and Union Minister of State and the Members of the Commission will enjoy a rank of Secretary to the Government of India.

Backward Class Commission

Pursuant to the direction of the Supreme Court in the Mandal case judgement, the Government of India enacted the National Commission for Backward Classes Act, 1993 (Act No. 27 of 1993) for setting up a National Commission for Backward Classes at the Centre as a permanent body.

The Act came into effect on the 2nd April, 1993. Section 3 of the Act provides that the Commission shall consist of five Members, comprising of a Chairperson who is or has been a judge of the Supreme Court or of a High Court; a social scientist; two persons, who have special knowledge in matters relating to backward classes; and a Member-Secretary, who is or has been an officer of the Central Government in the rank of a Secretary to the Government of India.

The Government of India constituted the Commission by its Notification No. 12011/34/BCC/Pt. 1 dated 14th August 1993 with a term of three years. The Commission was subsequently re-constituted on 28.2.1997. and 28.7.2000.

Minority Commission

The setting up of Minorities Commission was envisaged in the Ministry of Home Affairs Resolution dated 12.01.1978 which specifically mentioned that, "despite the safeguards provided in the Constitution and the laws in force, there persists among the Minorities a feeling of inequality and discrimination. In order to preserve secular traditions and to promote National Integration the Government of India attaches the highest importance to the enforcement of the safeguards provided for the Minorities and is of the firm view that effective institutional arrangements are urgently required for the enforcement and implementation of all the safeguards provided for the Minorities in the Constitution, in the Central and State Laws and in the government policies and administrative schemes enunciated from time to time.

Some time in 1984 the Minorities Commission was detached from Ministry of Home Affairs and placed under the newly created Ministry of Welfare.

National Commission for Minorities

With the enactment of the National Commission for Minorities Act, 1992, the Minorities Commission became a statutory body and renamed as National Commission for Minorities. The first Statutory National Commission was set up on 17th May 1993. Vide a Gazette notification issued on 23rd October 1993 by Ministry of Welfare, Government of India, five religious communities viz; the Muslims, Christians, Sikhs, Buddhists and Zoroastrians (Parsis) were notified as minority communities. As per the 2001 Census, these five religious minority communities constitute 18.42% of the country's population.

Functions of NCM

As per Section 9(1) of the NCM At, 1992, the Commission is required to perform following functions:-

(a) evaluation of the progress of the development of minorities under the Union and States;

(b) monitoring of the working of the safeguards for minorities provided in the Constitution and in laws enacted by Parliament and the State Legislatures;

(c) making recommendations for the effective implementation of safeguards for the protection of the interests of minorities by the Central Government or the State Governments;

(d) looking into specific complaints regarding deprivation of rights and safeguards of minorities and taking up such matters with the appropriate authorities;

(e) getting studies to be undertaken into the problems arising out of any discrimination against minorities and recommending measures for their removal;

(f) conducting studies, research and analysis on the issues relating to socio-economic and educational development of minorities;

(g) suggesting appropriate measures in respect of any minority to be undertaken by the Central Government or the State Governments;

(h) making periodical or special reports to the Central Government or any matter pertaining to minorities and in particular the difficulties confronted by them; and

(i) any other matter, which may be referred to it by the Central Government.

Section 2 (c) of NCM Act, 1992 stipulates that 'Minority' for the purposes of the Act, means a community notified as such by the Central Government. Therefore, all the functions of the Commission as laid down in Section 9(1) of the Act are related to the five notified communities.

Complaints from Notified Minority Communities

Since the financial year 2000-01, the Commission received the following number of complaints (year-wise):-

2000 – 01 2478

2001 – 02 2590

2002 – 03 3146

2003 – 04 3578

2004 – 05 3342

2005 – 06 2078 (as on 31.12.2005)

The complaints now being received are mostly related to police atrocities, service matters, minority educational institutions and encroachments to religious properties. Reports were called for from the concerned authorities under the Union and State Governments. On receipt of the reports, the Commission made appropriate recommendations to the respective authorities for redressal of the grievances.

Non-governmental Organization

Non-governmental organization (**NGO**) is a term that has become widely accepted for referring to a legally constituted, non-business organization created by natural or legal persons with no participation or representation of any government. In the cases in which NGOs are funded totally or partially by governments, the NGO maintains its non-governmental status therefore it excludes government representatives from membership in the organization. Unlike the term *intergovernmental organization*, "non-governmental organization" is a term in generalized use but not a legal definition, in many jurisdictions these type of organizations are defined as "civil society organizations" or alternative terms.

The number of internationally operating NGOs is estimated at 40,000. National numbers are even higher: Russia has 277,000 NGOs. India is estimated to have between 1 million and 2 million NGOs.

History

International non-governmental organizations have a history dating back to at least 1839. Rotary, later Rotary International, was founded in 1904. It has been estimated that by 1914 there were 1083 NGOs. International NGOs were important in the anti-slavery movement and the movement for women's suffrage, and reached a peak at the time of the World Disarmament Conference. However, the phrase "non-governmental organization" only came into popular use with the establishment of the United Nations Organization in 1945 with provisions in Article 71 of Chapter 10 of the United Nations Charter for a consultative role for organizations which are neither governments nor member states—see Consultative Status. The definition of "international NGO" (INGO) is first given in resolution 288 (X) of ECOSOC on February 27, 1950: it is defined as "any international organization that is not founded by an international treaty". The vital role of NGOs and other "major groups" in sustainable development was recognized in Chapter 27 of Agenda 21, leading to intense arrangements for a consultative relationship between the United Nations and non-governmental organizations.

Rapid development of nongovernmental sector occurred in western countries as a result of the processes of restructurization of the welfare state. Further globalisation of that process occurred after a fall of communist system and was important part of Washington consensus.

Globalization during the 20th century gave rise to the importance of NGOs. Many problems could not be solved within a nation. International treaties and international organizations such as the World Trade Organization were perceived as being too centred on the interests of capitalist enterprises. Some argued that in an attempt to counterbalance this trend, NGOs have developed to emphasize humanitarian issues, developmental aid and sustainable development. A prominent example of this is the World Social Forum which is a rival convention to the World Economic Forum held annually in January in Davos, Switzerland. The fifth World Social Forum in Porto Alegre, Brazil, in January 2005 was attended by representatives from more than 1,000 NGOs. Some have argued that in forums like these, NGOs take the place of what should belong to popular movements of the poor. Others argue that NGOs are often imperialist in nature, that they sometimes operate in a racialized manner in dominated countries, and that they fulfil a similar function to that of the clergy during the high colonial era. The philosopher Peter Hallward argues that they are an aristocratic form of politics. Whatever the case, NGO transnational networking is now extensive.

Types of NGOs

Apart from "NGO", often alternative terms are used as for example: independent sector, volunteer sector, civil society, grassroots organizations, transnational social movement organizations, private voluntary organizations, self-help organizations and non-state actors (NSA's).

Non-governmental organizations are a heterogeneous group. A long list of acronyms has developed around the term "NGO".

These include:

- BINGO is short for business-oriented international NGO, or big international NGO;
- CSO, short for civil society organization;
- DONGO: Donor Organized NGO;
- ENGO: short for environmental NGO, such as Global 2000;

- GONGOs are government-operated NGOs, which may have been set up by governments to look like NGOs in order to qualify for outside aid or promote the interests of the government in question;
- INGO stands for international NGO; Education charter international is an international NGO
- QUANGOs are quasi-autonomous non-governmental organizations, such as the International Organization for Standardization (ISO). (The ISO is actually not purely an NGO, since its membership is by nation, and each nation is represented by what the ISO Council determines to be the 'most broadly representative' standardization body of a nation. That body might itself be a nongovernmental organization; for example, the United States is represented in ISO by the American National Standards Institute, which is independent of the federal government. However, other countries can be represented by national governmental agencies; this is the trend in Europe.)
- TANGO: short for technical assistance NGO;
- GSO: Grassroots Support Organization

There are also numerous classifications of NGOs. The typology the World Bank uses divides them into Operational and Advocacy:

The primary purpose of an operational NGO is the design and implementation of development-related projects. One frequently used categorization is the division into :relief-oriented: or :development-oriented: organizations; they can also be classified according to whether they stress service delivery or participation; or whether they are religious or secular; and whether they are more public or private-oriented. Operational NGOs can be community-based, national or international.

The primary purpose of an Advocacy NGO is to defend or promote a specific cause. As opposed to operational project management, these organizations typically try to raise awareness, acceptance and knowledge by lobbying, press work and activist events.

USAID refers to NGOs as *private voluntary organisations*. However many scholars have argued that this definition is highly problematic as many NGOs are in fact state and corporate funded and managed projects with professional staff. Furthermore it has often been argued that USAID is in fact a key arm of American imperialism and that it sets up and supports NGOs in order to further imperial agendas.

NGOs exist for a variety of reasons, usually to further the political or social goals of their members or funders. Examples include improving the state of the natural environment, encouraging the observance of human rights, improving the welfare of the disadvantaged, or representing a corporate agenda. However, there are a huge number of such organizations and their goals cover a broad range of political and philosophical positions. This can also easily be applied to private schools and athletic organizations.

Methods

NGOs vary in their methods. Some act primarily as lobbyists, while others conduct programs and activities primarily. For instance, an NGO such as Oxfam, concerned with poverty alleviation, might provide needy people with the equipment and skills to find food and clean drinking water, whereas an NGO like the FFDA helps through investigation and documentation of human rights violations and provides legal assistance to victims of human rights abuses.

Public Relations

Non-governmental organizations need healthy relationships with the public to meet their goals. Foundations and charities use sophisticated public relations campaigns to raise funds and employ standard lobbying techniques with governments. Interest groups may be of political importance because of their ability to influence social and political outcomes.

Consulting

Many international NGOs have a consultative status with United Nations agencies relevant to their area of work. As an example, the Third World Network has a consultative status with the UN Conference on Trade and Development (UNCTAD) and the UN Economic and Social Council (ECOSOC). While in 1946, only 41 NGOs had consultative status with the ECOSOC, by 2003 this number had risen to 3,550.

Project Management

There is an increasing awareness that management techniques are crucial to project success in non-governmental organizations. Generally, non-governmental organizations that are private have either a community or environmental focus. They address varieties of issues such as religion, emergency aid, or humanitarian affairs. They mobilize public support and voluntary contributions for aid; they often have strong links with community groups in developing countries, and they often work in areas where government-to-government aid is not possible. NGOs are accepted as a part of the international relations landscape, and while they influence national and multilateral policy-making, increasingly they are more directly involved in local action.

Staffing

Not all people working for non-governmental organizations are volunteers. The reasons people volunteer are not necessarily purely altruistic, and can provide immediate benefits for themselves as well as those they serve, including skills, experience, and contacts.

There is some dispute as to whether expatriates should be sent to developing countries. Frequently this type of personnel is employed to satisfy a donor who wants to see the supported project managed by someone from an industrialized country. However, the expertise these employees or volunteers may have can be counterbalanced by a number of factors: the cost of foreigners is typically higher, they have no grassroot connections in the country they are sent to, and local expertise is often undervalued.

The NGO sector is an important employer in terms of numbers. For example, by the end of 1995, CONCERN worldwide, an international Northern NGO working against poverty, employed 174 expatriates and just over 5,000 national staff working in ten developing countries in Africa and Asia, and in Haiti.

Funding

Large NGOs may have annual budgets in the hundreds of millions or billions of dollars. For instance, the budget of the American Association of Retired Persons (AARP) was over US$540 million in 1999.. Funding such large budgets demands significant fundraising efforts on the part of most NGOs. Major sources of NGO funding include membership dues, the sale of goods and services, grants from international institutions or national governments, and private donations. Several EU-grants provide funds accessible to NGOs.

Even though the term "non-governmental organization" implies independence from governments, most NGOs depend heavily on governments for their funding. A quarter of the US$162 million income in 1998 of the famine-relief organization Oxfam was donated by the British government and the EU. The Christian relief and development organization World Vision collected US$55 million worth of goods in 1998 from the American government. Nobel Prize winner Medecins Sans Frontieres (MSF) (known in the USA as Doctors Without Borders) gets 46% of its income from government sources.

Monitoring and Control

In a March 2000 report on United Nations Reform priorities, former U.N. Secretary General Kofi Annan wrote in favor of international humanitarian intervention, arguing that the international community has a "right to protect" citizens of the world against ethnic cleansing, genocide, and crimes against humanity. On the heels of the report, the Canadian government launched the Responsibility to Protect R2PPDF (434 KiB) project, outlining the issue of humanitarian intervention. While the R2P doctrine has wide applications, among the more controversial has been the Canadian government's use of R2P to justify its intervention and support of the coup in Haiti.

Years after R2P, the World Federalist Movement, an organization which supports "the creation of democratic global structures accountable to the citizens of the world and call for the division of international authority among separate agencies", has launched Responsibility to Protect-Engaging Civil Society (R2PCS). A collaboration between the WFM and the Canadian government, this project aims to bring NGOs into lockstep with the principles outlined under the original R2P project. The governments of the countries an NGO works or is registered in may require reporting or other monitoring and oversight. Funders generally require reporting and assessment, such information is not necessarily publicly available. There may also be associations and watchdog organizations that research and publish details on the actions of NGOs working in particular geographic or program areas. In recent years, many large corporations have increased their corporate social responsibility departments in an attempt to preempt NGO campaigns against certain corporate practices. As the logic goes, if corporations work *with* NGOs, NGOs will not work *against* corporations.

In December 2007, The United States Department of Defense Assistant Secretary of Defense (Health Affairs) established an International Health Division under Force Health Protection & Readiness. Part of International Health's mission is to communicate with NGOs in areas of mutual interest. Department of Defense Directive 3000.05, in 2005, requires DoD to regard stability-enhancing activities as a mission of importance equal to warfighting. In compliance with international law, DoD has necessarily built a capacity to improve essential services in areas of conflict such as Iraq, where the customary lead agencies (State Department and USAID) find it difficult to operate. Unlike the "co-option" strategy described for corporations, the OASD(HA) recognizes the neutrality of health as an essential service. International Health cultivates collaborative relationships with NGOs, albeit at arms-length, recognizing their traditional independence, expertise and honest broker status. While the goals of DoD and NGOs may seem incongruent, the DoD's emphasis on stability and security to reduce and prevent conflict suggests, on careful analysis, important mutual interests.

Unit-VI

Human Rights and Marginalised Sections

The Rights of Ethnic and Racial Minorities

Introduction

One of the fundamental bedrocks of human rights is the principle that all human beings are born free and equal in dignity and rights. Discrimination and persecution on the grounds of race and ethnicity are clear violations of this principle. Racial discrimination can take many forms from the most brutal and institutional form of racisms-genocide and *apartheid*, to more covert forms whereby certain racial and ethnic groups are prevented from enjoying the same civil, political, economic, social and cultural rights as other groups in society.

Racial and ethnic discrimination continues to be a major human rights problem in the world today facing both minority and sometimes even majority populations. Much of the early focus of international attention was on apartheid in South Africa which came to an end in 1994. However, the struggle against ethnic and racial hatred has continued with the decade of the 1990's being riven with some of the worst ethnic conflicts the world has ever seen in the Balkans and the Great Lakes region in Africa.

Race is defined as "a group of people of common ancestry, distinguished from others by physical characteristics such as hair type, colour of eyes and skin, stature etc". (Collins English

Dictionary) Ethnic is defined as "relating to or characteristic of a human group having racial, religious, linguistic and certain other traits in common". (Collins English dictionary)

In international human rights law the term race is generally used in a broader sense and often blurs with other distinctions between groups of people based on religion, ethnicity, social groupings, language and culture. The term "race" in human rights law is sometimes used to encompass groups which may not fall into distinctive biological racial groupings, for example caste systems in India and Japan.

The International Convention on the Elimination of Racial Discrimination (article 1) does not define "race" but it does define "racial discrimination" to mean "any distinction, exclusion, restriction or preference based on race, colour, descent, or national or ethnic origin which has the purpose or effect of nullifying or impairing the recognition, enjoyment or exercise, on an equal footing, of human rights and fundamental freedoms in the political, economic, social, cultural or any other field of public life." Ethnicity is explicitly subsumed under this definition by the term "race". Most human rights treaties simply refer to "race" and do not use the terminology of "ethnicity".

Rights at Stake

The rights of ethnic and racial minorities are protected in international human rights law are as follows:

The Right to be Protected from Racial Discrimination, Hatred and Violence

International human rights law requires states not to engage in acts of racial discrimination and to carry out a variety of measures to prevent racial discrimination by public institutions, organisations and individuals. The nature of the measures required varies from treaty to treaty but can include: an obligation to review laws and policies to ensure they are not discriminatory; the eradication of racial segregation and apartheid; outlawing of propaganda espousing racial superiority; and banning of organisations promoting racial discrimination and hatred.

Right to Equal Protection before the Law Irrespective of Racial or Ethnic Origin

Racial and ethnic minorities have equal rights and the law should be equally applied of various civil, political, economic, social and cultural rights to these groups. Most human rights treaties (even those not specifically dealing with issues of race and ethnicity) specifically contain non-discriminatory provisions requiring states to apply principles of human rights law equally to all peoples irrespective of race, religion, social origin, etc.

Unequal treatment in the criminal justice system has been a particular area of concern in a number of countries with practices such as racial profiling (stop and search of suspects on the basis of racial origin) or uneven treatment in the arrest, prosecution and sentencing of offenders. Inequalities in health care provision, housing, education and employment for racial and ethnic minorities are common areas of concern.

The Right of Racial and Ethnic Groups to Enjoy Their Own Culture, Practice Their Own Religion and Use Their Own Language

This right appears in a several international human rights treaties and is an acknowledgement that racial and ethnic groups are free to act in accordance with their cultural heritage. There can sometimes be a conflict between the cultural, religious and linguistic practices and values of the state and the practices of minority groups. Some states have responded by insisting on a certain level of knowledge of the dominant culture and language.

Right to Benefit from Positive Steps Taken by the State to Promote Racial Harmony and the Rights of Racial Minorities

Governments are obliged to take special measures to ensure the adequate development and protection of racial groups. This includes affirmative action programmes. States are also required to promote racial understanding through the education system.

Right to Seek Asylum for Reasons of a Well-founded Fear of Persecution on the Grounds of Race, Religion, Nationality, Membership of a Particular Social Group or Political Opinion

This provision in international refugee law allows individuals to seek asylum in another state if the country of their nationality is unable to protect them from persecution on inter alia racial grounds. This is one of the few cases where the failure of a state to uphold human rights law creates the right for its individuals to seek the protection of another state. Moreover, states are required to apply the provisions of international refugee law in such a way that it does not discriminate on the grounds of race.

The Right to Remedies

Governments must ensure that effective protection and remedies are provided through competent national tribunals and other state institutions. Individuals also have the right to seek just and adequate reparation from such tribunals for damage done. This article may hold true for individual cases but is highly controversial when it comes to reparations for entire groups of people. The question of remedies was the main sticking point at the 2001 World Conference Against Racism with some countries insisting on a right to reparation, both financial and other, and some Western governments (former colonial powers and the USA) resisting any obligation to remedy past abuses. This debate is similar to the one surrounding issues of reparation to former slaves.

International and Regional Instruments for Protection and Promotion

International legal instruments take the form of a *treaty* (also called agreement, convention, or protocol) that binds the contracting states to the negotiated terms. When negotiations are completed, the text of a treaty is established as authentic and definitive and is "signed" by the representatives of states. A state can agree to be bound to a treaty in various ways. The most common are *ratification* or *accession*. A new treaty is ratified by those states that have negotiated the instrument.

A state that has not participated in the negotiations may, at a later stage, accede to the treaty. The treaty *enters into force*, or becomes valid, when a pre-determined number of states have ratified or acceded to the treaty.

When a state ratifies or accedes to a treaty, that state may make *reservations* to one or more articles of the treaty, unless reservations are prohibited by the treaty. Reservations may normally be withdrawn at any time. In some countries, international treaties take precedence over national law; in others a specific law may be required to give a ratified international treaty the force of a national law. Practically all states that have ratified or acceded to an international treaty must issue decrees, change existing laws, or introduce new legislation in order for the treaty to be fully effective on the national territory.

The *binding treaties* can be used to force governments to respect the treaty provisions that are relevant for the human right to adequate food and water. The *non-binding instruments*, such as declarations and resolutions, can be used in relevant situations to embarrass governments by negative public exposure; governments who care about their international image may consequently adapt their policies.

The following are the international treaties, declarations and commitments that determine standards for the protection of ethnic and racial minorities:

United Nations

Universal Declaration of Human Rights (1948) (article 2, 7): The Universal Declaration of Human Rights (UDHR) stipulates that everyone is entitled to the rights and freedoms set forth in the Declaration irrespective of their status, including their *racial and social origin* (article 2). Article 7 further affirms that all are equal before the law and are entitled to the protection of the law without discrimination.

Convention Relating to the Status of Refugees (1951) (article 1, 3): The Refugee Convention gives individuals the right to seek asylum on the grounds of well-founded fear of persecution based on *race*, religion, nationality, membership of a particular social group. Under article 3, states are required to implement these provisions "without discrimination as to *race*, religion or country of origin".

United Nations Declaration on the Elimination of All Forms of Racial Discrimination (1963): This declaration prepared the way for the treaty on the elimination of racial discrimination in 1965. States express their to intention to eliminate "racial discrimination throughout the world, in all its forms and manifestations, and of securing understanding of and respect for the dignity of the human person" and intend to adopt "national and international measures to that end, including teaching, education and information".

International Convention on the Elimination of All Forms of Racial Discrimination (1965): This treaty entered into force in 1969. This is the most comprehensive treaty concerning the rights of racial and ethnic minorities. It lays down in detail the steps required by states to prevent racial discrimination and violence and to foster greater racial harmony.

The convention is monitored by the Committee on the Elimination of Racial Discrimination (CERD) comprised of 18 experts. States are obliged to submit periodic progress reports on the implementation of the convention. Governments must submit reports irrespective of whether they believe they have a problem if racial discrimination. They are also obliged to give effect to the convention by taking preventive and educational measures etc. even if they believe the problem does not currently exist in their country. The committee is able to receive communications from individuals and groups claiming violations of the rights set forth in the convention.

International Covenant on Economic, Social and Cultural Rights (1966) (article 2): Article 2 emphasises that the rights protected in this treaty shall be exercised without distinction of social status or *race*.

International Covenant on Civil and Political Rights (1966) (article 2, 20, 26, 27): This main human rights treaty on civil and political rights obliges states to guarantee the rights set forth the Covenant "without distinction of any kind, such as race, colour, sex, language, religion, political or other opinion, national or social origin, property, birth or other status" (article 2). The treaty also requires governments to probihit by law any "national, racial or religious hatred that constitutes incitement to discrimination, hostility or violence" (article 20). ICCPR also stipulates that all persons are equal before the law and are entitled without any discrimination to the equal protection of the law (article 26). Minorities shall not be denied the right, in community with the other members of their group, to enjoy their own culture, to profess and practise their own religion, or to use their own language (article 27).

Rome Statute of the International Criminal Court (1998) (article 6, 7j): The statute of the International Criminal Court (ICC) gives the court jurisdiction over acts of genocide of specific national, ethnic, racial or religious groups under article 6. *Apartheid* is further defined as a crime against humanity in article 7(j).

UN treaties relating to specific categories of persons can also be used to protect racial and ethnic rights:

Convention on the Elimination of All Forms of Discrimination Against Women (1979): Discrimination against women from racial and ethnic minorities may also constitute breaches of this treaty and can be taken up with the Committee on the Elimination of Discrimination Against Women.

Convention on the Rights of the Child (1989) (article 30): This treaty protects the rights of children from ethnic, religious or linguistic minorities to enjoy their culture and to practice their religion and language. Violations of these rights can be taken up with the UN Committee on the Rights of the Child.

There are numerous other UN treaties and declarations aimed at combating the problem of discrimination against various racial, religious, social, ethnic groups etc. Examples include, the International Convention on the Suppression and Punishment of the Crime of *Apartheid* (1973), International

Convention against *Apartheid* in Sports (1985). UNESCO has adopted the Convention against Discrimination in Education (1960), which protects the rights of minority groups to education, the Declaration on Race and Racial Prejudice (1978) and the Declaration on Fundamental Principles concerning the Contribution to the Mass Media to Strengthening Peace and International Understanding, to the Promotion of Human Rights and to Countering Racialism, Apartheid and Incitement to War (1978).

The United Nations has taken a number of steps since its inception to combat the problem of racial discrimination. In addition to a number of declarations and conventions, efforts have been made to mobilise public opinion and awareness. 1971 was designated United Nations International Year for Action to Combat Racism and Racial Discrimination followed by two consecutive Decades for Action to Combat Racism and R acial Discrimination. World conferences to combat racism have been held under UN auspices in 1978, 1983 and 2001.

World Conference against Racism

The World Conference Against Racism, Racial Discrimination, Xenophobia and Related Intolerance, held in September 2001 in South Africa. The documents from the conference contain the latest pronouncements on government consensus concerning issues of race. The Commission on Human Rights established an Intergovernmental working group under its auspices in 2002 to make recommendations on the implementation of the Durban Declaration and Programme of Action and to prepare complementary international standards to update existing instruments.

Religious Minorities

Every woman, man, youth and child has the human right to freedom of thought, conscience and religion. These fundamental human rights are explicitly set out in the Universal Declaration of Human Rights, the International Covenant on Civil and Political Rights, the Declaration on the Elimination of All Forms of Intolerance and of Discrimination Based on

Religion or Belief and other widely adhered to international human rights treaties and Declarations.

- The Human Right to Freedom of Religion includes the following indivisible, interdependent and interrelated human rights:
- The human right to freedom of thought, conscience and religion.
- The human right to manifest one=s religion or belief in worship, observance, practice and teaching.
- The human right to freedom from discrimination based on religious beliefs or activities, or because of refusal to conform to a certain religion.
- The human right to freedom of expression and of association.
- The human right to conscientious objection on grounds of religious belief.
- The human right of parents to choose schools for their children which ensure the religious and moral education of their children in conformity with their own convictions.

Human Rights and Refugees

Asylum seekers and refugees are entitled to all the rights and fundamental freedoms that are spelled out in international human rights instruments. The protection of the refugee must therefore be seen in the broader context of the protection of human rights. The creation by States, in the aftermath of the Second World War, of two separate organizations to deal with human rights and refugees respectively, does not mean that these issues are not interrelated.

The work of the United Nations in the field of human rights and that of the High Commissioner for Refugees is inextricably linked in the sense that both entities share a common purpose which is the safeguarding of human dignity. The human rights programme of the United Nations deals with the rights of individuals in the territory of States. The refugee organization was established in order to restore minimum rights to persons after they leave their countries of origin.

The substantive link between human rights and refugees raises several questions:

In the first place, who is a refugee and what are his or her rights under international law? What are the rights of those asylum seekers who fail to qualify as refugees under the 1951 Convention and the 1967 Protocol? How can refugees be distinguished from economic migrants? Can the international community deny protection to those who claim not to receive protection from their country of origin?

Moreover, what exactly is the link between violations of human rights and movements of refugees? To what extent are those violations the causes of mass exoduses? In what ways can the rights of refugees be violated in the process of asylum-seeking in host countries?

Finally, what is the relationship between repatriation and human rights? Can repatriation be truly voluntary when the country of origin is unable, or unwilling, to guarantee respect for the civil, political, economic, social and cultural rights of its citizens?

Rights of Refugees

The present concept of international protection has evolved gradually and today implies a series of institutional and legal responses. Projecting refugees and seeking durable solutions to their problems are the two main functions of the High Commissioner for Refugees.

In practical terms, the task of international protection includes the prevention of refoulement, assistance in the processing of asylum seekers, providing legal counsel and aid, promoting arrangements for the physical safety of refugees, promoting and assisting voluntary repatriation, and helping refugees to resettle (article 8 of the Statute of the Office of the UNHCR).

Thus, the international protection function has a legal basis, and its exercise is mandatory for the High Commissioner. The right to protection, although not defined as a separate right as such, is implicit in the 1951 Convention and its fundamental provisions, particularly the principle of non-refoulement.

In addition, many universally recognized human rights are directly applicable to refugees. These include the right to life, protection from torture and ill-treatment, the right to a nationality, the right to freedom of movement, the right to leave any country, including one's own, and to return to one's country, and the right not to be forcibly returned.

These rights are affirmed, among other civil, political, economic, social and cultural rights, for all persons, citizens and non-citizens alike, in the Universal Declaration of Human Rights, the International Covenant on Civil and Political Rights, and the International Covenant on Economic, Social and Cultural Rights which together make up the International Bill of Human Rights.

(a) *"No one shall be subject to* arbitrary arrest, detention or exile" (Universal Declaration of Human Rights, article 9);

(b) "Everyone has the *right to seek and to enjoy in other countries asylum from persecution."* (Universal Declaration of Human Rights, article 14);

(c) "Everyone has the *right to a nationality"* (Universal Declaration of Human Rights, article 15);

(d) "Everyone has the *right to freedom of movement and residence within the borders of each State*" (Universal Declaration of Human rights, article 13; International Covenant on Civil and Political Rights, article 12).

Non-refoulement

Not all of the important rights for refugees are mentioned specifically in the International Bill of Human Rights. A central element of international protection is the right not to be forcibly returned or expelled to a situation which would threaten ones life or freedom. This is the principle of non-refoulement which is embodied in article 33 of the 1951 Convention.

The principle of non-refoulement finds further expression in article 3 of the United Nations Convention against Torture and Other Cruel, Inhuman or Degrading Treatment or Punishment which stipulates that "No State Party shall expel, return ("refouler") or extradite a person to another State where there are substantial grounds for believing that he would be in danger of being subjected to torture". Furthermore, "for the purpose of determining whether there are such grounds, the competent authorities shall take into account all relevant considerations including, where applicable, the existence in the State concerned of a consistent pattern of gross, flagrant or mass violations of human rights".

Refugee or Economic Migrant?

Some countries contend that the majority of asylum seekers are in fact not refugees but economic migrants. Currently, only an estimated 10 to 20 per cent of asylum seekers are granted refugee status in these countries. Contemporary refugee movements are different from those of the period immediately following the Second World War. Reasons for leaving are very often complex and not simply the result of immediate persecution. Persons flee because of civil conflicts, massive violations of their human rights, foreign aggression and occupation, poverty, famine, disease and ecological disasters. Many do not qualify as refugees on the basis of the United Nations definition.

In order to qualify, the person must be a "political" refugee. The 1951 Convention relating to the Status of Refugees places emphasis on "fear of persecution" but it does not define the term clearly. Its article 33 refers to threats to life and freedom of the individual "on account of his race, religion, nationality, membership of a particular social group or political opinion". This definition was drawn up in the context of the post-war years and does not correspond to many of today's refugee situations.

As a result some countries, especially in Africa and Latin America have expanded the definition of the term "refugee". In many other countries, however, the majority of applications for asylum are rejected on a strict reading of the 1951 definition.

From a human rights perspective, this situation raises great concern. It will not always be possible to distinguish, with certainty, between a refugee and an economic migrant. It may be argued that if the emphasis is placed on threats to life and freedom, there is little to distinguish between a person facing death through starvation and another threatened with arbitrary execution because of her political beliefs.

These considerations aside, the fact remains that regardless of whether a person is a refugee or an economic migrant, a citizen or a non-citizen, whether he or she is fleeing persecution, armed conflict, threats to his or her life or abject poverty, that person is entitled to minimum humanrights and minimum standards of treatment.

Violations of Human Rights and Refugees

Violations of Human Rights as Origins of Mass Exodus: Since 1980, both the United Nations General Assembly and the Commission on Human Rights have focused on ways to prevent mass exoduses. The Commission has included the question of human rights and mass exoduses in its agenda annually and in a number of resolutions it has emphasized the linkage between human rights violations and refugee movements. In recent years the Commission has also considered the plight of the internally displaced.

These two bodies, through various resolutions, have requested the Secretary-General to prepare reports on "International Cooperation to Avert New Flows of Refugees", appointed a Special Rapporteur to study the question of human ri-ghts and mass exoduses. and set up a 17 member Group of Governmental Experts on International Cooperation to Avert New Flows of Refugees.

The Special Rapporteur presented his study to the thirty-eighth session of the Commission on Human Rights in 1982. According to the report, mass exoduses do not only cause human deprivation and misery, but also place increasingly heavy burdens on the international community. In the light of the changing nature of refugee problems, the three traditional solutions of voluntary repatriation, local settlement and resettlement continue to be viable but must also be supplemented by other approaches.

The Special Rapporteur highlighted the multiplicity and complexity of the origins of mass exoduses. He identified violations of human rights as a major cause of mass exoduses:

"It is abundantly clear that unless ways can be found to counteract the withholding, of, or outright violations of, human rights, unless there is a more equitable sharing of the world's resources, more restraint and tolerance, the granting to everyone, regardless of race, religion, membership of a particular social group or political party, the right to belong or alternatively to move in an orderly fashion to seek work, decent living conditions and freedom from strife the world will continue to have to live with the problem of mass exodus. This problem, if left unchecked, will increasingly pose a threat to peace and stability around the globe.

The final report of the Group of Governmental Experts also stressed the complex and often interrelated political, economic, social and natural causes of mass exoduses. In its recommendations, the Group proposed that the General Assembly call upon Member States to avert new massive flows of refugees by respecting the principles of the Charter, in particular by not resorting to the threat or use of force, by settling their disputes peacefully, by promoting human rights and refraining from creatling conditions which could lead to massive flows of refugees, by cooperating with one another in order to prevent future flows of refugees, and by respecting international laws governing the treatment of refugees.

Following a recommendation by the Special Rapporteur in his report, the Secretary-General set up the Office for Research and the Collection of Information (ORCI) from 1987 to 1991. The Office served as a focal point for undertaking early warning activities to avert new and massive flows of refugees, for monitoring factors related to possible flows of refugees and displaced persons and comparable emergencies, as well as for preparing plans for possible responses. These functions are now being undertaken by the United Nations Department of Political Affairs. Such activities are an important part of the new and comprehensive approaches being considered by the international community to prevent massive flows of refugees. Prevention requires dealing with the root causes of problems. There is now increasing focus on political and economic conditions of countries of origin of refugees, including internal and external conflict, violations of human rights and level of development and economic performance. These issues are all interrelated. States have repeatedly emphasized that human rights are interdependent and include not only civil and political rights, but also economic, social and cultural rights. Respect for all these rights is the necessary condition for the attainment of human development and the preservation of human dignity.

In addition to its work on preventing mass exoduses, the Commission on Human Rights has, in recent years, also considered the plight of the internally displaced. In 1992, a representative of the Secretary-General was appointed inter alia to gather information on the human rights issues related to internally displaced persons and to examine existling international human rights, humanitarian and refugee laws and standards and their applicability to internally displaced persons. The Representative's report was presented to the Commission the following year, at its forty-ninth session.

The report recommended that a comprehensive mechanism be established within the international system to address the problems of displaced persons recognizing that the human rights aspect of this issue intersects with the humanitarian, the political and the economic dimensions. One important function of this mechanism would be the monitoring of situations with a view to detecting early signs of displacement. This early warning system could be the first step in a coordinated process aimed at ameliorating the suffering of displaced masses and averting further displacements.

Violations of Rights of Refugees

The international community has now recognized that human rights violations are a major cause of mass exoduses.

While efforts continue to remedy the problem at its source, attention is turning to the difficulties that asylum-seekers encounter after they leave their countries of origin. Three issues are giving rise to concern. The first is the disturbing tendency to close doors to asylum-seekers. The second relates to violations of the minimum rights of asylum-seekers during the process of applying for sylum and also after refugee status has been granted. Intolerance, racism, xenophobia, aggressioni, national and ethnic tensions and conflicts are on the rise in many places and affect many groups, in particular asylum-seekers and refugees. The third issue is the persistence of human rights violations in countries of origin and the need to address those violations before refugees can be voluntarily repatriated.

Restrictive Measures

There is a growing tendency to close doors to asylum-seekers. Some Governments, faced with an influx of asylum-seekers, economic migrants and illegal aliens, have introduced restrictive measures that hinder access to their territories. These measures include complicated or burdensome visa requirements for nationals of some countries and fines imposed on airlines that carry undocumented aliens.

Ill-Treatment of Asylum-seekers

In some cases the minimum standards of treatment of asylums seekers are not respected. Inadequate refugee-determination procedures and refoulement at airports and borders cause enormous problems for some asylum-seekers. At times refoulement takes inhumane forms such as the forcible return of asylum-seekers to the countries of origin where their lives, liberties and security may be threatened. Boats of asylum-seekers have even been pushed back to sea to die of hunger or make an easy prey for pirates and sharks when they have attempted to land on certain shores.

Other examples of ill-treatment include physical assaults, the detention of asylum-seekers for extended periods and without legitimate reasons and harsh interrogation procedures.

A Government may also fail to provide adequate protection to refugees and asylum-seekers-thereby exposing them to physical danger from racist and xenophobic aggression.

Human Rights of Political Dissidents

Almost 44 years after Cuban dictator Fidel Castro assumed power, the Cuban people still dream of free elections, freedom of expression, and economic and political rights. During the 1940s, democracy—and the economy—flourished in Cuba. In 1940, Cuba had adopted a constitution considered one of the most democratic and progressive in the region. Presidential elections almost universally regarded as free and fair took place in 1940, 1944 and 1948. By the 1950s, Cuban health care was the envy of the region, with infant mortality rates on a par with the United States and Canada, and superior to such countries as France and Belgium. Cuba's rate of 128 physicians and dentists per 100,000 people in 1957 placed the nation at the same health care level as the Netherlands and ahead of the United Kingdom and Finland. The 1950 UN Statistical Yearbook rated Cuba third among Latin American countries in per capita daily caloric consumption.

Literacy rates were among the highest in Latin America, surpassed only by Chile and Argentina. Cubans had a free public education system from kindergarten to university. Cubans had an 8-hour workday, peasant farmers received land rights under an advanced land reform program, and university access was widely available. Women formed a significant percentage of the Cuban judiciary, the diplomatic service, and municipal officers. The 1940 Constitution had extended social security, provided equal pay for equal work, protected individual and social rights, and outlawed the "latifundia" plantation system of land ownership. According to UN statistics, in 1958 Cuba ranked fifth in the region in per capita GDP, outpaced only by regional powerhouses such as Venezuela, Argentina, Uruguay, and Chile.

This promising advance toward the Cuban dream of freedom and material well-being was suddenly halted in 1952 when former President Fulgencio Batista found himself running third in the polls for the presidential elections scheduled for that year and decided to take the matter out of the hands of the voters. The Batista coup met with widespread opposition within Cuba, including that of political parties, unions, businessmen and students. Those opposed to Batista's dictatorship-which grew more brutal and repressive as the 1950s progressed-called for a return to the 1940 Constitution, to assurances of civil liberties and free elections. Indeed, this also was the platform of the July 26 Movement, headed by Fidel Castro and a small band of guerrillas who became a symbol of the widespread rejection of Batista's regime.

When Batista suddenly fled Cuba on New Year's Day 1959, a triumphant Cuban population eagerly awaited the restoration of civil liberties and free elections. The Cuban economy had weathered the political repression surprisingly well, remaining the envy of Latin America. Fidel Castro, capturing the sentiment of the moment, promised the eager population an early return to democratic elections and the restoration of civil liberties, forswearing any personal ambition to hold public office.

What the Cuban people instead got in Fidel Castro was a regime that conducted the summary trials and executions of thousands; suppressed political opposition; closed independent media outlets; ended independent economic activity; and made itself an economic dependency and military agent of the Soviet Union.

Today, Cuba, shorn of Soviet subsidies, is one of the poorest countries in the hemisphere. The country ranks last among the countries examined in the 1950 UN report-its citizens have less access to critical cereals, tubers, and meats than they had in the 1940s. And almost 44 years after Fidel Castro assumed power, the Cuban people still dream of free elections, freedom of expression, and the economic and political rights they once fought so hard to attain.

Castro's War on Freedom

Freedom of Expression and of Speech

"Ideas have a price, which you will now have to pay."

Cuban Government interrogators, to one of the 78 men and women arrested in a 2003 crackdown on human rights activists and journalists.

Ideological conformity in Cuba is imposed at the cost of an elaborate and pervasive system of undercover agents, informers, and neighborhood "committees" who detect and suppress dissent. Police and state security officials regularly harass, threaten, and otherwise abuse human rights advocates in public and private as a means of intimidation and control. Freedom of expression and the press are protected only insofar as they conform to the aims of socialist society. Independent voices can and have been arrested on charges as vague as "dangerousness," defined in the Cuban Penal Code as a "special proclivity of a person to commit crimes, demonstrated by his conduct in manifest contradiction of socialist norms." The Inter-American Commission on Human Rights characterized this as a subjective criterion used to justify violations of individual freedoms and due process for individuals whose sole crime was to hold a view different from the official view.

The government tightly controls distribution of information within Cuba, including access to the Internet, and reinforcement of revolutionary ideology and discipline is emphasized over any freedom of expression. All print and electronic media are considered state property under the control of the Communist Party, and independent journalists and librarians are subjected to arbitrary and periodic detentions, harassment, and seizure of equipment and books. Cuban citizens have no access to foreign magazines or newspapers, since many such mainstream publications are outlawed as enemy propaganda, as is the Universal Declaration of Human Rights. Under the 1999 Law to Protect National Independence and the Economy, anyone possessing or disseminating "subversive" literature faces possible prison terms as long as 20 years.

...The government has detained, summarily judged, and sentenced more than 70 human rights activists and independent journalists. These sentences range from 6 to 28 years in prison. The vast majority of those sentenced are promoters and organizers of the Varela Project, a citizens' initiative supported by the constitution, which collected more than 11,000 signatures from Cuban citizens. A year ago, we presented these signatures to the National Assembly of Popular Power, asking for a referendum. In this way Cubans could decide to make changes to the laws to guarantee fundamental human rights.

The majority of the peaceful opposition representing multiple organizations and ideologies-Liberal, Socialist, and Christian Democrat-support this initiative.... The day before the war in Iraq started, the Cuban regime initiated a terrible campaign of repression creating total uncertainty on the island. Peaceful activists were accused of conspiring against the independence and territorial integrity of the nation. However, none were found to possess arms, subversive plans, or secret information. All their actions were public and consisted of writing their ideas, defending human rights, and promoting the Varela Project. These are the prisoners of the Cuban Spring. Their lives and ours are in danger....

Human Rights of Aged Persons

Human Rights are universal, and civil, political, economic, social and cultural rights belong to all human beings, including older people. The Human Rights of the Aged are explicitly set out in the Universal Declaration of Human Rights, the International Covenants, the Convention on the Elimination of All Forms of Discrimination Against Women, and other widely adhered to international human rights treaties and Declarations.

The Human Rights of the Aged include the following indivisible, interdependent and interrelated human rights:

- The human right to an adequate standard of living, including adequate food, shelter and clothing.
- The human right to adequate social security, assistance, and protection.
- The human right to freedom from discrimination based on age or any other status, in all aspects of life including employment and access to housing, health care, and social services.

- The human right to the highest possible standard of health.
- The human right to be treated with dignity.
- The human right to protection from neglect and all types of physical or mental abuse.
- The human right to full and active participation in all aspects of political, economic, social and cultural life of society.
- The human right to full and effective participate in decision-making concerning their well-being.

Women's Rights

The term **women's rights** refers to freedoms and entitlements of women and girls of all ages. These rights may or may not be institutionalized, ignored or suppressed by law, local custom, and behavior in a particular society. These liberties are grouped together and differentiated from broader notions of human rights because they often differ from the freedoms inherently possessed by or recognized for men and boys, and because activists for this issue claim an inherent historical and traditional bias against the exercise of rights by women and girls.

Issues commonly associated with notions of women's rights include, though are not limited to, the right: to bodily integrity and autonomy; to vote (universal suffrage); to hold public office; to work; to fair wages or equal pay; to own property; to education; to serve in the military or be conscripted; to enter into legal contracts; and to have marital, parental and religious rights. Women and their supporters have campaigned and in some places continue to campaign for the same rights as modern men.

Historical Background

Until the mid-nineteenth century, writers assumed that a patriarchal order was a natural order that had existed as John Stuart Mill wrote, since "the very earliest twilight of human society". This was not seriously challenged until the eighteenth century when Jesuit missionaries found matrilineality in native North American peoples.

In the Middle Ages, an early effort to improve the status of women in Islam occurred during the early reforms under Islam, when women were given greater rights in marriage, divorce and inheritance. Women were not accorded with such legal status in other cultures, including the West, until centuries later. *The Oxford Dictionary of Islam* states that the general improvement of the status of Arab women included prohibition of female infanticide and recognizing women's full personhood. "The dowry, previously regarded as a bride-price paid to the father, became a nuptial gift retained by the wife as part of her personal property." Under Islamic law, marriage was no longer viewed as a "status" but rather as a "contract", in which the woman's consent was imperative. "Women were given inheritance rights in a patriarchal society that had previously restricted inheritance to male relatives." Annemarie Schimmel states that "compared to the pre-Islamic position of women, Islamic legislation meant an enormous progress; the woman has the right, at least according to the letter of the law, to administer the wealth she has brought into the family or has earned by her own work." According to Professor William Montgomery Watt, when seen in such historical context, Muhammad "can be seen as a figure who testified on behalf of women's rights."

Some have claimed that women generally had more legal rights under Islamic law than they did under Western legal systems until more recent times. English Common Law transferred property held by a wife at the time of a marriage to her husband, which contrasted with the Sura: "Unto men (of the family) belongs a share of that which Parents and near kindred leave, and unto women a share of that which parents and near kindred leave, whether it be a little or much-a determinate share" (Quran 4:7), albeit maintaining that husbands were solely responsible for the maintenance and leadership of his wife and family. "French married women, unlike their Muslim sisters, suffered from restrictions on their legal capacity which were removed only in 1965."

In the 16th century, the Reformation in Europe allowed more women to add their voices, including the English writers Jane Anger, Aemilia Lanyer, and the prophetess Anna Trapnell. However, it has been claimed that the Dissolution and resulting closure of convents had deprived many such women of one path to education. Giving voice in the secular context became more difficult when deprived of the rationale and protection of divine inspiration. Queen Elizabeth I demonstrated leadership amongst women, even if she was unsupportive of their causes, and subsequently became a role model for the education of women.

The Enlightenment and a Vindication of the Rights of Woman

The Age of Enlightenment was characterized by secular intellectual reasoning, and a flowering of philosophical writing. The most important feminist writer of the time was Mary Wollstonecraft, often described as the first feminist philosopher. In *A Vindication of the Rights of Woman* (1792) Wollstonecraft argued that it was the education and upbringing of women that created limited expectations. Despite some inconsistencies (Brody refers to the "Two Wollestoncrafts") reflective of problems that had no easy answers, this book remains a foundation stone of feminist thought.

In other parts of Europe, Hedvig Charlotta Nordenflycht was writing in Sweden, and what is thought to be the first scientific society for women was founded in Middelburg, in the south of Holland in 1785. This was the Natuurkundig Genootschap der Dames (Women's Society for Natural Knowledge). Which met regularly until 1881, finally dissolving in 1887. However Deborah Crocker and Sethanne Howard point out that women have been scientists for 4,000 years. Journals for women which focused on science became popular during this period as well.

Suffrage, the Right to Vote

The ideas that were planted in the late 1700s took root during the 1800s. Women began to agitate for the right to vote and participate in government and law making. The ideals of

Women's suffrage developed alongside that of universal suffrage, and women's movements took lessons from those in other countries. Today women's suffrage is considered a right (under the Convention on the Elimination of All Forms of Discrimination Against Women), although a few countries, mainly in the Middle East, continue to deny voting rights to women.

Modern Movement

In the subsequent decades women's rights again became an important issue in the English speaking world. By the 1960s the movement was called "feminism" or "women's liberation." Reformers wanted the same pay as men, equal rights in law, and the freedom to plan their families or not have children at all. Their efforts were met with mixed results.

In the UK a public groundswell of opinion in favour of legal equality had gained pace, partly through the extensive employment of women in men's traditional roles during both world wars. By the 1960s the legislative process was being readied, tracing through MP Willie Hamilton's select committee report, his Equal Pay For Equal Work Bill, the creation of a Sex Discrimination Board, Lady Sear's draft sex anti-discrimination bill, a government Green Paper of 1973, until 1975 when the first British Sex Discrimination Act, an Equal Pay Act, and an Equal Opportunities Commission came into force. With encouragement from the UK government, the other countries of the EEC soon followed suit with an agreement to ensure that discrimination laws would be phased out across the European Community.

In the USA, the US National Organization for Women (NOW) was created in 1966 with the purpose of bringing about equality for all women. NOW was one important group that fought for the Equal Rights Amendment (ERA). This amendment stated that "equality of rights under the law shall not be denied or abridged by the United States or any state on account of sex." But there was disagreement on how the proposed amendment would be understood. Supporters believed it would guarantee women equal treatment. But critics feared it might deny women the right be financially supported by their husbands. The amendment died in 1982 because not enough states had ratified it. ERAs have been included in subsequent Congresses, but have still failed to be ratified.

In the last three decades of the 20th century, Western women knew a new freedom through birth control, which enabled women to plan their adult lives, often making way for both career and family. The movement had been started in the 1910s by US pioneering social reformer Margaret Sanger and in the UK and internationally by Marie Stopes.

Over the course of the 20th century women took on a greater role in society. For example, many women served in government. In the U.S. government some served as U.S. Senators and others as members of the U.S. Cabinet. Many women took advantage of opportunities to become educated. In the United States at the beginning of the 20th century less than 20% of all college degrees were earned by women. By the end of the century this figure had risen to about 50%.

Opportunities also expanded in the workplace. Fields such as medicine, law, and science opened to include more women. At the beginning of the 20th century about 5% of the doctors in the United States were women. As of 2006, over 38% of all doctors in the United States were women, and today, women make almost 50% of the medical student population. While the numbers of women in these fields increased, many women still continued to hold clerical, factory, retail, or service jobs. For example, they worked as office assistants, on assembly lines, or as cooks.

United Nations and Womens' Rights

In 1946 the United Nations established a Commission on the Status of Women. Originally as the Section on the Status of Women, Human Rights Division, Department of Social Affairs, and now part of the Economic and Social Council (ECOSOC). Since 1975 the UN has held a series of world conferences on women's issues, starting with the World Conference of the International Women's Year in Mexico City. These conferences created an international forum for women's rights, but also illustrated divisions between women of different cultures and the difficulties of attempting to apply principles universally Emerging from the 1985 Nairobi conference was a realization that feminism is not monolithic but "*constitutes the political expression of the concerns and interests of women from different regions, classes, nationalities, and ethnic backgrounds. There is and must be a diversity of feminisms, responsive to the different needs and concerns of women, and defined by them for themselves.* This diversity builds on a common opposition to gender oppression and hierarchy which, however, is only the first step in articulating and acting upon a political agenda." At the Fourth World Conference on Women in Beijing, *The Platform for Action* was signed. This included a commitment to achieve "gender equality and the empowerment of women".

Convention on the Elimination of All Forms of Discrimination against Women

The Universal Declaration of Human Rights, adopted in 1948, enshrines "the equal rights of men and women", and addressed both the equality and equity issues. In 1979 the United Nations General Assembly adopted the **Convention on the Elimination of All Forms of Discrimination against Women** (**CEDAW**). Described as an international bill of rights for women, it came into force on 3 September 1981. The United States is the only developed nation that has not ratified the CEDAW.

The Convention defines discrimination against women in the following terms:

> *Any distinction, exclusion or restriction made on the basis of sex which has the effect or purpose of impairing or nullifying the recognition, enjoyment or exercise by women, irrespective of their marital status, on a basis of equality of men and women, of human rights and fundamental freedoms in the political, economic, social, cultural, civil or any other field.*

It also establishes an agenda of action for putting an end to sex-based discrimination: States ratifying the Convention are required to enshrine gender equality into their domestic legislation, repeal all discriminatory provisions in their laws, and enact new provisions to guard against discrimination against women. They must also establish tribunals and public institutions to guarantee women effective protection against discrimination, and take steps to eliminate all forms of discrimination practiced against women by individuals, organizations, and enterprises.

The CEDAW has been controversial for statements seen by some as promoting radical feminism. Particularly referenced is a 2000 report which said that in Belarus, "the Committee is concerned by the continuing prevalence of sex-role stereotypes and by the reintroduction of such symbols as a Mothers' Day and a Mothers' Award, which it sees as encouraging women's traditional roles."

Maputo Protocol

The **Protocol to the African Charter on Human and Peoples' Rights on the Rights of Women in Africa**, better known as the **Maputo Protocol**, was adopted by the African Union on 11 July 2003 at its second summit in Maputo, Mozambique. On 25 November 2005, having been ratified by the required 15 member nations of the African Union, the protocol entered into force. The protocol guarantees comprehensive rights to women including the right to take part in the political process, to social and political equality with men, and to control of their reproductive health, and an end to female genital mutilation

Reproductive Rights

Reproductive rights are rights relating to sexual reproduction and reproductive health. "Reproductive rights" are not recognised in international human rights law and is used as an umbrella term that may include some or all of the following rights: the right to legal or safe abortion, the right to control one's reproductive functions, the right to access quality reproductive healthcare, and the right to education and access in order to make reproductive choices free from coercion, discrimination, and violence. Reproductive rights may also be understood to include education about contraception and sexually transmitted infections, and freedom from coerced sterilization and contraception, protection from gender-based practices such as female genital cutting, or FGC, and male genital mutilation, or MGM.

Reproductive rights are understood as rights of both men and women, but are most frequently advanced as women's rights. The United Nations Population Fund (UNPF) and the World Health Organization (WHO) advocate for reproductive rights with a primary emphasis on women's rights. The idea of these rights were first discussed as a subset of human rights at the United Nation's 1968 International Conference on Human Rights. The sixteenth article of the Proclamation of Teheran recognises reproductive rights as a subset of human rights and states, "Parents have a basic human right to determine freely and responsibly the number and the spacing of their children."

Abortion

Women's access to safe and legal abortions is restricted in law or in practice in most countries in the world. Even where abortion is permitted by law, women may only have limited access to safe abortion services. Only a small number of countries prohibit abortion in all cases. In most countries and jurisdictions, abortion is allowed to save the pregnant woman's life, or where the pregnancy is the result of rape or incest.

Human Rights Watch considers abortion within the context of human rights, arguing:

> *"Abortion is a highly emotional subject and one that excites deeply held opinions. However, equitable access to safe abortion services is first and foremost a human right. Where abortion is safe and legal, no one is forced to have one. Where abortion is illegal and unsafe, women are forced to carry unwanted pregnancies to term or suffer serious health consequences and even death. Approximately 13% of maternal deaths worldwide are attributable to unsafe abortion—between 68,000 and 78,000 deaths annually."*

They furthermore argue that "...international human rights legal instruments and authoritative interpretations of those instruments compel the conclusion that women have a right to decide independently in all matters related to reproduction, including the issue of abortion." Human Rights Watch argues that "the denial of a pregnant woman's right to make an independent decision regarding abortion violates or poses a threat to a wide range of human rights." Basing its analysis on the authoritative interpretations of international human rights instruments by UN expert bodies Human Rights Watch states that where women's access to safe and legal abortion services are restricted, the following human rights may be at risk: the right to life, the right to health (or health care), right to freedom from discrimination, right to security of person, the right to liberty, the right to privacy, the right to information, the right to be free from cruel, inhuman, or degrading treatment, the right to decide the number and spacing of children (reproductive rights), the right to freedom of thought, and the right to freedom of religion.

Other groups however, such as the Catholic Church, regard abortion not as a right but as a 'moral evil'. (Catechism para 2271.)

Rape and Sexual Violence

Rape, sometimes called sexual assault, is an assault by a person involving sexual intercourse with or sexual penetration of another person without that person's consent. Rape is generally considered a serious sex crime as well as a civil assault. When part of a widespread and systematic practice rape and sexual slavery are now recognised as crime against humanity and war crime. Rape is also now recognised as an element of the crime of genocide when committed with the intent to destroy, in whole or in part, a targeted group.

Rape as an Element of the Crime of Genocide

In 1998, the International Criminal Tribunal for Rwanda established by the United Nations made landmark decisions that rape is a crime of genocide under international law. The trial of Jean-Paul Akayesu, the mayor of Taba Commune in Rwanda, established precedents that rape is a element of the crime of genocide. The Trial Chamber held that "sexual assault formed an integral part of the process of destroying the Tutsi ethnic group and that the rape was systematic and had been perpetrated against Tutsi women only, manifesting the specific intent required for those acts to constitute genocide."

Judge Navanethem Pillay said in a statement after the verdict: "From time immemorial, rape has been regarded as spoils of war. Now it will be considered a war crime. We want to send out a strong message that rape is no longer a trophy of war." An estimated 500,000 women were raped during the 1994 Rwandan Genocide.

The Akayesu judgement includes the first interpretation and application by an international court of the 1948 Convention on the Prevention and Punishment of the Crime of Genocide. The Trial Chamber held that rape, which it defined as "a physical invasion of a sexual nature committed on a person under circumstances which are coercive", and sexual assault constitute acts of genocide insofar as they were committed with the intent to destroy, in whole or in part, a targeted group, as such. It found that sexual assault formed an integral part of the process of destroying the Tutsi ethnic group and that the rape was systematic and had been perpetrated against Tutsi women only, manifesting the specific intent required for those acts to constitute genocide.

Rape and Sexual Enslavement as Crime against Humanity

The Rome Statute, which defines the jurisdiction of the International Criminal Court, recognises rape, sexual slavery, enforced prostitution, forced pregnancy, enforced sterilization, "or any other form of sexual violence of comparable gravity" as crime against humanity if the action is part of a widespread or systematic practice.

Rape was first recognised as crime against humanity when the International Criminal Tribunal for the former Yugoslavia issued arrest warrants based on the Geneva Conventions and

Violations of the Laws or Customs of War. Specifically, it was recognised that Muslim women in Foca (southeastern Bosnia and Herzegovina) were subjected to systematic and widespread gang rape, torture and enslavement by Bosnian Serb soldiers, policemen and members of paramilitary groups after the takeover of the city in April 1992.

The indictment was of major legal significance and was the first time that sexual assaults were investigated for the purpose of prosecution under the rubric of torture and enslavement as a crime against humanity. The indictment was confirmed by a 2001 verdict of the International Criminal Tribunal for the former Yugoslavia that rape and sexual enslavement are crimes again humanity. This ruling challenged the widespread acceptance of rape and sexual enslavement of women as intrinsic part of war. Children's rights

Children's rights are the perceived human rights of children with particular attention to the rights of special protection and care afforded to the young, including their right to association with both biological parents, human identity as well as the basic needs for food, universal state-paid education, health care and criminal laws appropriate for the age and development of the child. Interpretations of children's rights range from allowing children the capacity for autonomous action to the enforcement of children being physically, mentally and emotionally free from abuse, though what constitutes "abuse" is a matter of debate. Other definitions include the rights to care and nurturing.

"A child is any human being below the age of eighteen years, unless under the law applicable to the child, majority is attained earlier." According to Cornell University, a child is a person, not a *subperson*, and the parent has absolute interest and possession of the child, but this is very much an American view. The term "child" does not necessarily mean minor but can include adult children as well as adult nondependent children. There are no definitions of other terms used to describe young people such as "adolescents", "teenagers," or "youth" in international law.

The field of children's rights spans the fields of law, politics, religion, and morality.

Rationale

As minors by law children do not have autonomy or the right to make decisions on their own for themselves in any known jurisdiction of the world. Instead their adult caregivers, including parents, social workers, teachers, youth workers and others, are vested with that authority, depending on the circumstances. Some believe that this state of affairs gives children insufficient control over their own lives and causes them to be vulnerable. Louis Althusser has gone so far as describe this legal machinery, as it applies to children, as "repressive state apparatuses".

Structures such as government policy have been held by some commentators to mask the ways adults abuse and exploit children, resulting in child poverty, lack of educational opportunities, and child labor. On this view, children are to be regarded as a minority group towards whom society needs to reconsider the way it behaves. However, there is no evidence that such views are widely shared in society.

Researchers have identified children as needing to be recognized as participants in society whose rights and responsibilities need to be recognized at all ages.

Children's Rights

Consensus on defining children's rights has become clearer in the last fifty years. A 1973 publication by Hillary Clinton (then an attorney) stated that children's rights were a "slogan in need of a definition". According to some researchers, the notion of children's rights is still not well defined, with at least one proposing that there is no singularly accepted definition or theory of the rights held by children.

Children's rights law is defined as the point where the law intersects with a child's life. That includes juvenile delinquency, due process for children involved in the criminal justice system, appropriate representation, and effective rehabilitative services;

care and protection for children in state care; ensuring education for all children regardless of their origin, race, gender, disabilities, or abilities, and; health care and advocacy.

Types of Rights

Children's rights are defined in numerous ways, including a wide spectrum of civil, cultural, economic, social and political rights. Rights tend to be of two general types: those advocating for children as autonomous persons under the law and those placing a claim on society for protection from harms perpetrated on children because of their dependency. These have been labeled as the **right of empowerment** and as the **right to protection**. One Canadian organization categorizes children's rights into three categories:

- *Provision:* Children have the right to an adequate standard of living, health care, education and services, and to play. These include a balanced diet, a warm bed to sleep in, and access to schooling.
- *Protection:* Children have the right to protection from abuse, neglect, exploitation and discrimination. This includes the right to safe places for children to play; constructive child rearing behavior, and acknowledgment of the evolving capacities of children.
- *Participation:* Children have the right to participate in communities and have programs and services for themselves. This includes children's involvement in libraries and community programs, youth voice activities, and involving children as decision-makers.

In a similar fashion, the Child Rights Information Network, or CRIN for short, categorizes rights into two groups:

- Economic, social and cultural rights, related to the conditions necessary to meet basic human needs such as food, shelter, education, health care, and gainful employment. Included are rights to education, adequate housing, food, water, the highest attainable standard of health, the right to work and rights at work, as well as the cultural rights of minorities and indigenous peoples.

- Environmental, cultural and developmental rights, which are sometimes called "third generation rights," and including the right to live in safe and healthy environments and that groups of people have the right to cultural, political, and economic development.

Amnesty International openly advocates four particular children's rights, including the end to juvenile incarceration without parole, an end to the recruitment of military use of children, ending the death penalty for people under 21, and raising awareness of human rights in the classroom. Human Rights Watch, an international advocacy organization, includes child labor, juvenile justice, orphans and abandoned children, refugees, street children and corporal punishment.

Scholarly study generally focuses children's rights by identifying individual rights. The following rights "allow children to grow up healthy and free":

- Freedom of speech
- Freedom of thought
- Freedom from fear
- Freedom of choice and the right to make decisions
- Ownership over one's body

A Canadian organization identifies several other issues affecting children's rights, including fetal rights, infanticide, child abandonment, child identity rights, paternity fraud, paternity testing, age of consent, shaken baby syndrome, genital mutilation, bullying, corporal punishment, parental alienation, children's rights in family law, youth suicide, anorexia nervosa, ADHD, smoking, and childhood pregnancy. Other issues affecting children's rights include the sale of children, child prostitution and child pornography.

Difference between Children's Rights and Youth Rights

"In the majority of jurisdictions, for instance, children are not allowed to vote, to marry, to buy alcohol, to have sex, or to engage in paid employment." Within the youth rights movement, it is believed that the key difference between *children's* rights and *youth* rights is that children's rights supporters generally advocate the establishment and enforcement of protection for children and youths, while youth rights (a far smaller movement) generally advocates the expansion of freedom for children and/or youths and of rights such as suffrage.

Child's Right to be Parented by Biological Parents

The U.N. Convention on the Rights of the Child supports the right of a child to be parented by his /her biological parents) unless the parent(s) is/are either neglectful or abusive to the child in which case the state must protect the child from the parent by means of removing the child or monitoring the parents' actions. The society of the child with the biological parent(s) is commonly identified as an essential child right. This includes the notion that children should not be denied relationships and benefits provided by the relationships and upbringing afforded by their biological parents. The only exception is unless the government must interfere for the purpose of protecting a child from parental abuse or neglect. These cases are generally addressed by an immediate judicial review with the caveat that "all interested parties shall be given an opportunity to participate in the proceedings and make their views known".

Parents affect the lives of children in a unique way, and as such their role in children's rights has to be distinguished in a particular way. Particular issues in the child-parent relationship include child neglect, child abuse, freedom of choice, corporal punishment and child custody. There have been theories offered that provide parents with rights-based practices that resolve the tension between "commonsense parenting" and children's rights. The issue is particularly relevant in legal proceedings that affect the potential emancipation of minors, and in cases where children sue their parents.

A child's rights to a relationship with both their parents is increasingly recognized as an important factor for determining the best interests of the child in divorce and child custody proceedings. Some governments have enacted laws creating a rebuttable presumption that shared parenting is in the best interests of children.

Movement

The 1796 publication of Thomas Spence's *The Rights of Infants* is among the earliest English-language assertions of the rights of children. Throughout the 1900s children's rights activists organized for homeless children's rights and public education. The 1927 publication of *The Child's Right to Respect* by Janusz Korczak strengthened the literature surrounding the field, and today dozens of international organizations are working around the world to promote children's rights.

Opposition

The opposition to children's rights far outdates any current trend in society, with recorded statements against the rights of children dating to the 1200s and earlier. Opponents to children's rights believe that young people need to be protected from the adultcentric world, including the decisions and responsibilities of that world. In the dominate adult society, childhood is idealized as a time of innocence, a time free of responsibility and conflict, and a time dominated by play. The majority of opposition stems from concerns related to national sovereignty, states' rights, the parent-child relationship. Financial constraints and the "undercurrent of traditional values in opposition to children's rights" are cited, as well. The concept of children's rights has received little attention in the United States.

International Law

The Universal Declaration of Human Rights is seen as a basis for all international legal standards for children's rights today. There are several conventions and laws that address children's rights around the world. A number of current and historical documents affect those rights, including the 1923 Declaration of the Rights of the Child, drafted by Eglantyne Jebb and her sister Dorothy Buxton in London, England in 1919, endorsed by the League of Nations and adopted by the

United Nations in 1946. It later served as the basis for the Convention on the Rights of the Child.

Convention on the Rights of the Child

The United Nations' 1989 Convention on the Rights of the Child, or CRC, is the first legally binding international instrument to incorporate the full range of human rights—civil, cultural, economic, political and social rights. Its implementation is monitored by the Committee on the Rights of the Child. National governments that ratify it commit themselves to protecting and ensuring children's rights, and agree to hold themselves accountable for this commitment before the international community. The CRC, along with international criminal accountability mechanisms such as the International Criminal Court, the Yugoslavia and Rwanda Tribunals, and the Special Court for Sierra Leone, is said to have significantly increased the profile of children's rights worldwide.

Enforcement

A variety of enforcement organizations and mechanisms exist to ensure children's rights and the successful implementation of the [[Union. They include the Child Rights Caucus for the United Nations General Assembly Special Session on Children. It was set up to promote full implementation and compliance with the Convention on the Rights of the Child, and to ensure that child rights were given priority during the UN General Assembly Special Session on Children and its Preparatory process. The United Nations Human Rights Council was created "with the hope that it could be more objective, credible and efficient in denouncing human rights violations worldwide than the highly politicised Commission on Human Rights." The NGO Group for the Convention on the Rights of the Child is a coalition of international non-governmental organisations originally formed in 1983 to facilitate the implementation of the United Nations Convention on the Rights of the Child.

Many countries around the world have children's rights ombudspeople or children's commissioners whose official, governmental duty is to represent the interests of the public by investigating and addressing complaints reported by individual citizens regarding children's rights. Children's ombudspeople can also work for a corporation, a newspaper, an NGO, or even for the general public.

Human Rights and Differently-Abled Persons

What are the Human Rights of Differently-Abled Persons?

Human Rights are universal, and civil, political, economic, social and cultural rights belong to all human beings, including differently-abled persons. Differently-abled persons are entitled to the realization of all human rights and fundamental freedoms on equal terms with others in society, without discrimination of any kind. They also enjoy certain human rights specifically linked to their status.

The Human Rights at Issue

The human rights of differently-abled persons include the following indivisible, interdependent and interrelated human rights:

The human right to freedom from any distinction, exclusion, restriction or preference based on the status of differently-abled, which has the purpose or effect of impairing the enjoyment of human rights and fundamental freedoms.

The human right to freedom from discrimination in access to housing, education, social services, health care or employment.

The human right to active participation in all aspects of social, economic, political and cultural life of society, and in shaping decisions and policies affecting him-or herself and community, at the local, national and international levels.

The human right to equality of opportunity.

The human right to full equality before the law and equal protection of the law.

The human right to the highest attainable standard of health, to medical, psychological and functional treatment, including prosthetic and orthetic appliances, to medical and social rehabilitation, and other services necessary for the maximum development of capabilities, skills and self-reliance.

The human right to work, according to capabilities, to receive wages that contribute to an adequate standard of living, and to receive equal remuneration for equal work.

The human right to economic and social security, and to an adequate standard of living.

The human right to be treated with dignity and respect.

Governments' Obligations to Ensuring the Human Rights of Differently-Abled Persons:

What Provisions of Human Rights Law Guarantee the Human Rights of Differently-abled Persons?

"All human beings are born free and equal in dignity and rights.... Everyone is entitled to all ... rights and freedoms ... without distinction of any kind.... All are equal before the law and are entitled without any discrimination to equal protection of the law. All are entitled to equal protection against any discrimination ... and against any incitement to ... discrimination.... Everyone has the right to a standard of living adequate for ... health and well-being .. Including ... the right to security in the event of ... disability...." —Universal Declaration of Human Rights, Articles 1, 2, 7, and 25

"The States Parties ... undertake to guarantee that ... rights ... will be exercised without discrimination of any kind.... The States Parties recognize the right to work.... The right of everyone to ... equal remuneration for work of equal value.... the right of everyone to an adequate standard of living.... to the highest attainable standard of physical and mental health.... to education.... [Education] shall enable all persons to participate effectively in a free society.... Primary education shall be ... available to all; Secondary education ... shall be made generally available and accessible to all...; Higher education shall be made equally accessible to all.... States Parties ... recognize the right of everyone ... to take part in cultural life; to enjoy the benefits of scientific progress...." —International Covenant on Economic, Social, and Cultural Rights, Articles 2, 6, 7, 11, 12, 13, and 15

"Each State Party ... undertakes to ... ensure ... rights ... without distinction of any kind...; to ensure that any person whose rights or freedoms ... are violated shall have an effective remedy.... No one shall be subjected to torture or to cruel, inhuman or degrading treatment or punishment.... no one shall be subjected without his free consent to medical or scientific experimentation.... All persons shall be equal before the courts.... Everyone shall have the right to recognition everywhere as a person before the law.... No one shall be subjected to ... unlawful interference with his privacy, family, home.... The right of men and women ... to marry and to found a family shall be recognized.... Every citizen shall have the right and the opportunity ... to take part in the conduct of public affairs...; to vote...; to have access, on ... terms of equality, to public service.... All persons are equal before the law and are entitled without any discrimination to the equal protection of the law.... [The] law shall prohibit any discrimination and guarantee to all persons equal and effective protection against discrimination on any ground...." —International Covenant on Civil and Political Rights, Articles 2, 7, 14, 16, 17, 23, and 26

"Each Member shall ... formulate, implement ... a national policy on vocational rehabilitation and employment of disabled persons.... The ... policy shall aim at ensuring that appropriate vocational rehabilitation measures are made available to all categories of disabled persons, and at promoting employment opportunities for disabled persons in the open labour market.... The ... policy shall be based on the principle of equal opportunity between disabled workers and workers generally. Equality of opportunity and treatment for disabled men and women workers shall be respected.... The competent authorities shall take measures with a view to providing ... vocational guidance, vocational training, placement, employment and other related services to enable disabled persons to secure, retain and advance in employment.... Measures shall be taken to promote the establishment and development of vocational rehabilitation and employment services for disabled persons in rural areas and remote communities." — ILO Vocational Rehabilitation and Employment (Disabled Persons) Convention, No. 159, Articles 2, 3, 4, 7, and 8

"States Parties shall respect and ensure ... rights ... to each child within their jurisdiction without discrimination of any kind.... States Parties shall take all appropriate ... measures to protect the child from all forms of physical or mental violence, injury or abuse..., maltreatment or exploitation.... States Parties recognize that a mentally or physically disabled child should enjoy a full and decent life, in conditions which ensure dignity, promote self-reliance, and facilitate the child=s active participation in the community. States Parties recognize the right of the disabled child to special care and shall encourage and ensure the extension ... to the eligible child and those responsible for his or her care, of assistance ... which is appropriate to the child=s condition.... [A]ssistance ... shall be designed to ensure that the disabled child has effective access to and receives education, training, health care services, rehabilitation services, preparation for employment and recreation opportunities in a manner conducive to the child=s achieving the fullest possible social integration and individual development...." —Convention on the Rights of the Child, Articles 2, 19, and 23

Governments' Commitments to Ensuring the Human Rights of Differently-Abled Persons

What commitments have governments made to ensuring the realization of the human rights of differently-abled persons?

"Disabled persons shall enjoy ... rights ... without any exception whatsoever and without distinction or discrimination.... Disabled persons have the inherent right to respect for their human dignity. Disabled persons, whatever the origin, nature and seriousness of their handicaps and disabilities, have the same fundamental rights as their fellow-citizens..., which implies first and foremost the right to enjoy a decent life, as normal and full as possible.... Disabled persons have the same civil and political rights as other human beings.... Disabled persons are entitled to the measures designed to enable them to become as self-reliant as possible.... Disabled persons have the right to medical, psychological and functional treatment, including prosthetic and orthetic appliances, to medical and social rehabilitation, education, vocational training and rehabilitation, aid, counselling, placement services and other services which will enable them to develop their capabilities and skills to the maximum and will hasten the processes of their social integration or reintegration.... Disabled persons have the right to economic and social security and to a decent level of living. They have the right, according to their capabilities, to secure and retain employment or to engage in a useful, productive and remunerative occupation.... Disabled persons are entitled to have their special needs taken into consideration at all stages of economic and social planning.... Disabled persons have the right to live with their families ... and to participate in all social, creative or recreational activities. No disabled person shall be subjected ... to differential treatment other than that required by his or her condition or by the improvement which he or she may derive therefrom. If the stay of a disabled person in a specialized establishment is indispensable, the environment and living conditions therein shall be as close as possible to those of the normal life of a person of his or her age.... Disabled persons shall be protected against all exploitation, all regulations and all treatment of a discriminatory, abusive or degrading nature." —Declaration on the Rights of Disabled Persons, Articles 2, 3, 4, 5, 6, 7, 8, 9, and 10.

"More than 500 million people in the world are disabled as a consequence of mental, physical or sensory impairment. They are entitled to the same rights as all other human beings and to equal opportunities.... Governments must ... ensure that [disabled] people ... have an opportunity to achieve a standard of living equal to that of their fellow citizens.... A strategy of prevention is essential for reducing the incidence of impairment and disability.... Measures should be taken for the earliest possible detection of ... symptoms ... of impairment, to be followed immediately by ... curative or remedial action, which can prevent disability or ... lead to significant reductions in the severity of disability.... For early detection it is important to ensure adequate education ... of families and technical assistance to them by medical social services.... The principle of equal rights for the disabled and non-disabled implies that the needs of each and every individual are of equal importance, that these needs must be made the basis for the planning of societies, and that all resources must be employed in such a way as to ensure, for every individual, equal opportunity for participation...." —World Programme of Action Concerning Disabled Persons, paras. 2, 3, 13, 14, and 25.

"Special attention needs to be paid to ensuring non-discrimination, and the equal enjoyment of all human rights and fundamental freedoms by disabled persons, including their active participation in all aspects of society.... The World Conference on Human Rights reaffirms that all human rights and fundamental freedoms are universal and thus unreservedly include persons with disabilities. Every person is born equal and has the same rights to life and welfare, education and work, living independently and active participation in all aspects of society. Any direct discrimination or other negative discriminatory treatment of a disabled person is therefore a violation of his or her rights.... The place of disabled persons is everywhere. Persons with disabilities should be guaranteed equal opportunity through the elimination of all socially determined barriers, by they physical, financial, social or psychological, which exclude or restrict full participation in society." —Vienna Declaration, Part I, para. 22, and Part II, paras. 63 and 64.

"Objectives ...: To ensure the realization of the rights of all persons with disabilities, and their participation in all aspects of social, economic and cultural life; To create, improve and develop necessary conditions that will ensure equal opportunities for persons with disabilities and the valuing of their capabilities in the process of economic and social development; To ensure the dignity and promote the self-reliance of persons with disabilities.... Actions: ... Governments at all levels should promote mechanisms ensuring the realization of the rights of persons with disabilities and reinforce their capabilities of integration."—Cairo Programme of Action, paras. 6.29 and 6.32

"We heads of State and Government ... will create ... action to: ... Ensure that disadvantaged and vulnerable persons and groups are included in social development, and that society acknowledges and responds to the consequences of disability by securing the legal rights of the individual and by making the physical and social environment accessible.... We will ... Ensure equal education opportunities at all levels for children, youth and adults with disabilities.... Strive to ensure that persons with disabilities have access to rehabilitation and other independent living services and assistive technology to enable them to maximize their well-being, independence and full participation in society."—Copenhagen Declaration, para. 26(I), and Commitments 2(d), 6(f), and (n)

"Broadening the range of employment opportunities for persons with disabilities requires: ... Ensuring that laws and regulations do not discriminate against persons with disabilities.... Making appropriate adjustments in the workplace to accommodate persons with disabilities.... Developing alternative forms of employment, such as supported employment, for persons with disabilities who need these services.... Governments, in collaboration with organizations of people with disabilities and the private sector, should work towards the equalization of opportunities so that people with disabilities can contribute to and benefit from full participation in society. Policies concerning people with disabilities should focus on their abilities rather than their disabilities and should ensure their dignity as citizens...." —Copenhagen Programme of Action, paras. 62(a), (c), (d), and 75(k)

"Actions to be taken: ... Design and implement ... gender-sensitive health programmes ... that address the needs of women throughout their lives and take into account ... the special needs of ... women with disabilities.... Ensure that girls and women of all ages with any form of disability receive supportive services...." —Beijing Platform for Action, paras. 106 (c) and (o)

"As human beings are at the centre of our concern for sustainable development, they are the basis for our actions in implementing the Habitat Agenda.... We shall intensify our efforts to eradicate ... discrimination, to promote and protect all human rights and fundamental freedoms for all, and to provide for basic needs.... We shall promote full accessibility for people with disabilities ... in policies, programmes and projects for shelter and sustainable human settlements development...." —Istanbul Declaration, para. 7

"... Persons with disabilities have not always had the opportunity to participate fully and equally in human settlements development and management, including decision-making, often owing to social, economic, attitudinal and physical barriers, and discrimination. Such barriers should be removed and the needs and concerns of persons with disabilities should be fully integrated into shelter and sustainable human settlement plans and policies to create access for all.... We ... commit ourselves to ...: Promoting shelter and supporting basic services and facilities for education and health for ... persons with disabilities... and people belonging to vulnerable and disadvantaged groups.... We ... commit ourselves to ... Promoting equal access and full participation of persons with disabilities in all spheres of human settlements and providing adequate policies and legal protection against discrimination on grounds of disabilities...." —Habitat Agenda, paras. 16, 40(l), and 43(v)

Minorities of Sexual Orientation

Understanding Lesbian, Gay, Bisexual and Transgender Rights as Human Rights

In 1948, the 56 members of the United Nations adopted the Universal Declaration of Human Rights (UDHR). Recognized as one of the most influential and inspirational statements of human rights, the UDHR proclaims that recognizing the inherent dignity and. .. the equal and inalienable rights of all members of the human family is the foundation of freedom, justice and peace in the world.

Human rights are the rights a person has simply because he or she is a human being. Human rights are **inalienable**: you cannot lose these rights any more than you can cease being human. Human rights are **indivisible**: you cannot be denied a right because it is less important than another right. Human rights are **interdependent**: all human rights are part of a complementary framework. For example, the right to participate in government is directly affected by the right to free expression, to get an education, and even to obtain the necessities of life.

Human rights are also defined as those basic standards people need to live in dignity. To violate someone's human rights is to treat that person as less than a human being. To advocate for human rights is to demand that the human dignity of all people be respected. In claiming these rights, everyone also accepts the responsibility not to infringe on the rights of others and to support those whose rights are abused or denied.

Since the adoption of the UDHR, the concept of human rights has entered international law and popular consciousness in much of the world. At the same time, many governments around the world continue to violate the human rights of their citizens. Consider the following news items from 1998, the year of the UDHR's fiftieth anniversary:

- In Afghanistan, at least five men convicted of homosexuality were placed next to walls and then buried as the walls were toppled on top of them.
- In Mexico, the Citizen's Commission Against Homophobic Hate Crimes documented 125 murders of homosexuals, many including extreme violence. Many of the murders were dismissed by police who refused to investigate them.
- In the United States, Matthew Shepard, a 21-year-old student at the University of Wyoming, was brutally beaten in an attack motivated in part by his homosexuality. His skull was smashed, his face and head mutilated, and his body tied to a wooden ranch fence in freezing weather. He died several days after being found by bicyclists who, at first, mistook his body for a scarecrow.

1. This definition is taken from Nancy Flowers (ed.), *Human Rights Here and Now: Celebrating the Universal Declaration of Human Rights.* Minneapolis: Human Rights Resource Center, 1998. This curriculum guide contains more information on the history of human rights and lessons introducing human rights to K-12 students.
2. The bullet points in this and the following two sections are taken from 'The International Gay and Lesbian Human Rights Commission Celebrates the 50th Anniversary of the Universal Declaration of Human Rights.' Press release, December 1998.

As these cases highlight, lesbian, gay, bisexual, and transgender (LGBT) persons are subject to human rights abuse in countries in every region of the world. The violations they face include killing as well as imprisonment, torture, and abuses aimed specifically at sexual minorities, such as practices aimed at forcibly 'changing' their sexual orientation. These violations of UDHR Article 3, 'the right to life, liberty, and security of person,' are only the most extreme examples of violations of the rights of sexual minorities.

Also during 1998:

- In Argentina, Buenos Aires police raided gay bars during October detaining over 100 persons. (Article 20 of the UDHR states that everyone has the 'right to freedom of peaceful assembly and association.')
- In Sweden, authorities deported a gay asylum seeker from Iran. Repatriated Iranian gays face possible imprisonment or death in Iran. (Article 14 of the UDHR declares the 'right to seek and to enjoy in other countries asylum from persecution.')
- In India, theaters showing *Fire,* are attacked because of the movie's lesbian story line. Many theaters subsequently refuse to screen the film. (Article 27 of the UDHR holds that all have the 'right freely to participate in the cultural life of the community.')

- In the United States, two adult men are arrested in Houston under Texas' sodomy law for consensual homosexual conduct in private. Though rarely enforced, about half of all U.S. states have similar laws. (Article 7 of the UDHR states that 'All are equal before the law and are entitled without any discrimination to equal protection of the law.' In addition, Article 12 maintains, 'No one shall be subjected to arbitrary interference with his privacy, family, home or correspondence, nor to attacks upon his honor and reputation.')

These cases demonstrate how human rights violations of LGBT persons extend beyond their rights to life and liberty and include the full spectrum of rights accorded in the UDHR.

Not all the news fifty years after passage of the UDHR is so bleak, however.

- In South Africa and Ecuador, newly adopted constitutions pledge equality before the law (Article 7 of the UDHR) regardless of sexual orientation. Also in South Africa, the highest constitutional court struck down laws criminalizing homosexuality as a violation of the right to privacy (Article 12 of the UDHR) and because they affected the 'dignity, personhood, and identity of lesbian and gay people.'
- In Canada, that nation's Supreme Court ruled that when the Alberta legislature omitted 'sexual orientation' from the province's anti-discrimination laws, it was violating the Canadian Charter of Rights and Freedoms. The court ruled that such protection should be read into the law. (Article 8 of the UDHR describes the 'right to an effective remedy by the competent national tribunals for acts violating the fundamental human rights granted by the constitution or the law.')
- In Colombia, the Constitutional Court decreed that private religious schools cannot ban gay students and that firing gay teachers is unconstitutional. (Article 26 of the UDHR says everyone has the 'right to education.')

These last three snapshots from 1998 illustrate that the rights of sexual minorities are increasingly being seen as human rights. Many of those who drafted the UDHR probably would not have considered the rights of sexual minorities in 1948, given the homophobia and general lack of consciousness about LGBT issues at that time.

The Universal Declaration of Human Rights was drafted in reaction to the inhumanity committed during World War II. Like Jews, gypsies, and the disabled, gay men and lesbians were singled out by the Nazis for slave labor and extermination. As many as 100,000 gay men were sent to the concentration camps where they were killed or worked to death. They were required to wear pink triangles, a symbol that has since come to stand for the international gay rights movement. Several thousand lesbians, considered 'anti-social elements' and forced to wear black triangles, met similar fates. Despite these atrocities, the UDHR contains no specific guarantees of fundamental human rights regardless of sexual orientation.

While subsequent human rights documents have addressed discrimination of other specific groups based on age, race, or sex, no international human rights document explicitly mentions sexual orientation or gender identity. As the examples describing abuses against sexual minorities at the beginning of this introduction suggest, such protection is needed and deserved. For this reason, evolving conceptions of human rights that come to include sexual orientation, such as those in South Africa, Ecuador, Canada, and Colombia, are especially significant.

In theory, general human rights documents protecting the rights of all should also protect the rights of sexual minorities. In fact, many persons opposing specific protections of the rights of lesbian, gay, bisexual, and transgender persons often argue that sexual minorities are already covered by existing law and thus no further mention is needed. In some cases, general human rights laws have been used specifically to secure rights for lesbians and gays. For example, based on the European Convention for the Protection of Human Rights and

Fundamental Freedoms, laws against homosexual acts between consenting adults were struck down in Ireland and Cyprus.

While lesbian, gay, bisexual, and transgender persons are winning victories based on general human rights law, just as often these laws fail to provide sexual minorities with necessary protection from human rights abuses for a number of reasons. Sexual minorities often fail to report violence against them. They may fear their sexual orientation will be made public, making them or their families targets for further violence. They may fear that their complaints will not be taken seriously or that such complaints will be used as reprisals against them. For good reason, they may lack trust in the authorities who are supposed to protect them. In many countries, police are some of the worst violators of sexual minorities' human rights. For example, as this is being written, Amnesty International reports that Entre Amigos, an organization in El Salvador that provides sex education to gay, lesbian, bisexual, and trans gender persons, as well as the general public, is the target of intimidation and violence, including killings and death threats from members of the National Civilian Police.

3. Amnesty International Urgent Action, Extra 159/99, Fear for Safety/Death threats, El Salvador, 12 November 1999.

In many countries, sexual minorities are so marginalized, they lack the most basic resources to defend themselves, publicize abuses, or rally support. For example, such an environment made it easier for the President of Zimbabwe, Robert Mugabe, to compare lesbians and gays to pigs. In 1996 his government prevented a gay and lesbian organization from participating in an international book fair in Harare, the capital. He said, I find it extremely outrageous and repugnant to my human conscience that such repulsive organizations, like those of homosexuals, who offend both against the laws of nature and the morals and religious beliefs espoused by our society, should have any advocate in our midst and even elsewhere in the world.'

Governments also hide their persecution of sexual minorities using the cover of other legal charges. Men and women who are imprisoned, tortured, and even executed for no reason other than their sexual orientation or gender identity are often falsely charged with other crimes such as 'vagrancy,' 'hooliganism,' and 'causing a public disturbance.' In some countries, declaring oneself gay is seen as 'causing a public disturbance.' Once arrested, sexual minorities are sometimes subjected to cruel and unusual forms of punishment, including bogus 'medical treatments' to 'cure' them of their 'disease.

As a result of cultural and religious taboos, some governments are reluctant even to admit the existence of gays and lesbians. Not surprisingly, these same governments are even less willing to protect their human rights. They claim that abuses against sexual minorities are carried out by individuals and that the government cannot control such actions, ignoring that most countries have laws that do protect individuals from persecution based on religion or race by other individuals.

In some countries, protection for gays and lesbians may be labeled a foreign, 'western' concept being forced upon them. In other countries, governments maintain the right to discriminate against lesbian, gay, bisexual, and transgender persons based on religious authority and criminal law. Such laws, however, are vulnerable to challenge under international law. In 1994, the UN Human Rights Committee ruled that laws criminalizing homosexual acts in the Australian state of Tasmania violated Australia's obligations under Articles 2 (non-discrimination) and 17 (right to privacy) of the International Covenant on Civil and Political Rights. In 1997, Tasmania repealed its anti-gay law.

One of the most powerful ways to promote the continued evolution of LGBT rights as human rights and to interrupt the cycle of abuses against sexual minorities is through human rights education. Such education includes learning about human rights (for example, violations of rights and international laws protecting rights) and learning how to respect others and support and defend their human rights. Obviously, schools can play a key role in creating a culture that supports the human rights of all, including lesbian, gay, bisexual, and transgender persons.

Ironically, schools are sometimes among the least safe environments for LGBT youth.

Human Rights Watch, the largest U.S.-based human rights organization, is currently investigating whether the treatment of LGBT youth in schools constitutes a violation of fundamental

4. Quoted in Amnesty International, *Breaking the Silence: Human Rights Violations Based on Sexual Orientation.* London, 1997: 38.

Human Rights: Their investigation was initiated after a conversation with representatives from the Gay, Lesbian and Straight Education Network (GLSEN) and the Lambda Legal Defense and Education Fund. Lambda and GLSEN argued that youth under the age of 16 are legally required to attend school and that parents turn over their responsibility for the safety and well-being of their children to teachers and administrators. Schools, therefore, become custodial settings, responsible for the well-being of those placed in their charge. While human rights organizations have paid careful attention to the treatment of those placed in custodial institutions such as prisons and psychiatric hospitals, no human rights organization has looked at schools in the same way using a human rights perspective.

Such attention is needed in schools. GLSEN has collected compelling evidence that homophobia in schools is destructive to the education of all students, not only LGBT students who are direct targets. Straight students have been abused after being mistaken for gay, and all straight students are shortchanged a lesson in respect when school culture routinely marginalizes some students because of their sexual orientation or gender identity. In addition to the right to an education (Article 26 of the UDHR), all students in school have the right to be free from violence (Article 3), the right to freedom of expression (Article 19), and the right to freedom of assembly (Article 20). Statistics compiled by GLSEN suggest that violence against LGBT youth is pervasive. Recent school board decisions in Salt Lake City, Utah and Orange County, California to ban gay-straight alliances from meeting at public schools demonstrate threats to the rights to assembly and free expression.

In addition to the unsafe environment for LBGT youth, school curriculum routinely ignores sexual minorities. Writers' sexual orientation is rarely mentioned, even when such information is crucial to understanding their work. LGBT persons are left out of almost every history textbook. Few teachers ask students to consider sexual minorities in the context of lessons about civil or human rights.

Lesbian, Gay, Bisexual, and Transgender Rights: A Human Rights Perspective is intended to help teachers introduce thoughtful examination and responsible action among high school students about the rights of sexual minorities. Unlike other curricula, however, this discussion is not set in the context of civil or political rights but in the broader context of human rights at the international level as well as at the most local level-school. By learning to examine thoughtfully the human rights of lesbian, gay, bisexual, and transgender persons and by gaining practice in the skills needed to prevent abuses and secure human rights, we can face the fear and shatter the silence that allows sexual minorities to be killed, tortured, and arbitrarily detained in countries throughout the world. We can also create schools where the human rights of all are respected.

Unit-VII

Human Rights and Other Issues

Ragging

Ragging is a form of abuse on newcomers to educational institutions in Australia, Britain, India, Sri Lanka and in many other Commonwealth countries. It is similar to the American form, known as hazing, but is commonly much more severe.

Some senior students force the unorganized newcomers to undergo several forms of mental, physical and sexual abuses. The juniors are usually too frightened to resist their organized group of tormentors.

Legal Definition

The legal definition is seen as:

"'Ragging' means the doing of any act which causes, or is likely to cause any physical, psychological or physiological harm of apprehension or shame or embarrassment to a student, and includes– (a) teasing or abusing of playing Practical joke on, or causing hurt to any student. or (b) asking any student to do any act, or perform any thing, which he/she would not, in the ordinary course, be willing to do or perform."

Current Situation

The torture on innocent students often run for months, and involve the same batch of students being physically and mentally abused by same and/or different group of seniors (including those from the opposite sex) over and over again.

Anti Ragging organization, SAVE, stated in a recent publication that in some institutions it has been reportedly turned into a tool for extorting money from the juniors.

Ragging is different from other crimes because the motive is solely to get perverse pleasure. Ragging is also different from other crimes as it is actively promoted by certain sections of the society.

The following criminal activities can be categorised under ragging (especially if they take place inside a school or college):

- unlawful coercion
- criminal intimidation
- assault
- battery
- sexual abuse
- rape
- murder

Legal and Sociological Aspects

Ragging has a long history, and has been highlighted in literature (*e.g.*, in Britain, Tom Brown's Schooldays, or Boy by Roald Dahl, and in India, Chetan Bhagat's *Five Point Someone*). Another example can be seen in C.S. Lewis's "The Silver Chair" in which the main characters attend a school in which ...*what ten or fifteen of the biggest boys and girls liked best was bullying the other children*".

In recent years, it has been the focus of a number of legal actions. For example, the Supreme Court of India defined it in a 2001 judgement as:

> *Any disorderly conduct whether by words spoken or written or by an act which the effect of teasing, treating or handling with rudeness any other student, Indulging in rowdy or indisciplined activities which causes or is likely to cause annoyance, hardship or psychological*

harm or to raise fear or apprehension thereof in a fresher or a junior student or asking the students to do any act or perform something which such student will not do in the ordinary course and which has the effect of causing or generating a sense of shame or embarrassment so as to adversely affect the physique or psyche of a fresher or a junior student.

Ragging can be thought of in terms verbal, physical and sexual aggression. A single act may be a combination of more than one of these.

A report from 2007 by the Indian anti-ragging group Coalition to Uproot Ragging from Education analyzed 64 ragging complaints, and found that over 60% of these were related to physical ragging, and 20% were sexual in nature.

While India's only registered Anti Ragging NGO, Society Against Violence in Education (SAVE) has noted 7 reported ragging deaths in the year 2007 alone and 31 reported deaths in the period 2000-2007:

Ragging is usually conducted during a fixed period in most institutions, which may range from one day to almost the whole year. Once this period is over, 'seniors' suddenly become "friends" (apparently): the beginning of this new relationship is often a "fresher's party". However, it often turns like a Dracula story, where the seniors incorporate some of the willing juniors to their gang, so that they may continue ragging (which is often used also as a tool for financial exploitations). Next these "incorporated" or "befriended" juniors also rag their juniors when the formers become seniors in the next year.

In any event, innumerable freshers under severe stress may then leave the system, or may be suffering from serious psychological trauma, which may continue to take its toll through post-traumatic stress disorders. Occasionally, there may be physical injury, and some may even commit suicide.

It has been observed that often, after the ragging season, the friendship between juniors & seniors is only apparent, possibly due to the fact the junior still remains dependent on the seniors in many respects. It has also been pointed out by many that the apparent friendship between the seniors and the juniors is only an eyewash. Respect can never be earned with threats, therefore the apparent respect the juniors show to their seniors is because of the fear (though they cherish hatred for their tormentors).

Human Rights and Ragging

Ragging in India's educational system is widespread, yet ragging is far from being recognized as an issue under human rights by Indian government and Human Rights fraternity. This article attempts to establish "ragging" as an issue of "Human rights in Education" with the help of authoritative reports from the United Nations, and calls upon human rights fraternities to address the issue of ragging from a human rights perspective.

Ragging, a colonial legacy, is widespread in India's education. Various State Legislatures in India have been passing anti-ragging legislations, yet the issue is far from being resolved. Indian legal fraternity has yet to approach the problem of ragging from a perspective other than that of "crime." In the absence of any serious research to that effect, ragging is hardly recognized as an issue under human rights; human rights fraternities in India do not seem to bother about "ragging."

Ragging, though widely believed to be a major factor for campus violence and suicides in educational institutions in India, has yet to be recognized as traditional and systematic human rights abuse in education, and such human right violations in education have not been given the proper attention in India that they deserve. However, within the United Nations, ragging has been considered as an issue of human rights in education.

Katarina Tomasevski, the Special Rapporteur with Commission on Human Rights, Economic and Social Council, United Nations, in her Annual Report in 2001, advocates a 4-A scheme, whereby governmental human rights obligations to make education available, accessible, acceptable, and adaptable have been recognized. The Commission on Human Rights had asked the Special Rapporteur to focus on overcoming obstacles and difficulties in the realization of the right to worldwide education and, in keeping this direction in view, the Special Rapportuer made specific mention of "Ragging" in Chapter V, "STREAMLINING THE HUMAN RIGHTS FRAMEWORK FOR EDUCATION."

"75... The Supreme Court of Sri Lanka decided in April 1998 on the constitutionality of a law that aimed to outlaw and suppress inter alia, verbal abuse (recognized as ragging, bullying, or harassment) within educational institutions. The victimization of students, especially newcomers, through verbal abuse should be outlawed, the Court affirmed, adding that "ragging has far too long been cruel, inhuman and degrading. Our society has been unable to deal with the root causes of ragging, and the anxieties, fears and frustrations of youth on which ragging has fed and flourished."

Appreciating domestic courts' increasing recognition of human rights in education, the Special Rapportuer expressed her satisfaction about the entry of human rights in education law. The report's recommendation section says:

> *"81. the international and domestic human rights law protecting the right to education and guaranteeing human rights in education should be used as a corrective for all education strategies." The Special Rapporteur recommends to all international actors involved in promoting education to review their approach using human rights as the yardstick."*

Making a particular reference to India, the report says:

> *"24...While fully aware of the allocations of responsibility within education between central and State governments, the special rapportuer emphasized the responsibility of the State in ensuring the full implementation of international human rights law binding upon it..."*

This mean that State needs to take up the task of making education acceptable to all and elimination of ragging should be construed to be a necessary step in this direction.

The Special Rapportuer's report calls for:

1. Mainstreaming of human rights in educational strategies
2. The full mobilization of the existing human rights standards for education in order to enable the human rights community to provide a timely contribution to developments which were, until recently, deemed to lie beyond the reach of human rights safeguards.

Ragging as a form of Misandry

Some feel that ragging is another form of misandry, which has evolved over time since it affects males much more severely.

Eve Teasing

Eve teasing is a euphemism used in India, Bangladesh and Pakistan for public sexual harassment (Street harassment) or molestation of women by men, with eve being a reference to the biblical eve. Considered a problem related to delinquency in the youth a form of sexual aggression, and a growing menace throughout the Indian subcontinent; eve teasing ranges in severity from sexually suggestive remarks, inadvertent brushing in public places, catcalls, to outright groping, and sometimes with a coy suggestion of "innocent fun", just as euphemism used to describe it in the region, making it appear innocuous and hence warrant no liability on the part of the perpetrator, that is why, many feminists and voluntary organizations have suggested that the expression 'Eve Teasing' be replaced by a more appropriate expression. According to them, considering the semantic roots of the term in Indian English, eve-teasing refers to the temptress nature of eves, making teasing a norm rather than an aberration.

It is a crime easy to commit, but difficult to prove, as eve-teasers often devise ingenious ways to attack women, even though many feminist writers term it as "little rapes", and usually occur in public places, streets, and public transport.

Some guidebooks to the region warn female tourists that eve teasing may be avoided by wearing conservative clothing, though eve teasing is reported both by Indian women and by conservatively-dressed foreign women.

History

Though the problem received public and media attention in 1960s, it was in the coming decades, when more and more women started going out to colleges and work, independently which meant no longer accompanied by a male escort which had been a norm in traditional society, that the problem grew to an alarming proportion. Soon that the Indian government had to take remedial measures, both judicial and law enforcement, to curb the menace and efforts were made to sensitize the police about the issue, and police started rounding up eve teasers. The deployment of plain-clothed female police officers for the purpose has been particularly effective, other measures seen in various states were setting up of Women's Helpline in various cities, Women Police stations, and special anti-eve-teasing cells by the police.

Also, seen during this period was a marked rise of not just the number women coming forward to report incidence of eve-teasing like cases of sexual harassment due to changing public opinion against eve-teasers. What also grew in this period was the severity of eve-teasing incidences, which in some cases led to acid throwing, which led to states like Tamil Nadu, making eve-teasing a non-bailable offense. The number of women's organization and those working for womens rights also saw a rise, especially as this period also saw the rise of another social evil of bride burning, this meant previous lackadaisical attitude towards women's right had to be abandoned by law makers, who now had to sit up and take action. In the coming years, such organizations played a key role in lobbying for the eventual passing of several women-centric legislation, during this period, including 'The Delhi Prohibition of Eve-teasing Bill 1984'.

The death of a female student, Sarika Shah, in Chennai in 1998, caused by Eve teasing, brought some tough laws to counter the problem in South India. After this case, there has been about half-a-dozen reports of suicide that have been attributed to pressures caused by eve teasing. In 2007, an eve-teasing resulted in the death of Pearl Gupta, a college student in Delhi. In Feb 2009, Girl students of M.S. University (MSU) Vadodara thrashed four boys near the family and community sciences faculty, after they passed lewd comments on a girl student staying in SD Hall hostel.

Many other cases go unreported for fear of reprisals and exposure to public shame. In some cases police let the offenders go, after public humiliation through the Murga Punishment. In 2008, a Delhi court ordered a 19-year-old youth, after he was caught eve-teasing, to distribute 500 handbills, detailing the consequences of indecent conduct, to youngsters outside schools and colleges.

Depiction in Popular Culture

Traditionally, Indian cinema has depicted eve teasing as a part of flirtatious beginnings of a courtship, along with the usual accompaniment of song and dance routines, which invariably results in the heroine submitting to the hero's advances towards the end of the song, and young men tend to emulate the example, depicted so flawlessly on screen and which gave rise to the *Roadside Romeo* which even made it a film version in *Roadside Romeo* (2007).

Legal Redressal

Though Indian law doesn't use the term 'eve-teasing', victims usually take recourse to Section 298 (A) and (B) of the Indian Penal Code (IPC), which sentences a man found guilty of making a girl or woman the target of obscene gestures, remarks, songs or recitation for a maximum tenure of three months. Section 292 of the IPC clearly spells out that showing pornographic or obscene pictures, books or slips to a woman or girl draws a fine of Rs.2000 with two years of rigorous imprisonment for first offenders. In case of repeated offence, when and if proved, the offender will be slapped with a fine of Rs.5000 with five years imprisonment. Under Section 509 of the IPC, obscene gestures, indecent body language and acidic comments directed at any woman or girl carries a penalty of rigorous imprisonment for one year or a fine or both.

The 'National Commission for Women' (NCW) has also proposed No 9. Eve Teasing (New Legislation) 1988.

Public Response

'Fearless Karnataka' or 'Nirbhaya Karnataka' is a coalition of many individuals and groups including 'Alternative Law Forum', 'Blank Noise', 'Maraa', 'Samvada' and 'Vimochana'. After rise of eve teasing cases in 2000s, it organized several public awareness campaigns, including 'Take Back the Night', followed by another public art project titled, The Blank Noise Project, starting in Bangalore in 2003.. A similar program to fight eve-teasing was also hosted in Mumbai in 2008.

Human Trafficking

Human trafficking is the commerce and trade in the movement or migration of people, legal and illegal, including both legitimate labor activities as well as forced labor. The term is used in a more narrow sense by advocacy groups to mean the recruitment, transportation, harbouring, or receipt of people for the purposes of slavery, forced labor (including bonded labor or debt bondage), and servitude. It is the fastest growing criminal industry in the world, with the total annual revenue for trafficking in persons estimated to be between $5 billion and $9 billion. The Council of Europe states that "people trafficking has reached epidemic proportions over the past decade, with a global annual market of about $42.5 billion." Trafficking victims typically are recruited using coercion, deception, fraud, the abuse of power, or outright abduction. Threats, violence, and economic leverage such as debt bondage can often make a victim consent to exploitation.

Exploitation includes forcing people into prostitution or other forms of sexual exploitation, forced labour or services, slavery or practices similar to slavery and servitude. For children, exploitation may also include forced prostitution, illicit international adoption, trafficking for early marriage, or recruitment as child soldiers, beggars, for sports (such as child camel jockeys or football players), or within certain religious groups.

Overview

Human trafficking differs from people smuggling. In the latter, people voluntarily request smuggler's service for fees and there may be no deception involved in the (illegal) agreement. On arrival at their destination, the smuggled person is usually free. On the other hand, the trafficking victim is enslaved, or the terms of their debt bondage are highly exploitative. The trafficker takes away the basic human rights of the victim.

Victims are sometimes tricked and lured by false promises or physically forced. Some traffickers use coercive and manipulative tactics including deception, intimidation, feigned love, isolation, threat and use of physical force, debt bondage, or other abuse. People who are seeking entry to other countries may be picked up by traffickers, and misled into thinking that they will be free after being smuggled across the border. In some cases, they are captured through slave raiding, although this is increasingly rare.

Trafficking is a fairly lucrative industry. In some areas, like Russia, Eastern Europe, Hong Kong, Japan, and Colombia, trafficking is controlled by large criminal organizations. However, the majority of trafficking is done by networks of smaller groups that each specialize in a certain area, like recruitment, transportation, advertising, or retail. This is very profitable because little startup capital is needed, and prosecution is relatively rare.

Trafficked people are usually the most vulnerable and powerless minorities in a region. They often come from the poorer areas where opportunities are limited, they often are ethnic minorities, and they often are displaced persons such as runaways or refugees (though they may come from any social background, class or race).

Women are particularly at risk from sex trafficking. Criminals exploit lack of opportunities, promise good jobs or opportunities for study, and then force the victims to become prostitutes. Through agents and brokers who arrange the travel and job placements, women are escorted to their destinations and delivered to the employers. Upon reaching their destinations, some women learn that they have been deceived about the nature of the work they will do; most have been lied to about the financial arrangements and conditions of their employment; and find themselves in coercive or abusive situations from which escape is both difficult and dangerous.

Trafficking of children often involves exploitation of the parents' extreme poverty. The latter may sell children to traffickers in order to pay off debts or gain income or they may be deceived concerning the prospects of training and a better life for their children. In West Africa, trafficked children have often lost one or both parents to the African AIDS crisis.. Thousands of male (and sometimes female) children have also been forced to be child soldiers.

The adoption process, legal and illegal, results in cases of trafficking of babies and pregnant women between the West and the developing world. In David M. Smolin's papers on child trafficking and adoption scandals between India and the United States, he cites there are systemic vulnerabilities in the intercountry adoption system that makes adoption scandals predictable.

Thousands of children from Asia, Africa, and South America are sold into the global sex trade every year. Often they are kidnapped or orphaned, and sometimes they are actually sold by their own families.

Men are also at risk of being trafficked for unskilled work predominantly involving forced labor which globally generates $31bn according to the International Labour Organization. Other forms of trafficking include forced marriage, and domestic servitude.

Extent

Due to the illegal nature of trafficking and differences in methodology, the exact extent is unknown. According to United States State Department data, an "estimated 600,000 to 820,000 men, women, and children [are] trafficked across international borders each year, approximately 70 percent are women and girls and up to 50 percent are minors. The data also illustrates that the majority of transnational victims are trafficked into commercial sexual exploitation." However, they go on to say that "the alarming enslavement of people for purposes of labor exploitation, often in their own countries, is a form of human trafficking that can be hard to track from afar." Thus the figures for persons trafficked for labor exploitation are likely to be greatly underestimated.

Reporters have witnessed a rapid increase in prostitution in Cambodia, Bosnia, and Kosovo after UN and, in the case of the latter two, NATO peacekeeping forces moved in. Peacekeeping forces have been linked to trafficking and forced prostitution. Proponents of peacekeeping argue that the actions of a few should not incriminate the many participants in the mission, yet NATO and the UN have come under criticism for not taking the issue of forced prostitution linked to peacekeeping missions seriously enough.

A common misconception is that trafficking only occurs in poor countries. But every country in the world is involved in the underground, lucrative system. A "source country" is a country that girls are trafficked from. Usually, these countries are destitute and may have been further weakened by war, corruption, natural disasters or climate. Some source countries are Nepal, Guatemala, the former Soviet territories, and Nigeria, but there are many more. A "transit country", like Mexico or Israel, is a temporary stop on trafficked victims' journey to the country where they will be enslaved. A "destination country" is where trafficked persons end up. These countries are generally affluent, since they must have citizens with enough "disposable income" to "buy the traffickers' 'products'". Japan, India, much of Western Europe, and the United States are all destination countries.

In a 2006 report the Future Group, a Canadian humanitarian organization dedicated to combatting human trafficking and the child sex trade, ranked eight industrialized nations. In the report, titled "Falling Short of the Mark: An International Study on the Treatment of Human Trafficking Victims", Canada received an F rating, the United Kingdom received a D, while the United States received a B+ and Australia, Norway, Sweden, Germany and Italy all received grades of B or B-.

North America

According to the National Human Rights Center in Berkeley, California, there are currently about 10,000 forced laborers in the U.S., around one-third of whom are domestic servants and some portion of whom are children. The Associated Press reports, based on interviews in California and in Egypt, that trafficking of children for domestic labor in the U.S. is an extension of an illegal but common practice in Africa. Families in remote villages send their daughters to work in cities for extra money and the opportunity to escape a dead-end life. Some girls work for free on the understanding that they will at least be better fed in the home of their employer. This custom has led to the spread of trafficking, as well-to-do Africans accustomed to employing children immigrate to the U.S.

Research conducted by University of California at Berkeley on behalf of the anti-trafficking organisation Free the Slaves found that less than half of people in slavery in the United States, about 46%, are forced into prostitution. Domestic servitude claims 27%, agriculture 10%, and other occupations 17%.

An estimated 14,000 people are trafficked into the United States each year, although again because trafficking is illegal, accurate statistics are difficult. According to the Massachusetts based Trafficking Victims Outreach and Services Network (project of the nonprofit MataHari: Eye of the Day) in Massachusetts alone, there were 55 documented cases of human trafficking in 2005 and the first half of 2006 in Massachusetts. In 2004, the Royal Canadian Mounted Police (RCMP) estimated that 600-800 persons are trafficked into Canada annually and that additional 1,500-2,200 persons are trafficked through Canada into the United States. In Canada, foreign trafficking for prostitution is estimated to be worth $400 million annually.

According to the Future Group report, Canada in particular has a major problem with modern-day sexual slavery, giving

Canada an F for its "abysmal" record treating victims. The report concluded that Canada "is an international embarrassment" when it comes to combating this form of slavery.

The report's principal author Benjamin Perrin wrote, "Canada has ignored calls for reform and continues to re-traumatize trafficking victims, with few exceptions, by subjecting them to routine deportation and fails to provide even basic support services." The report criticizes former Liberal Party of Canada cabinet ministers Irwin Cotler, Joe Volpe and Pierre Pettigrew for "passing the buck" on the issue.

Commenting on the report, the then Minister of Citizenship and Immigration, Monte Solberg told Sun Media Corporation, "It's very damning, and if there are obvious legislative or regulatory fixes that need to be done, those have to become priorities, given especially that we're talking about very vulnerable people."

Asia

In Asia, Japan is the major destination country for trafficked women, especially from the Philippines and Thailand. The US State Department has rated Japan as either a 'Tier 2' or a 'Tier 2 Watchlist' country every year since 2001 in its annual *Trafficking in Persons* reports. Both these ratings implied that Japan was (to a greater or lesser extent) not fully compliant with minimum standards for the elimination of human trafficking trade. There are currently an estimated 300,000 women and children involved in the sex trade throughout Southeast Asia. It is common that Thai women are lured to Japan and sold to Yakuza-controlled brothels where they are forced to work off their price. By the late 1990s, UNICEF estimated that there are 60,000 child prostitutes in the Philippines, describing Angeles City brothels as "notorious" for offering sex with children. UNICEF estimates many of the 200 brothels in the notorious Angeles City offer children for sex.

Many of the Iraqi women fleeing the Iraq War are turning to prostitution, while others are trafficked abroad, to countries like Syria, Jordan, Qatar, the United Arab Emirates and Turkey.

In Syria alone, an estimated 50,000 Iraqi refugee girls and women, many of them widows, are forced into prostitution. Cheap Iraqi prostitutes have helped to make Syria a popular destination for sex tourists. The clients come from wealthier countries in the Middle East. High prices are offered for virgins.

As many as 200,000 Nepali girls, many under 14, have been sold into the sex slavery in India. Nepalese women and girls, especially virgins, are favored in India because of their light skin.

Africa

In parts of Ghana, a family may be punished for an offense by having to turn over a virgin female to serve as a sex slave within the offended family. In this instance, the woman does not gain the title of "wife." In parts of Ghana, Togo, and Benin, shrine slavery persists, despite being illegal in Ghana since 1998. In this system of slavery of ritual servitude, sometimes called *trokosi* (in Ghana) or *voodoosi* in Togo and Benin, young virgin girls are given as slaves in traditional shrines and are used sexually by the priests in addition to providing free labor for the shrine.

Europe

Since the fall of the Iron Curtain, the impoverished former Eastern bloc countries such as Albania, Moldova, Romania, Bulgaria, Russia, Belarus and Ukraine have been identified as major trafficking source countries for women and children. Young women and girls are often lured to wealthier countries by the promises of money and work and then reduced to sexual slavery.

It is estimated that 2/3 of women trafficked for prostitution worldwide annually come from Eastern Europe, three-quarters have never worked as prostitutes before. The major destinations are Western Europe (Germany, Italy, Netherlands, Spain, UK, Greece), the Middle East (Turkey, Israel, the United Arab Emirates), Asia, Russia and the United States. An estimated 500,000 women from Central and Eastern Europe are working in prostitution in the EU alone.

In the United Kingdom, the Home Office has stated that 71 women were trafficked into prostitution in 1998. They also suggest that the actual figure could be up to 1,420 women trafficked into the UK during the same period. However, the figures are problematic as the definition used in the UK to identify cases of sex trafficking-derived from the Sexual Offences Act 2003-does not require that victims have been coerced or misled. Thus, any individual who moves to the UK for the purposes of sex work can be regarded as having been trafficked-even if they did so with their knowledge and consent. The Home Office do not appear to be keeping records of the number of people trafficked into the UK for purposes other than sexual exploitation.

In Russia, many women have been trafficked overseas for the purpose of sexual exploitation, Russian women are in prostitution in over 50 countries. Annually, thousands of Russian women end up as prostitutes in Israel, China, Japan or South Korea. Russia is also a significant destination and transit country for persons trafficked for sexual and labor exploitation from regional and neighboring countries into Russia, and on to the Gulf states, Europe, Asia, and North America.

In poverty-stricken Moldova, where the unemployment rate for women ranges as high as 68% and one-third of the workforce live and work abroad, experts estimate that since the collapse of the Soviet Union between 200,000 and 400,000 women have been sold into prostitution abroad—perhaps up to 10% of the female population. In Ukraine, a survey conducted by the NGO La Strada Ukraine in 2001–2003, based on a sample of 106 women being trafficked out of Ukraine found that 3% were under 18, and the U.S. State Department reported in 2004 that incidents of minors being trafficked was increasing. It is estimated that half a million Ukrainian women were trafficked abroad since 1991 (80% of all unemployed in Ukraine are women).

The ILO estimates that 20 percent of the five million illegal immigrants in Russia are victims of forced labor, which is a form of trafficking. However even citizens of Russian Federation have become victims of human trafficking. They are typically kidnapped and sold by police to be used for hard labor, being regularly drugged and chained like dogs to prevent them from escaping. There were reports of trafficking of children and of child sex tourism in Russia. The Government of Russia has made some effort to combat trafficking but has also been criticized for not complying with the minimum standards for the elimination of trafficking.

Causes of Trafficking

Trafficking in people has been facilitated by porous borders and advanced communication technologies, it has become increasingly transnational in scope and highly lucrative. Unlike drugs or arms, people can be "sold" many times. The opening up of Asian markets, porous borders, the end of the Soviet Union and the collapse of the former Yugoslavia have contributed to this globalization.

Some causes and facilitators of trafficking include:

- Lack of employment opportunities
- Organized crime
- Regional imbalances
- Economic disparities
- Social discrimination
- Corruption in government
- Political instability
- Armed conflict
- Mass resettlement for large projects without proper Resettlement and Rehabilitation packages.
- Profitability
- Insufficient penalties against traffickers
- Minimal law enforcement on global sex tourism industry
- Legal processes that prosecute victims for prosecution instead of the traffickers
- Poor international border defence

Relation to Other Vulnerability Issues

Human trafficking is not a stand alone issue. It is closely related other issues that threaten security well being of the victims. Victims are exposed to continuous threats of physical violence by traffickers to ensure compliance. Many are held in bondage and beaten to suppress resistance. Other threats include absolute poverty due to wage deprivation.

They are unprotected by labor laws, and long working hours as well as lack of holiday is common. For example, 15 is the standard working hours per day among Chinese victims in France. In Japan, Thai trafficking victims also complained of breach of work contracts, non-payment of wages, mandatory night work and poor accommodation.

Human Trafficking and Sexual Exploitation

There is no universally accepted definition of trafficking for sexual exploitation. The term encompasses the organized movement of people, usually women, between countries and within countries for sex work with the use of physical coercion, deception and bondage through forced debt. However, the issue becomes contentious when the element of coercion is removed from the definition to incorporate facilitating the willing involvement in prostitution. For example, In the United Kingdom, The Sexual Offences Act, 2003 incorporated trafficking for sexual exploitation but did not require those committing the offence to use coercion, deception or force, so that it also includes any person who enters the UK to carry out sex work with consent as having being trafficked.

Save the Children stated “The issue gets mired in controversy and confusion when prostitution itself is considered as a violation of the basic human rights of both adult women and minors, and equal to sexual exploitation per se..... trafficking and prostitution become conflated with each other.... On account of the historical conflation of trafficking and prostitution both legally and in popular understanding, an overwhelming degree of effort and interventions of anti-trafficking groups are concentrated on trafficking into prostitution”.

Sexual trafficking includes coercing a migrant into a sexual act as a condition of allowing or arranging the migration. Sexual trafficking uses physical coercion, deception and bondage incurred through forced debt. Trafficked women and children, for instance, are often promised work in the domestic or service industry, but instead are usually taken to brothels where their passports and other identification papers are confiscated. They may be beaten or locked up and promised their freedom only after earning – through prostitution – their purchase price, as well as their travel and visa costs.

The main motive of a woman (in some cases an underage girl) to accept an offer from a trafficker is better financial opportunities for herself or her family. In many cases traffickers initially offer 'legitimate' work or the promise of an opportunity to study. The main types of work offered are in the catering and hotel industry, in bars and clubs, modeling contracts, or au pair work. Traffickers sometimes use offers of marriage, threats, intimidation and kidnapping as means of obtaining victims. In the majority of cases, the women end up in prostitution.

Also some (migrating) prostitutes become victims of human trafficking. Some women know they will be working as prostitutes, but they have an inaccurate view of the circumstances and the conditions of the work in their country of destination. In Japan the prosperous entertainment market had created huge demand for commercial sexual workers, and such demand is being met by trafficking women and children from the Philippines, Colombia and Thailand. Women are forced into street prostitution, based stripping and live sex acts. However, from information obtained from detainees or deportees from Japan, about 80 percent of the women went there with the intention of working as prostitutes.

The Fundamentalist Church of Jesus Christ of Latter Day Saints, in the US and Canada, has also been implicated in the trafficking of underage women across state and international boundaries (US/Canada). In most cases, this is for the continuation of polygamous practices, in the form of plural marriage.

Trafficking victims are also exposed to different psychological problems. They suffer social alienation in the host and home countries. Stigmatization, social exclusion and intolerance make reintegration into local communities difficult. The governments offer little assistance and social services to trafficked victims upon their return. As the victims are also pushed into drug trafficking, many of them face criminal sanctions.

Efforts to Reduce Human Trafficking

Governments, international associations, and nongovernmental organizations have all tried to end human trafficking with various degrees of success.

Government Actions

Actions taken to combat human trafficking vary from government to government. Some have introduced legislation specifically aimed at making human trafficking illegal. Governments can also develop systems of co-operation between different nation's law enforcement agencies and with non-government organizations (NGOs). Many countries though have come under criticism for inaction, or ineffective action. Criticisms include failure of governments in not properly identifying and protecting trafficking victims, that immigration policies might re-victimize trafficking victims, or insufficient action in helping prevent vulnerable people becoming trafficking victims.

A particular criticism has been the reluctance of some countries to tackle trafficking for purposes other than sex.

Other actions governments could take is raise awareness. This can take on three forms. Firstly in raising awareness amongst potential victims, in particular in countries where human traffickers are active. Secondly, raising awareness amongst police, social welfare workers and immigration officers. And in countries where prostitution is legal or semi-legal, raising awareness amongst the clients of prostitution, to look out for signs of a human trafficking victim.

Raising awareness can take on different forms. One method is through the use of awareness films or through posters

International Law

In 2000 the United Nations adopted the Convention against Transnational Organized Crime, also called the Palermo Convention, and two Palermo protocols there to:

- Protocol to Prevent, Suppress and Punish Trafficking in Persons, especially Women and Children; and
- Protocol against the Smuggling of Migrants by Land, Sea and Air.

All of these instruments contain elements of the current international law on trafficking in human beings.

Council of Europe

The Council of Europe Convention on Action against Trafficking in Human Beings was adopted by the Council of Europe on 16 May 2005. The aim of the convention is to prevent and combat the trafficking in human beings. The Convention entered into force on 1 February 2008. Of the 47 member states of the Council of Europe, so far 21 have signed the convention and 17 have ratified it.

United Kingdom

In the United Kingdom, after intense pressure from Human Rights organisations, trafficking for labour exploitation was made illegal in 2004 (trafficking for sexual exploitation being criminalised many years previously). However, the 2004 law has been used very rarely and by mid-2007 there had not been a single conviction under these provisions.

Australia

Human trafficking in Australia.

United States Law

Laws against trafficking in the United States exist at the federal and state levels. Over half of the states now criminalize human trafficking though the penalties are not as tough as the federal laws. Related federal and state efforts focus on regulating the tourism industry to prevent the facilitation of sex tourism and regulate international marriage brokers to ensure criminal background checks and information on how to get help are given to the potential bride.

The United States federal government has taken a firm stance against human trafficking both within its borders and beyond. Domestically, human trafficking is a federal crime under Title 18 of the United States Code. Section 1584 makes it a crime to force a person to work against his will, whether the compulsion is effected by use of force, threat of force, threat of legal coercion or by "a climate of fear" (an environment wherein individuals believe they may be harmed by leaving or refusing to work); Section 1581 similarly makes it illegal to force a person to work through "debt servitude." Human trafficking as it relates to involuntary servitude and slavery is prohibited by the 13th Amendment. Federal laws on human trafficking are enforced by the United States Department of Justice Civil Rights Division, Criminal Section.

The Victims of Trafficking and Violence Protection Act of 2000 allowed for greater statutory maximum sentences for traffickers, provided resources for protection of and assistance for victims of trafficking and created avenues for interagency cooperation. It also allows many trafficking victims to remain in the United States and apply for permanent residency under a T-1 Visa.. The act also attempted to encourage efforts to prevent human trafficking internationally, by creating annual country reports on trafficking and tying financial non-humanitarian assistance to foreign countries to real efforts in addressing human trafficking.

The United States Department of State has a high-level official charged with combating human trafficking, the Director of the Office to Monitor and Combat Trafficking in Persons ("anti-trafficking czar"). The current director is Mark P. Lagon.

International NGOs such as Human Rights Watch and Amnesty International have called on the United States to improve its measures aimed at reducing trafficking. They recommend that the United States more fully implement the United Nations Convention against Transnational Organized Crime Protocol to Prevent, Suppress and Punish Trafficking in

Persons, especially Women and Children and for immigration officers to improve their awareness of trafficking and support the victims of trafficking.

Several state governments have taken action to address human trafficking in their borders, either through legislation or prevention activities. For example, Florida state law prohibits forced labor, sex trafficking, and document servitude, and provides for mandatory law enforcement trainings and victim services. A 2006 Connecticut law prohibits coerced work and makes trafficking a violation of the Connecticut RICO Act.

Non-Governmental Organizations

Human rights organisations, including Amnesty International, Anti-Slavery International and Human Rights Watch have campaigned against human trafficking. Several non-governmental organizations (NGOs) and human rights organizations have been formed to combat human trafficking. Some of these include:

> ***Somaly Mam Foundation****, founded in 2007 at the United Nations with the support of UNICEF, UNIFEM, and IOM, the Somaly Mam Foundation is known for empowering victims of human trafficking to become activists and agents of change. With the leadership of world renowned Cambodian activist, Somaly Mam, the organization has garnered support from influential leaders and celebrities such as Susan Sarandon, Daryl Hannah, Diane von Furstenberg, and Hillary Clinton. The foundation also runs activities to support Rescue and Rehabilitation of victims in Southeast Asia and works to increase global awareness to inspire action.*

Redlight Children Campaign, founded in 2002 is a non-profit organization created by New York lawyer and president of Priority Films Guy Jacobson and Israeli actress Adi Ezroni in 2002, to combat worldwide child sexual exploitation and human trafficking. Its mission is to decrease the demand side of the international sex trade through legislation and enforcement while raising awareness utilizing mass media and grassroots outreach. Through its partnership with Priority

Films, Redlight Children has recently launched the K11 Project—three films which attempt to expose real life experiences of the underage sex trade. K11 consists of two documentaries and a feature-length narrative, Holly (film), which were all filmed on location in Cambodia. Red Light also began working the Somaly Mam Foundation in 2003. A comprehensive blueprint outlines three phases of the attack on this crime against humanity: raising awareness, correcting, improving, and enforcing current legislation, followed by allocating the appropriate resources to mirror the size and scope of the epidemic. The hope is that utilizing both film and mass media will put the issue on the international agenda, inciting action from the general public and policy makers, thereby leading to an allocation of appropriate resources and stricter enforcement that will effectively reduce demand.

Not For Sale, founded in 2007, equips and mobilizes Smart Activists to deploy innovative solutions to re-abolish slavery in their own backyards and across the globe. Headquartered in Montara, CA, Not For Sale has 42 regional chapters across the United States. Through the innovation and implementation of 'open-source activism', the campaign identifies trafficking rings inside the United States, and collaborates with local law enforcement and community groups to shut them down and provide support for the victims. Internationally, the campaign partners with poorly resourced abolitionist groups to enhance their capacity.

Polaris Project, founded in 2002, is an international anti-human trafficking organization with offices in Washington DC, New Jersey, Colorado, and Japan. Polaris Project's comprehensive approach includes operating local and national human trafficking hotlines, conducting direct outreach and victim identification, providing social services and housing to victims, advocating for stronger state and national anti-trafficking legislation, and engaging community members in grassroots efforts.

Tiny Stars, Using the Protect Act of 2003, Tiny Stars works closely with Federal Law enforcement agencies to capture

American child predators. Founded by Jake Collins in 1997, Tiny Stars focuses on identifying, tracking, and capturing pedophiles who victimize girls between the ages of 8–14 years old. To advance its mission, the organization has developed a network of undercover agents, often former agents of the CIA, FBI, or Navy SEALS. Tiny Stars has more recently begun conducting operations and fundraising under the name Global Centurion.

National Human Trafficking Resource Center (NHTRC) is a program funded by the Department of Health and Human Services. The NHTRC operates the National Human Trafficking Resource Center Hotline 24-hours a day, 365 days a year.

Made By Survivors (MBS)[6] is a division of **The Emancipation Network** (TEN) and is an organization that uses economic empowerment to help survivors of trafficking and people at high risk to rebuild their lives. MBS's handicraft programs offer these survivors a job that enables them to support themselves and live a meaningful, independent life. For those still living at the shelter, handicrafts programs provide therapeutic benefits, job training, literacy, social interaction, and a stipend for part-time work.

MBS partners with 18 anti-slavery organizations around the world, including Thailand, Cambodia, Nepal, India, Ukraine, Uganda, the Philippines, Tanzania, and the United States. MBS also runs volunteer trips to India as a way to educate people who can use the experience to get more involved and educate the public. The trips also help the survivors to trust people again and reintegrate them back into a normal life. In addition, MBS offers people the opportunity to host parties at their homes to sell the handicrafts and educate friends and family.

Criticisms

Lack of Accurate Data and Possible Overestimation: Estimates of the number of people trafficked for sexual purposes is contentious-problems of definition can be compounded by the willingness of victims to identify as being trafficked.

Distinguishing trafficking from voluntary migration is crucial because the ability of women to purposefully and voluntarily migrate for work should be respected. In a 2003 report the Thai sex worker support organization EMPOWER stated that many anti-trafficking groups fail to see the difference between migrant sex workers and women forced to prostitute themselves against their will. They documented a May 2003 "raid and rescue" operation on a brothel in Chiang Mai that was carried out without the consent of the workers, resulting in numerous human rights violations.

In her 2007 book *Sex at the Margins: Migration, Labour Markets and the Rescue Industry*, sociologist Laura Mar'a Agust'n has likewise criticized what she calls the "rescue industry" for viewing most migrant sex workers as victims of trafficking that need to be saved, with the effect of severely restricting international freedom of movement. Agust'n does not deny human trafficking or forced prostitution takes place, but rather that the 'rescue industry' overestimates figures.

Much criticism of the recent publicity around sex trafficking and the associated demands for legal sanction against prostitutes or their customers, has come from sexual health / AIDS organisations. Their principle concern being that such measures hinder efforts to prevent the spread of HIV/AIDS. The epidemiologist Elizabeth Pisani, in her book *The Wisdom of Whores: Bureaucrats, Brothels, and the Business of AIDS*, examines the phenomenon of sex trafficking and its impact on HIV prevention in detail. She concludes that forced trafficking (as opposed to voluntary involvement in sex work) is wildly over estimated.

Focus on "Sex Trafficking"

Whilst most mainstream human rights groups acknowledge all forms of trafficking, there is growing criticism of the focus on trafficking for sexual exploitation at the expense of tackling other forms such as domestic or agricultural trafficking. Ambassador Nancy Elly Raphael, the first director of the U.S. Federal Trafficking in Persons Office, resigned over what she saw as misrepresentation of the issue in order to provide support for the anti-prostitution lobby. She says “It was so ideological. Prostitution, that’s what was driving the whole program. They kept saying, ‘If you didn’t have prostitution, you wouldn’t have trafficking.’ I was happy to leave.”

In many countries, particularly the United States and the United Kingdom, the overwhelming majority of interventions concentrate on sex trafficking. For example, on 8 July 2008, Fiona Mactaggart MP, a prominent UK government spokesperson on the issue, admitted that the UK government concentrated on disrupting sex trafficking. Quoting from Sigma Huda, UN special rapporteur on trafficking in persons, she said “For the most part, prostitution as actually practised in the world usually does satisfy the elements of trafficking...”

War and Terrorism

Since its independence in 1947, India has been facing the problem of insurgency and terrorism in different parts of the country. For the purpose of this column, insurgency has been taken to mean an armed violent movement, directed mainly against security forces and other government targets, to seek territorial control; terrorism has been taken to mean an armed violent movement directed against government as well as non-government targets, involving pre-meditated attacks with arms, ammunition and explosives against civilians, and resorting to intimidation tactics such as hostage-taking and hijacking, but not seeking territorial control.

India has faced exclusively terrorist movements in Punjab and Jammu and Kashmir, bordering Pakistan, and part insurgent-part terrorist movements in the northeast, bordering Myanmar and Bangladesh; in Bihar, bordering Nepal; and in certain interior states like Andhra Pradesh, Madhya Pradesh and Orissa that do not have international borders.

India has also faced terrorism of an ephemeral nature, which sprang suddenly due religious anger against either the government or the majority Hindu community or both and petered out subsequently. Examples of this would be the simultaneous explosions in Mumbai on March 12, 1993, which killed about 250 civilians, and the simultaneous explosions in Coimbatore, Tamil Nadu, in February 1998. Tamil Nadu has also faced the fallout of terrorism promoted by the Liberation Tigers of Tamil Eelam in Sri Lanka in the form of attacks by LTTE elements on its political rivals living in the state and in the assassination of former prime minister Rajiv Gandhi in May 1991.

India had also faced, for some years, Hindu sectarian terrorism in the form of the Anand Marg, which, in its motivation and irrationality, resembled to some extent the Aum Shinrikiyo of Japan. The Marg, with its emphasis on meditation, special religious and spiritual practices and use of violence against its detractors, had as many followers in foreign countries as it had in India. Its over-ground activities have petered out since 1995, but it is believed to retain many of its covert cells in different countries. However, they have not indulged in acts of violence recently.

Causes

The causes for the various insurgent/terrorist movements include:

***Political Causes*:** This is seen essentially in Assam and Tripura. The political factors that led to insurgency-cum-terrorism included the failure of the government to control large-scale illegal immigration of Muslims from Bangladesh, to fulfil the demand of economic benefits for the sons and daughters of the soil, etc.

***Economic Causes*:** Andhra Pradesh, Madhya Pradesh, Orissa and Bihar are prime examples. The economic factors include the absence of land reforms, rural unemployment, exploitation of landless labourers by land owners, etc. These economic grievances and perceptions of gross social injustice have given rise to ideological terrorist groups such as the various Marxist/Maoist groups operating under different names.

***Ethnic Causes*:** Mainly seen in Nagaland, Mizoram and Manipur due to feelings of ethnic separateness.

Religious Causes: Punjab before 1995 and in J&K since 1989.

In Punjab, some Sikh elements belonging to different organisations took to terrorism to demand the creation of an independent state called Khalistan for the Sikhs. In J&K, Muslims belonging to different organisations took to terrorism for conflicting objectives. Some, such as the Jammu & Kashmir Liberation Front, want independence for the state, including all the territory presently part of India, Pakistan and China. Others, such as the Hizbul Mujahideen, want India's J&K state to be merged with Pakistan. While those who want independence project their struggle as a separatist one, those wanting a merger with Pakistan project it as a religious struggle.

There have also been sporadic acts of religious terrorism in other parts of India. These are either due to feelings of anger amongst sections of the Muslim youth over the government's perceived failure to safeguard their lives and interests or due to Pakistan's attempts to cause religious polarisation.

The maximum number of terrorist incidents and deaths of innocent civilians have occurred due to religious terrorism. While the intensity of the violence caused by terrorism of a non-religious nature can be rated as low or medium, that of religious terrorism has been high or very high. It has involved the indiscriminate use of sophisticated Improvised Explosive Devices, suicide bombers, the killing of civilians belonging to the majority community with hand-held weapons and resorting to methods such as hijacking, hostage-taking, blowing up of aircraft through IEDs, etc.

Certain distinctions between the modus operandi and concepts/beliefs of religious and non-religious terrorist groups need to be underlined, namely:

Non-religious terrorist groups in India do not believe in suicide terrorism, but the LTTE does. Of the religious terrorist groups, the Sikhs did not believe in suicide terrorism. The indigenous terrorist groups in J&K do not believe in suicide terrorism either; it is a unique characteristic of Pakistan's pan-Islamic jihadi groups operating in J&K and other parts of

India. They too did not believe in suicide terrorism before 1998; in fact, there was no suicide terrorism in J&K before 1999. They started resorting to it only after they joined Osama bin Laden's International Islamic Front in 1998. Since then, there have been 46 incidents of suicide terrorism, of which 44 were carried out by bin Laden's Pakistani supporters belonging to these organisations.

Non-religious terrorist groups in India have not resorted to hijacking and blowing up of aircraft. Of the religious terrorists, the Sikh groups were responsible for five hijackings, the indigenous JKLF for one and the Pakistani jihadi group, the Harkat-ul-Mujahideen (which is a member of the IIF), for one. The Babbar Khalsa, a Sikh terrorist group, blew up Air India's *Kanishka* aircraft off the Irish coast on June 23, 1985, killing nearly 200 passengers and made an unsuccessful attempt the same day to blow up another Air India plane at Tokyo. The IED there exploded prematurely on the ground. The Kashmiri and the Pakistani jihadi groups have not tried to blow up any passenger plane while on flight. However, the JKLF had blown up an Indian Airlines aircraft, which it had hijacked to Lahore in 1971, after asking the passengers and crew to disembark.

All terrorist groups — religious as well as non-religious — have resorted to kidnapping hostages for ransom and for achieving other demands. The non-religious terrorist groups have targeted only Indians, whereas the religious terrorist groups target Indians as well as foreigners. The Khalistan Commando Force, a Sikh terrorist group, kidnapped a Romanian diplomat in New Delhi in 1991. The JKLF kidnapped some Israeli tourists in J&K in 1992. HUM, under the name Al Faran, kidnapped five Western tourists in 1995 and is believed to have killed four of them. An American managed to escape. Sheikh Omar, presently on trial for the kidnap and murder of American journalist Daniel Pearl in Karachi in January last year, had earlier kidnapped some Western tourists near Delhi. They were subsequently freed by the police.

Non-religious terrorist groups in India have not carried out any act of terrorism outside Indian territory. Of the religious terrorist groups, a Sikh organisation blew up an Air India plane off the Irish coast and unsuccessfully tried to blow up another plane at Tokyo the same day, plotted to kill then prime minister Rajiv Gandhi during his visit to the US in June 1985 (the plot was foiled by the Federal Bureau of Investigation), attacked the Indian ambassador in Bucharest, Romania, in October 1991, and carried out a number of attacks on pro-government members of the Sikh diaspora abroad. The JKLF kidnapped and killed an Indian diplomat in Birmingham, England, in 1984. In the 1970s, the Anand Marg had indulged in acts of terrorism in foreign countries.

None of the non-religious terrorist groups advocate the acquisition and use of Weapons of Mass Destruction. Of the religious groups, the Sikh and the indigenous Kashmiri terrorist groups did/do not advocate the acquisition and use of WMD. However, the Pakistani pan-Islamic groups, which are members of the IIF and which operate in J&K, support bin Laden's advocacy of the right and religious obligation of Muslims to acquire and use WMD to protect their religion, if necessary.

The Sikh terrorist groups did not cite their holy book as justification for their acts of terrorism, but the indigenous Kashmiri groups as well as the Pakistani jihadi groups operating in India cite the holy Koran as justification for their jihad against the government of India and the Hindus.

The Sikh and the indigenous Kashmiri groups projected/project their objective as confined to their respective state, but the Pakistani pan-Islamic terrorist groups project their aim as extending to the whole of South Asia — namely the 'liberation' of Muslims in India and the ultimate formation of an Islamic Caliphate consisting of the 'Muslim homelands' of India and Sri Lanka, Pakistan and Bangladesh.

The Sikh terrorist groups demanded an independent nation on the ground that Sikhs constituted a separate community and could not progress as fast as they wanted to in a Hindu-dominated country. They did not deride Hinduism and other non-Sikh religions. Nor did they call for the eradication of Hindu influences from their religion. The indigenous Kashmiri organisations, too, follow a similar policy. But the Pakistani pan-Islamic jihadi organisations ridicule and condemn Hinduism and other religions and call for the eradication of what they describe as the corrupting influence of Hinduism on Islam as practised in South Asia.

The Sikh and indigenous Kashmiri terrorist organisations believed/believe in Western-style parliamentary democracy. The Pakistani jihadi organisations project Western-style parliamentary democracy as anti-Islam since it believes sovereignty vests in people and not in God.

Religious as well as non-religious terrorist groups have external links with like-minded terrorist groups in other countries.

Examples: The link between the Marxist groups of India with Maoist groups of Nepal, Sri Lanka and Bangladesh; the link between the indigenous Kashmiri organisations with the religious, fundamentalist and jihadi organisations of Pakistan; the link between organisations such as the Students Islamic Movement of India with jihadi elements in Pakistan and Saudi Arabia; and the link between the Pakistani pan-Islamic jihadi organisations operating in India with bin Laden's Al Qaeda and the Taliban.

The Role of the Diaspora

Religious as well as non-religious terrorist groups draw moral support and material sustenance from the overseas diaspora. The Khalistan movement was initially born in the overseas Sikh community in the UK and Canada and spread from there to Punjab in India. The indigenous Kashmiri organisations get material assistance from the large number of migrants from Pakistan-occupied Kashmir, called the Mirpuris, who have settled in Western countries. The Marxist groups get support from the Marxist elements in the overseas Indian community.

Funding

The following are the main sources of funding for terrorist and insurgent groups:

Clandestine contributions from Pakistan's Inter-Services Intelligence.

Contributions from religious, fundamentalist and pan-Islamic jihadi organisations in Pakistan.

Contributions from ostensibly charitable organisations in Pakistan and Saudi Arabia.

Contributions from trans-national criminal groups, such as the mafia group led by Dawood Ibrahim who operates from Karachi, Pakistan.

Extortions and ransom payments for releasing hostages.

Collections — voluntary or forced — from the people living in the area where they operate.

Narcotics smuggling.

The funds are normally transmitted either through couriers or through the informal hawala channel. Rarely are funds transmitted through formal banking channels.

Sanctuaries

Religious terrorist organisations have their main external sanctuaries in Pakistan and Bangladesh, while non-religious terrorist organisations look to Nepal, Bhutan and Myanmar. Some northeast non-religious terrorist groups also operate from Bangladesh, while certain religious groups get sanctuary in Nepal.

Since 1956, Pakistan has been using its sponsorship of and support to different terrorist groups operating in India as a strategic weapon to keep India preoccupied with internal security problems. Before the formation of Bangladesh in 1971, the then East Pakistan was the main sanctuary for non-religious terrorist groups operating in India. Since 1971, the present Pakistan, called West Pakistan before 1971, has been the main sanctuary for all Sikh and Muslim terrorist groups.

Pakistan has given sanctuary to 20 principal leaders of Sikh and Muslim terrorist groups, including hijackers of Indian aircraft and trans-national criminal groups colluding with terrorists. Despite strong evidence of their presence in Pakistani territory and active operation from there, its government has denied their presence and refused to act against them. It has also ignored Interpol's notices for apprehending them and handing them over to India.

For some years after 1971, the Bangladesh authorities acted vigorously against Indian groups operating from their territory. This has gradually diluted due to the collusion of the pro-Pakistan elements in Bangladesh's military-intelligence establishment with Pakistan's military-intelligence establishment, the collusion of Bangladesh's religious fundamentalist parties with their counterparts in Pakistan and the unwillingness or inability of successive governments in Dhaka to act against these elements.

In Nepal, Bhutan and Myanmar, there is no collusion of the governments with the Indian terrorist groups operating from their territory. Their authorities have been trying to be help India as much as they can. However, their weak control over the territory from which the terrorists operate and their intelligence and security establishment does not allow for effective action against the terrorists.

Child Labour

The problem of child labour continues to pose a challenge before the nation. Government has been taking various pro-active measures to tackle this problem. However, considering the magnitude and extent of the problem and that it is essentially a socio-economic problem inextricably linked to poverty and illiteracy, it requires concerted efforts from all sections of the society to make a dent in the problem.

Way back in 1979, Government formed the first committee called Gurupadswamy Committee to study the issue of child labour and to suggest measures to tackle it. The Committee examined the problem in detail and made some far-reaching recommendations. It observed that as long as poverty continued, it would be difficult to totally eliminate child labour and hence, any attempt to abolish it through legal recourse would not be a practical proposition. The Committee felt that in the circumstances, the only alternative left was to ban child labour in hazardous areas and to regulate and ameliorate the conditions of work in other areas. It recommended that a multiple policy approach was required in dealing with the problems of working children.

Based on the recommendations of Gurupadaswamy Committee, the Child Labour (Prohibition & Regulation) Act was enacted in 1986. The Act prohibits employment of children in certain specified **hazardous occupations and processes** and regulates the working conditions in others. The list of hazardous occupations and processes is progressively being expanded on the recommendation of Child Labour Technical Advisory Committee constituted under the Act.

In consonance with the above approach, a **National Policy on Child Labour** was formulated in 1987. The Policy seeks to adopt a gradual & sequential approach with a focus on rehabilitation of children working in hazardous occupations & processes in the first instance. The Action Plan outlined in the Policy for tackling this problem is as follows:

- **Legislative Action Plan** for strict enforcement of Child Labour Act and other labour laws to ensure that children are not employed in hazardous employments, and that the working conditions of children working in non-hazardous areas are regulated in accordance with the provisions of the Child Labour Act. It also entails further identification of additional occupations and processes, which are detrimental to the health and safety of the children.
- **Focusing of General Developmental Programmes for Benefiting Child Labour**-As poverty is the root cause of child labour, the action plan emphasizes the need to cover these children and their families also under various poverty alleviation and employment generation schemes of the Government.
- **Project Based Plan of Action** envisages starting of projects in areas of high concentration of child labour. Pursuant to this, in 1988, the **National Child Labour Project** (NCLP) Scheme was launched in 9 districts

of high child labour endemicity in the country. The Scheme envisages running of special schools for child labour withdrawn from work. In the special schools, these children are provided formal/non-formal education along with vocational training, a stipend of Rs.100 per month, supplementary nutrition and regular health check ups so as to prepare them to join regular mainstream schools. Under the Scheme, funds are given to the District Collectors for running special schools for child labour. Most of these schools are run by the NGOs in the district.

Government has accordingly been taking proactive steps to tackle this problem through strict enforcement of legislative provisions along with simultaneous rehabilitative measures. State Governments, which are the appropriate implementing authorities, have been conducting regular inspections and raids to detect cases of violations. Since poverty is the root cause of this problem, and enforcement alone cannot help solve it, Government has been laying a lot of emphasis on the rehabilitation of these children and on improving the economic conditions of their families. The coverage of the NCLP Scheme has increased from 12 districts in 1988 to 100 districts in the 9 Plan to 250 districts during the 10 Plan.

Strategy for the Elimination of Child Labour under the 10 Plan

An evaluation of the Scheme was carried out by independent agencies in coordination with V. V. Giri National Labour Institute in 2001. Based on the recommendations of the evaluation and experience of implementing the scheme since 1988, the strategy for implementing the scheme during the 10 Plan was devised. It aimed at greater convergence with the other developmental schemes and bringing qualitative changes in the Scheme. Some of the salient points of the 10 Plan Strategy are as follows:

- Focused and reinforced action to eliminate child labour in the hazardous occupations by the end of the Plan period.

- Expansion of National Child Labour Projects to additional 150 districts.
- Linking the child labour elimination efforts with the Scheme of Sarva Shiksha Abhiyan of Ministry of Human Resource Development to ensure that children in the age group of 5-8 years get directly admitted to regular schools and that the older working children are mainstreamed to the formal education system through special schools functioning under the NCLP Scheme.
- Convergence with other Schemes of the Departments of Education, Rural Development, Health and Women and Child Development for the ultimate attainment of the objective in a time bound manner.

The Government and the Ministry of Labour & Employment in particular, are rather serious in their efforts to fight and succeed in this direction. The number of districts covered under the NCLP Scheme has been increased from 100 to 250, as mentioned above in this note. In addition, 21 districts have been covered under **INDUS**, a similar Scheme for rehabilitation of child labour in cooperation with US Department of Labour. Implementation of this Project was recently reviewed during the visit of Mr. Steven Law, Deputy Secretary of State, from the USA. For the Districts not covered under these two Schemes, Government is also providing funds directly to the NGOs under the Ministry's **Grants-in-aid Scheme** for running Special Schools for rehabilitation of child labour, thereby providing for a greater role and cooperation of the civil society in combating this menace.

Elimination of child labour is the single largest programme in this Ministry's activities. Apart from a major increase in the number of districts covered under the scheme, the priority of the Government in this direction is evident in the quantum jump in **budgetary allocation** during the 10 Plan. Government has allocated Rs. 602 crores for the Scheme during the 10 Plan, as against an expenditure of Rs. 178 crores in the 9 Plan. The resources set aside for combating this evil in the Ministry is around 50 per cent of its total annual budget.

The implementation of NCLP and INDUS Schemes is being closely monitored through periodical reports, frequent visits and meetings with the District and State Government officials. The Government's commitment to achieve tangible results in this direction in a time bound manner is also evident from the fact that in the recent Regional Level Conferences of District Collectors held in Hyderabad, Pune, Mussoorie and Kolkata district-wise review of the Scheme was conducted at the level of Secretary. These Conferences provided an excellent opportunity to have one-to-one interaction with the Collectors, who play a pivotal role in the implementation of these Schemes in the District. Besides, these Conferences also helped in a big way in early operationalisation of Scheme in the newly selected 150 districts.

The Government is committed to eliminate child labour in all its forms and is moving in this direction in a targeted manner. The multipronged strategy being followed by the Government to achieve this objective also found its echo during the recent discussions held in the Parliament on the Private Member's Bill tabled by Shri Iqbal Ahmed Saradgi. It was unanimously recognized therein that the problem of child labour, being inextricably linked with poverty and illiteracy, cannot be solved by legislation alone, and that a holistic, multipronged and concerted effort to tackle this problem will bring in the desired results.

Patriarchism

One of the rare truthful moments in one's life arrives when one is at her writing table putting together her cv that will officially announce her presence as an available adult in the employment world. Call them solipsist or honest, there are some queries on that paper that need enumeration when you write that resume.

Honorific: Mr/Mrs/Ms/Miss/Master. The last is archaic and is hence never included in the checkboxes. So, indeed, is the next, and the middle option sits on the fence in its timeliness (the term was first suggested as a convenience to writers of business letters by such publications as the '*Bulletin of the*

American Business Writing Association' (1951) and *'The Simplified Letter,'* issued by the National Office Management Association, the USA (1952)) and superfluity (especially if single/married checkboxes are going to appear later on the biodata although office romances are still mostly outlawed). What's the point of an honorific if one wants to withhold an idea of one's place in her own domestic life and, even if there is, doesn't it get somewhat limited? Why not then, being Hindu and Indian, use the more egalitarian Sri/Srimati (abbreviated Smt)/Kumar/Kumari version which is also based on age of consent/adulthood but not on marriedness/actual loss of virginity? Or, whether married or not, wear the timeless 'Mrs' as a universal feminine?

Name: Shakespeare was wrong and while a first name often gives out a persona to go with it (think Lucy (graceful), Tom (rakish), Walter (ineffectual), Emma (practical), Phil (sensitive)), a last name denotes your lineage (which is partly why some of you saw the light of day). And while most countries including our own (it is valid by our constitution) have married women keep their natural (born) surnames today as it would have been unfair (and incest-like?) to have done otherwise (and ridiculous to have men change theirs at marriage and pointless), mothers lose out when it comes to naming their children on their share of posterity, the easy answer to that naming game being letting women carry their mother's surnames and men their father's to accommodate both patrilineal and matrilineal realities. That is even infinitely better than handing out American Indian style names to individuals like Shining Water and Laughing Brook as suggested by certain poetic and literary circles of intellectuals to evade addressing heredity altogether. As the modern nuclear family made up of independent, adult children has satisfactorily resolved the unnecessary locality conundrum.

Address/Locality: Here's a regressive court ruling. An Italian court order passed in 2003 allows adult men to live with their parents if they are not employed or have no source of income. Here's another. The Calcutta High Court, in 2006, made it compulsory for fathers to provide for their grown, unmarried daughters in India's West Bengal. Here's a third.

This year (2008), Tamil Nadu down south legalises a pension for unmarriageable, unemployed spinsters above the age of 49.

Sex: Pointless unless job applied for is sex-specific *e.g.* surrogate motherhood. Which is still rare on the prospective wage earner's weekly news bulletin.

Subcaste: Quotas, anyone? (Somewhere down the line we have to strike a balance. It has to be noted that nowhere else in the world do castes, classes or communities queue up for the sake of gaining backward status. Nowhere else in the world is there competition to assert backwardness and then to claim we are more backward than you. Supreme Court. March 29, 2007)

Guardian's Name: Writer Gita Hariharan famously won guardianship rights for mothers in the Indian Supreme Court in 2000, the year many of us came to appreciate for the first time the meaning of the words, a landmark case. Hariharan had the apex court observe the mother is also, if secondary to the father (which is unjust and unjustified), the natural legal guardian of her child. That ruling triggered a change in official records from school applications to provident fund forms as also formats for cvs, making way for inclusion of the candidate's mother's name as an option next to the father's.

In 1910, German women won the right to work without the need of consent from their fathers or husbands. Indian adult women still need to provide the name of their father, husband or a legal guardian when applying for a stay at a guesthouse or a hostel. Forty per cent of them are beaten for stepping outdoors sans "the nod." How can a mother "guard" a child if the laws of the same land do not grant her the right and, authority that accrues thereof, to guard herself, community and family? Women have, can and do provide and protect as well as any other sex, some of them working to support the education and artistic projects of their spouses but 'Name of Wife' hardly figures in the professional records of such dependents, it is at best presented as a generic 'Name of Spouse(s).' It will take another enterprising couple to set right this account: Hariharan's victory merely bares the contradictions and shows the way.

Wear: Feeling 'empowered' in a sari? That's only because you are looked upon as a girl in other garb which accrues even less respect in Indian societal surrounds than an adult woman. If you aren't upto subverting others' ideas and responses to life for gain or fun from start-off right away and, rather than take the elevator, want to climb the learning ladder the innocent and sincere way, do not seriously wear one to your job interview. It is both overtly (in its flimsy midriff-baring uppers) and covertly (in its unreasonably restrictive lowers) sexual, informal, not-so-traditional (it is only just over two centuries old) and un-Indian (its idea was borrowed from Europe by the Tagorean women). Contrary to common opinion, pants are not so casual as much as practical and while not ethnic, are basic international attire.

Attitudes: Have you noticed how sometimes a generation gap doesn't exist outside a family? Humility is the first cousin of shyness. It is the awareness of thin wrists and heartbeats and of the eventuality of the need to pee, even if sans an urge once in a period of two days. It is hence a necessary evil. So is shyness because it stops us from getting into trouble. So is tolerance. It helps build fortitude. Which is far from the helpless resignation that masquerades as the value in some cultures. Religion is individual, it is prayers that are participatory. Don't get exploited for a bad reason. Don't be apologetic if you are. Anger is a virtue. It moves earth, creates and shakes the worlds. Tears should be involuntary. Wanting to cry is masochism. Homosexuals self-fertilise. It's better to be celibate. Female umpires will be the next good thing happening to cricket. Do not be quick to judge (if you don't know enough to do so) but do trust your judgment. Society is falling in love with mobile phones and gadgets and falling out of love with common sense and decency.

Abstractions: In 2006, the European Union did a rethink on some words pertaining to a religion, even planning to banish them from English vocabulary. Though the initiative did not work out, it was joyously appreciated by this writer who has borne since decades the same misgivings about the constant misuse of ideas and words leading to misnomenclature, both journalistic and academic, and unnecessary definition problems. Now is the time to reclaim for what they really mean some of the following words.

Fundamentalism Means: Rootedness. Once meant (subjectively): A movement in American Protestantism that arose in the early part of the 20th century in reaction to modernism and that stresses the infallibility of the Bible not only in matters of faith and morals but also as a literal historical record. Used to mean: Orthodox adherence to a set of principles considered, usually incorrectly, as basic to a faith because adherents are unaware that the teachings handed down to them had mutated over time.

Conservative Meaning: Disposed to preserve. Used to mean: One that preserves degenerated and degenerating systems and structures instead of truly everlasting ones. Suggested replacement in this form: Degenerative

Traditional Meaning: Established. Used to mean: Old-fashioned. Suggested replacements in this form. Conventional, customary

Social Meaning: Of or pertaining to the life, welfare and relations of human beings in a community. Used to mean: Of or pertaining to anti-life, malevolent and anti-relationship attitudes and mindsets within or outside a community if the same are widely accepted or conventional. Suggested replacement: Societal

Religious: Used to mean and should be replaced with godly and/or orthodox.

Patriarchy: Used to mean and should be replaced with misogyny. Or patriarchism. Patriarchy is good as is matriarchy as is egalitarianism provide the power is in the hands of those that deserve it and it is them who will use it the best.

Feminine: Used to mean weak, petty, vain, affected in specific ways and inferior to men but the word is not an oxymoron, contrary to expectations. Just two reasons why. The earliest life forms like the algae and the fungi have the least differentiation of sex, the humans, being the most developed among the living must have the most, so to be human must also equally mean to be feminine for one of the two opposite sexes. Second. Women's liberation and evolution in the latter part of the millennium must have been a natural response to beat a threat of extinction brought about by weakening of the genes by weakening the female of the species.

Differently Abled: Used to mean disabled.

Terrorism: Used to mean insurgency and should be written as such unless it takes the form of mercenary militantism.

Activism: Used to mean political activity and initiative in social engineering and reform.

Radical, Extremist: Used to mean rational or natural and should be written as such. For example, I do not, since decades, live off my parents' money, indeed, I take care of at least one person with the sum I make that is decidedly meagre, given my renunciations. Sage, even personally complacent to the point of boredom unless provoked, I do not whine and am not known to complain, indeed, I am so free of that anti-establishment paranoia that even those that compromise daily with the state of things and actually contribute in its maintenance are seen to fashionably share and display as an excuse for their behaviour, that I am often considered "dumb" or deliberately "naïve." Why is it then that I lack a voice? Why are agents for my book so hard to come by? Why am I so summarily dismissed whenever I seek to do anything that will touch the greater order, like study further or find the resources to raise the baby that I have never had for fear of its abject poverty, publish a book, mobilise social change, save the world?

Communal: Meaning common or for all as in a communal kitchen or a communal pencil sharpener but now denoting exclusivity to some who are privy to access of privileges as in a communal issue of conflict.

Discrimination: Used to mean unfounded prejudice or bias when, in reality, it means good judgment based on discerning of worth or merit.

Westernised: Variously used to mean rational, unorthodox, free-spirited, natural, international, egalitarian, effete or urban, depending on context of use, mostly by those who are the worst upholders of Oriental values who ignore and forget our individualistic and egalitarian texts, traditions, practices and schools, hence this is one of the most ironic and misused of all (mis)constructs.

Moral: Used to mean unliberated and judgmental.

Judgmental: Used, in its turn, to mean misjudgmental.

Myth: Used to mean a lie, unconscious or deliberate as opposed to a profound fable or a simple fairy tale.

Justify: Used to mean usually failed attempts at real justification. The 'judgmental' are said to 'justify' their judgment by 'myth' and not by fact.

Sex Worker: Used to mean prostitute. Who does not practise the "oldest profession in the world" because since when did crime (as in a confidence trick or dogma assisted robbery) become glorified to the status of paid work rather than a mere individual occupation and is there any reason why one party should pay the other for the benefit of the mutual pleasure derived from a consensual act even if that is solicited by either? Prostitutes also have little role to play in women's safety which can be only achieved through quashing of the "honour theory," awareness of women's equal strength and power and the real threat of the more vulnerable men's rape and castration.

Honour: Often used to mean just the opposite with regard to a woman whose pride is first vested in her soul (which is, physically, her actions and her brain) and last in her vagina which, again, is pregnable but equally often not and never violable.

Family: Often used to mean the sum of petty egotisms of the elderly and the male within or outside a domestic household and their spin-off effects on the vanities of its older female members which, taken as a whole, detracts from everyone's well being while accomplishing little else.

Guilt: Used to mean just so but is strangely devalued, even viewed as a vice, just to help evade consequences of one's actions instead of making amends for them or redressal. Have you just harmed somebody? Are you guilty? You should be if you cannot justify yourself.

Islamism: This is the word the Europeans sought to ban. Some of them believe that no true faith would justify acts of deliberate untruth and true terror. Does the same section uphold multiculturalism over universal humanity? Is Hirsi Ali right or is Irshad Manzi, strictly the religion's first and only reformer till date – the others have mostly deserted it including the 13 century Sufis, the real Mussalman?

Domestic Violence

The response to the phenomenon of domestic violence is a typical combination of effort between law enforcement agencies, social service agencies, the courts and corrections/probation agencies. The role of all these has progressed over last few decades, and brought their activities in public view.

The traditional attitude on issues related to domestic violence gave top priority to privacy. Police officers, government and other social forces were always reluctant to interfere in family matters in the past and preferred to simply counsel the couple even in extreme cases instead of making arrests and generating the process of criminal justice.

However in recent times, the spirit of activism shown by advocacy and feminist groups has brought the effect and scope of the criminal justice system to redress wrongs done by domestic abuse in sharp visibility.

Domestic violence is now being viewed as a public health problem of epidemic proportion world over-and many public, private and governmental agencies are seen making huge efforts to control it. Given below are the main bodies from the leading countries of the world that are rendering great service in this area. There are several organizations all over the world – government and non government – actively working to fight the problems generated by domestic violence to the human community.

Police intervention, law and justice, social workers and medical professionals are all tackling this sensitive problem in a more realistic manner now. United Kingdom, US, Canada, India and all other leading countries in the world have made rapid progress in this area.

In India-Sakshi – a violence intervention agency for women and children in Delhi works on cases of sexual assault, sexual harassment, child sexual abuse and domestic abuse and focuses on equality education for judges and implementation of the 1997 supreme Court Sexual Harassment Guidelines. Women's Rights Initiative – another organization in the same city runs a pro bono legal aid cell for cases of domestic abuse and work in collaboration with law enforcers in the area of domestic violence.

In Mumbai–the commercial capital of India, bodies like Majlis and Swaadhar are doing meaningful works in this field. Sneha in Chinnai and Vimochana in Bangalore are working on many women's issues arising from domestic abuse. They are also doing active work in issues related to labour. Services ranging from counseling, education and outreach, giving provisions, and mobilizing and organizing activism are provided by them. Anweshi is a women's counseling centre in Kozhikode that doubles up as meditation, resource and counseling center for battered women. Then there are several domestic violence redressal bodies in Calcutta like the Socio-Legal Aid Research and Training Center, Prgatisheel Mahila Manch and Swayam. All the above bodies have their own registered offices, contact numbers and websites for those who want to seek help.

In the United Kingdom Kiran Asian Women's Aid and Asiana operate as Asian Women's refuge center. They are run by women who understand the culture and needs of Asian women. There are various bodies in all the states of US to redress the wrongs done to human beings by domestic violence and abuse. They are situated in California, Connecticut, Georgia, Illinois, Louisiana, and Maryland. Michigan, Massachussetts, New York, New Jersey, North Carolina, Pennsylvania, Virginia, Texas, Oregon, Washington State and Washington DC. In Canada-Saskatchewan, Montreal and Vancouver house several bodies which provide redressal, safe services and shelter for victims of domestic violence.

Sexual Harassssment

According to the Protection of Human Right Act, 1993 "human rights" means the rights relating to life, liberty, equality and dignity of the individual guaranteed by the Constitution or embodied in the International Covenants and enforceable by courts in India. It is necessary and expedient for employers in work places as well as other responsible persons or institutions to observe certain guidelines to ensure the prevention of sexual harassment of women as to live with dignity is a human right guaranteed by our constitution.

It has been laid down by the Supreme Court that it is the duty of the employer or other responsible persons in work places or other institutions to prevent or deter the Commission of acts of sexual harassment and to provide the procedure for the resolution, settlement or prosecution of acts of sexual harassment by taking all steps required.

What Amounts to Sexual Harassment?

Sexual harassment includes such unwelcome sexually determined behaviour (whether directly or by implication) as:

(a) physical contact and advances

(b) a demand or request for sexual favours

(c) sexually coloured remarks

(d) showing pornography

(e) any other unwelcome physical, verbal or non-verbal conduct of sexual nature.

Where any of these acts is committed in circumstances where under the victim of such conduct has a reasonable apprehension that in relation to the victim's employment or work whether she is drawing salary, or honorarium or voluntary, whether in government, public or private enterprise such conduct can be humiliating and may constitute a health and safety problem it amounts to sexual harassment.

It is discriminatory for instance when the woman has reasonable grounds to believe that her objection would disadvantage her in connection with her employment or work including recruiting or promotion or when it creates a hostile work environment. Adverse consequences might be visited if the victim does not consent to the conduct in question or raises any objection thereto.

Steps to be Taken by the Employers

All Employers or persons in charge of work place whether in public or private sector should take appropriate steps to prevent sexual harassment. Without prejudice to the generality of this obligation they should take the following steps:

(a) Express prohibition of sexual harassment as defined, above at the work place should be notified, published and circulated in appropriate ways.

(b) The Rules/Regulations of Government and Public Sector bodies relating to conduct and discipline should include rules / regulations prohibiting sexual harassment and provide for appropriate penalties in such rules against the offender.

(c) As regards private employers steps should be taken to include the aforesaid prohibitions in the standing orders under the Industrial Employment (Standing Orders) Act, 1940.

(d) Appropriate work conditions should be provided in respect of work, leisure, health and hygiene to further ensure that there is no hostile environment towards women at work places and no employee woman should have reasonable grounds to believe that she is disadvantaged in connection with her employment.

Awareness

Awareness of the rights of female employees in this regard should be created in particular by prominently notifying the guidelines (and appropriate legislation when enacted on the subject) in a suitable manner.

Criminal Proceedings/Disciplinary Action

Where such conduct amounts to a specific offence under the Indian Penal Code or under any other law, the employer shall initiate appropriate action in accordance with law by making a complaint with the appropriate authority.

In particular, it should ensure that victims, or witnesses are not victimized or discriminated against while dealing with complaints of sexual harassment. The victims of sexual harassment should have the option to seek transfer of the perpetrator or their own transfer. Where such conduct amounts to misconduct in employment as defined by the relevant service rules, appropriate disciplinary action should be initiated by the employer in accordance with those rules.

Complaints

- Whether or not such conduct constitutes an offence under law or a breach of the service rules, an appropriate complaint mechanism should be created in the employer's organization for redress of the complaint made by the victim. Such complaint mechanism should ensure time bound treatment of complaints.
- The complaint mechanism, referred above, should be adequate to provide, where necessary, a Complaints Committee, a special counsellor or other support services, including the maintenance of confidentiality.
- The Complaints Committee should be headed by a woman and not less than half of its member should be a woman. Further, to prevent the possibility of any undue pressure or influence from senior levels, such Complaints Committee should involve a third party, either NGO or other body who is familiar with the issue of sexual harassment.
- Complaint procedure must be time bound.
- Confidentiality of the complaint procedure has to be maintained.
- Complainants or witnesses should not be victimised or discriminated against while dealing with complaints.
- The Complaints Committee must take an annual report to the Government department concerned of the complaints and action taken by them.

- The employers and person in charge will also report on the compliance with the aforesaid guidelines including on the reports of the Complaints Committee to the Government department.

Conducting Enquiry by the Complaints Committee

Any person aggrieved shall prefer a complaint before the Complaints Committee at the earliest point of time and in any case within 15 days from the date of occurrence of the alleged incident. The complaint shall contain all the material and relevant details concerning the alleged sexual harassment including the names of the contravener and the complaint shall be addressed to the Complaints Committee.

If the complainant feels that she cannot disclose her identity for any particular reason the complainant shall address the complaint to the head of the organisation and hand over the same in person or in a sealed cover.

Upon receipt of such complaint the head of the organisation shall retain the original complaint with him and send to the Complaints Committee a gist of the complaint containing all material and relevant details other than the name of the complainant and other details, which might disclose the identity of the complainant.

The Complaints Committee shall take immediate necessary action to cause an inquiry to be made discreetly or hold an inquiry, if necessary.

The Complaints Committee shall after examination of the complaint submit its recommendations to the head of the organisation recommending the penalty to be imposed.

The head of the organisation, upon receipt of the report from the Complaints Committee shall after giving an opportunity of being heard to the person complained against submit the case with the Committee's recommendations to the management.

The Management of the Organisation shall confirm with or without modification the penalty recommended after duly following the prescribed procedure.

Where the conduct of an employee amounts to misconduct in employment as defined in the relevant service rules the employer should initiate appropriate disciplinary action in accordance with the relevant rules.

Third Party Harassment

Where sexual harassment occurs as a result of an act or omission by any third party or outsider, the employer and person in charge will take all steps necessary and reasonable to assist the affected person in terms of support and preventive action.

The Central / State Governments are requested to consider adopting suitable measures including legislation to ensure that the guidelines laid down by this order are also observed by the employers in Private Sector

Laws under which a case can be filed

Section 209, IPC deals with obscene acts and songs and lays down:

Whoever, to the annoyance of others:

a) does any obscene act in any public place or

b) sings, recites or utters any obscene song, ballad or words in or near any public place, shall be punished with imprisonment of either description for a term, which may extend to 3 months or with fine or both. (Cognizable, bailable and triable offences).

Section 354, IPC deals with assault or criminal force to a woman with the intent to outrage her modesty and lays down that:

Whoever assaults or uses criminal force to any woman, intending to outrage or knowing it to be likely that he will thereby outrage her modesty, shall be punished with imprisonment of either description for a term which may extend to two years, or with fine or both.

Section 509, IPC deals with word, gesture or act intended to insult the modesty of a woman and lays down that:

Whoever intending to insult the modesty of any woman utters any word, makes any sound or gesture, or exhibits any object intending that such word or sound shall be heard, or that such gesture or object shall be seen by such woman, or intrudes upon the privacy of such woman, shall be punished with simple imprisonment for a term which may extend to one year, or with fine, or both. (Cognizable and bailable offences).

Civil suit can be filed for damages under tort laws. That is, the basis for filing the case would be mental anguish, physical harassment, loss of income and employment caused by the sexual harassment.

Under the Indecent Representation of Women (Prohibition) Act (1987) if an individual harasses another with books, photographs, paintings, films, pamphlets, packages, etc. containing "indecent representation of women"; they are liable for a minimum sentence of 2 years. Further section 7 (Offenses by Companies) holds companies where there has been "indecent representation of women" (such as the display of pornography) on the premises guilty of offenses under this act, with a minimum sentence of 2 years.

Exploitation of Labour

- In our country majority of companies not willing to pay proper salary to the workers. They are exploiting the worker beyond the limit of human tolerance. The industry only wants maximum profit with out any responsibility and liability. The workers are forced to work more than 8 hours a day with and any benefits. The minimum basic salary fixed by govt is just a peanut and eye wash.. The minimum salary should be at least 150 Rs to 200 Rs Per hour for unskilled worker. If the salary is less than the said amount, there no value for man power and he /she not able to buy minimum calories to keep body and soul together.

Many foreign multinational companies wish to invest in India is almost a for free labour destination. For example in USA per hour minimum labour cost is not less than 5 US dollar for a unskilled worker. Above that the industry wants everything free such as tax cut and labour reforms etc. etc to exploit maximum. Workers are not paid slaves or object of exploitation. If the industry wants quality work, the company should quality salary too. Most of the companies charging extremely for their service and products. Any householder can understand the meaning of inflation.

In India how many the so called industries pay salary to get minimum calorie per day?

You may find 80 to 90 % workers the take home salary is not even sufficient to buy or afford to purchase the minimum calorie of 10 days food, out of his/her one month salary. A worker need at least 1800 calorie daily in take. Forget the other needs of children's education, medical expenses of family and day to day expenses of the month etc.

In India the term salary is not only for individual worker, The salary is for one unit, (Means 1 to 5 persons.) Is it a salary or slavery? In India all are not CEOs, engineers, doctors, and industrialists!!!. Cheap labour does not mean the field and freedom for exploitation.

The cost of living is gone beyond salary limit. The industry & business community increase prices with out any interpretation and responsibility in the name industrial growth of nation and generate employment. It is only to exploit the people. The management of companies dismisses the work force, if they do not dance according the choice. The working class is not a puppets of India. The working class have all rights to demand, as the industry is carrying out business in India and with the PEOPLE OF INDIA and they are the end consumer of production too, The management have no right to dismiss a worker and forcing the workers to go labour courts, which may take years to get judgment. What will be the economically condition of working class? Is the Govt paying any attention to take care his family during the period of legal dispute?

If the working class forces the management to go court for their various actions, Then the so called exploiting industry may not survive. No political party or any establishment is not above the people of India. Why the working class form the Union? Because the industry or any establishment never paid any attention to the needs of working class, is long struggle in human history. Union demands, right to strike, is part of human expression against exploitation. It is not dada-giri or militancy as called by the exploiters of Nations man power wealth and people of India.

The minimum salary fixed by government is sufficient to eat one time food in this days? The concept welfare state for whom ? Is it only for few rich peoples of India or for all citizen of India? The government should impose strong rule and regulation, If management dismiss a worker, the company should be closed on the same day, unless the dispute settle in the court of law or pay salary up to the day of court judgment. The company may claim the closer of the company may deteriorate the finical conditions, the same logic will apply to the working class too. Which may prevent illegal actions, strikes, and unpleasant incidents.

Female Infanticide

In rural areas where a lot of people do not have access to sex determination facilities, female infanticide is shockingly common. The parents wait until the mother gives birth, and when they find out that a daughter is born, they go ahead and kill the baby by adopting various means such as strangling the baby, giving her poison, dumping her in a garbage bin, drowning her, burying her alive, starving her, stuffing her mouth with salt, or leaving her outdoors overnight so she dies of exposure.

What is disturbing is that female infanticide is not considered a big crime and rarely do culprits get convicted. Once in while there is a harsh conviction of the parent followed by some publicity, and it isn't long before the news dies down. Surprisingly, mothers are the ones who often perpetrate the crime, with the support of other women in her network. Since the mother is the one who has given birth to the unwanted female, she is the one who must do away with it. She is forced to do so at times, and willingly does so at others since she herself desires a male child. How much the mother, another victim of atrocities, is really to blame though, is anybody's guess.

Where the daughter's life is spared, parents often neglect her and expect her to work around the house serving her brothers and father. Girls are rarely sent to school, and if they are, they are removed after a few years of education and put to work-perhaps sent to cities to work as maids in homes, and send back money earned by them. In all probability, they are treated far better at the homes they work in as maids than they are in their own homes-but instances of harsh ill-treatment and abuse of such girls are also just as common.

Rural life is far removed from city life. Although we may have come across villagers who perhaps now work under us as office boys, peons, waiters in restaurants, drivers, cooks and household help, rarely do we ever try and bring about a change in their mindset. Sadly though, educated, urban and fairly wealthy people too often nurse a desire for a male child, and although they may not kill their daughter after she is born, they do try and find out the sex of their child, and abort female fetuses.

Although disclosing the gender of a foetus is illegal, there are numerous doctors that disclose the child's sex for an enhanced fee, and then offer to arrange for the abortion. Thus although there is a good law in place, its implementation is not as effective as it should be.

Although all of us take pride in our Indian culture, we need to recognize that there is something fundamentally wrong with a culture that assumes the superiority of males, and that celebrates Indian women for being meek, submissive and sacrificial. One way you can help counter this mindset is by being proud of the women in your life, and by taking pride in yourself if you are a woman.

Unit-VIII

Human Rights Related to Education

Human Rights Education: Meaning, Objectives and Principles

Today education is one of the most important functions of State and local governments. It is required in the performance of our most basic responsibilities. It is the principal instrument in awakening the human beings to cultural values, non-judgementalism, tolerance, and in preparing them to adjust to complex environments where rights and duties cooperate. There is growing consensus that education in and for human rights is essential and can contribute to both the reduction of human rights violations and the building of free, just and peaceful societies. Human rights education is also increasingly recognized as an effective strategy to prevent human rights abuses.

To receive Human Rights Education is also a Human Right to which everyone is entitled to by virtue of being a human being. In the present Indian society poor people have been ignored as far as education is concerned. They too are entitled to Human Rights Education so that they become aware of all the rights to sustain a life, full of dignity.

The irony of our times is that on the one hand we have a human rights jurisprudence which has reached its peak of glory and on the other we see human rights violations all around and this keeps happening in newer and newer forms-ethnic, displacement from homeland, etc. to name a few.

Last decade was dedicated to the concept of Education For All and it primarily focused on access to education. However, after a decade of action, the results show that access to education is not enough. More than that a right to access education, each person has a right to participate in a quality education. There is growing consensus that education in and for Human Rights is essential and can contribute to both the reduction of Human Rights violations and the building of free, just and peaceful societies. Human rights education is also increasingly recognized as an effective strategy to prevent human rights abuses.

Human Rights Education is stressed in all human rights documents as "an essential contribuion to the development of a global human rights culture".

Universally, Human Rights Education is defined as training, dissemination, and information efforts aimed at building a universal culture of Human Rights by imparting knowledge and skills, and moulding attitudes. This kind of education is needed to identify and eliminate from the school system all that is prejudicial to the human rights. Moreover, it would lay down certain guidelines to translate conceptual clarity and focus for each stage.

Under the present conditions of market mechanisms in economy, the greatest part of the society considers it impossible to achieve rule of law and form a civil society without creating new ideology, which should combine revival or our national ideals with the universal democratic values. Just Human Rights and freedoms represent the main values and fundamental elements of rule of law. The strategic line of modern civilization's spiritual development is to consider Human Rights the supreme value and bring up the society to respect and protect Human Rights. The society which is based on violence, hostility and hatred, lacks vitality, it has no prospects. Since the adoption of the World declaration on Human Rights in 1948 UN and UNESCO constantly appeal to the governments of different countries to give more information about human rights in the society, spread various international documents in primary and secondary educational institutions.

Human Rights Education-Problem and Prospects

A second decade on Human Rights Education is proposed, which would:

provide a sense of common collective vision, goals and action, as well as an opportunity to increase partnership at all levels;

provide international support for regional and national programmes created in line with the first Decade, an incentive to continue them and to start new ones;

represent the commitment of the international community (including the United Nations, Governments and civil society) to continue to pursue human rights education'.

Therefore, it is hoped that the importance of the Human Rights education will be realized and our country will be able to overcome the Human Rights violations.

Research in Human Right Education

Over the last five decades, the process of internationalization and globalization of the concept of human rights has generated the movement "All Human Rights for All." In a complex country such as India, violations of human rights at all levels necessitate human rights education at all school levels in general and teacher education in particular. Hence, human rights education should find its rightful place in the school curriculum, teacher training courses—pre-and in-service, textbooks, supplementary reading materials, educational policies, and school administration. Human rights education must exert its influence from early childhood education onward and through a broad range of disciplines to build a human rights culture. India even after fifty years of legislative functioning has not been able to fill the dearth of Human Rights law. Therefore, the future sounds promising with the greater commitment from all sectors. And preparation of a sound, realistic plan of action can help us achieve human rights education for all and transform the human rights movement into a mass movement to achieve a better social order and peaceful coexistence. Indeed, this is one of the greatest challenges in the 21st century.

National Human Rights Commission's Guidelines for Sponsoring Research

Scope: Non-recurring assistance may be given for undertaking research studies in the field of human rights. A suggestive list of broad areas for research studies in subjects related to human rights is enclosed **(Annexure-I).** The detailed guidelines for giving financial assistance for research projects will be as follows:

Funds for Research

(1) Funds for research projects will be made to an institution or a group of institutions for carrying out a specific research project. An institution which is associated in any manner with any aspect of protection and promotion of human rights with good track record and which is not run for profit, shall be eligible to be considered for entrusting the research project, such as:

1. a research and training institution set up and fully funded by the Central Government/State Government/Public Sector Undertaking;
2. an institution/organisation registered under the Societies Registration Act, 1860 (Act XXI of 1860);
3. a registered public trust;
4. a registered institution exclusively devoting itself to the espousal of the cause of human rights;
5. a university or a deemed university;
6. a State Human Rights Commission.

(2) *Research Project:* The project should be submitted by the Director/Head of the Institution as follows:

1. A brief outline of the project indicating objectives, methodology, stages of research work proposed, item-wise budget, number of personnel required, time frame, etc. should be submitted by the Director/Head of the Institution to the Commission.
2. It should be clearly mentioned whether a similar proposal has been submitted to any other organisation for financial assistance and, if so,

whether any assistance is received/expected to be received.

3. The Project Director shall give a declaration that he/she will undertake and complete the work as per the terms and conditions specified by the Commission.

(3) The project would be granted to individuals who have ample research experience and would take the responsibility of completing it. However, the grant for the project will be made available to him/her only through the institution which, while forwarding the proposal shall agree to:

1. Administer and manage the finance by opening a separate bank account in the name of the project in any nationalised bank to be operated jointly by the Project Director and one other person nominated by the institution. All funds released by the NHRC will be credited to this account.
2. Provide accommodation and furniture and other logistic support required for the project.
3. Make available all its research facilities, such as library and other facilities.
4. Arrange all other assistance necessary for the project.
5. Ensure that the project is completed within the specified time.
6. Also make sure that the funds are utilized for the purpose for which it is sanctioned.

(4) In addition to the above, the Project Director will enclose a detailed note on the work done so far on the subject and the precise contribution which the research project is expected to make to the existing body of knowledge.

(5) *Items covered under the Fund:* The following items would be covered under the Fund:

1. Fixed fee/allowance to the minimum required project staff.
2. Travel undertaken in relation to the project.

3. Consultancy charges.
4. Contingency.
5. Overhead Charges, wherever necessary.
6. Printing and Publication.
7. Stationery.

No asset should be generated out of the funds provided by the NHRC for the project. The funds shall be spent exclusively for the purpose for which they are released.

Note: Payment for the work already done before the submission of the research proposal will not be allowed.

(6) *Time Frame:* The duration of the research study proposed to be conducted should not normally exceed two years.

(7) *Scrutiny:* Every research proposal submitted to the Commission will be scrutinized and,

1.1 After scrutiny of the project the Commission may call for any clarification or suggest modifications therein.

1.2 If the research project satisfies the criteria laid down by the Commission from time to time, the Commission will approve the proposal.

The decision of the Commission to accept or reject the proposal shall be final.

2. The institution receiving funds will confirm in writing that the conditions applied by the Commission are acceptable to it.

3. The institution will maintain separate accounts in respect of the research project. The accounts will remain open to inspection of the Commission or its representative.

(8) *Release of Funds:* The project will clearly indicate the different stages of implementation of the project along with objectives, activities and the outcome in each phase. The funds will be released in installments depending on the completion of the various phases of the project. The directions of the Commission shall be complied

with and the unspent funds available at the time of termination would then have to be refunded to the Commission immediately.

(9) *Progress Reports:* The Project Director will submit to the Commission progress reports of the project periodically through the Head of the Institution as may be decided by the Commission along with Utilization Certificate of the funds released by that time.

(10) *Changes in Approved Projects:* The Project Director will have to obtain prior approval of the Commission in case any change is to be made in the research project already approved by the Commission.

(11) *Termination of the Project:* If the Commission is not satisfied with the progress of the project, or if it finds that its rules are violated in any manner, it reserves the right to terminate the research project without any notice.

(12) *Final Report:*

1. The draft final report of the project will be submitted by the Project Director to the Commission (two copies) upon completion of the project period and in no case later than one month thereafter. The draft report will be scrutinized in the Commission and on the basis of that scrutiny, the Commission may suggest some changes. 20 copies of the final report, after incorporating suggestions made by the Commission, if any, should be submitted to the Commission at the earliest. The final report should be comprehensive enough to serve as a definite record and should generally cover the following points:

   I. The problem studied/objectives.

   II. Methodology of the study :

      (a) The design of research.

      (b) The selection of the universe and the units for study, considerations that governed the selection of the universe, size of the sample and the procedure for the sample drawn.

(c) Tools used: detailed account of the exercise of tool construction, special contribution made by the project in devising new tools or sharpening existing ones.

(d) Field work: the manner in which field work was conducted including division of labour among the project staff, problems encountered.

(e) The schedule of the project.

(f) Organisational structure and problems.

(g) Methodological gains.

(h) Limitations of the study.

(i) Other observations.

III. Description and analysis of data.

IV. Findings and conclusion:

(a) Summary of findings.

(b) Conclusion.

(c) Implications for further research.

(d) Recommendations.

2. The Project Director will submit, along with the final report, 20 copies of the summary of the report.

3. The report of the research will be the exclusive property of the Commission.

(13) *Finalisation of Accounts:* When the project is completed the institution will submit a statement of accounts with a Utilization Certificate for the expenditure incurred, within three months of the date of acceptance/clearance of the project report. 15% of the funds shall be released only after full accounts are furnished to the Commission.

(14) *Conditions for Publication:* NHRC shall have exclusive right over the project report, which shall be mentioned in the report itself. The Commission reserves the exclusive right to publish the final report of the research project financed by it. The Commission will give directions with regard to publication/dissemination of the final report. The Commission's approval shall be

necessary to the use of the report/publication in any manner.

(15) *Preservation of Data:* The institution receiving funds for a project should also submit to the Commission the entire project in a floppy.

Broad Areas for Undertaking Research in Human Rights

1. Gender Justice :

1.1 Collect and analyse the available studies on the conditions of widows in general and in particular, in Mathura, Vrindavan and Varanasi; nature of their human rights violations; review the working of social security programmes for vulnerable sections and in particular for widows and destitute women; review the effectiveness of various plans and programmes and suggest new ones where necessary.

1.2 Review the safeguards to protect human rights of women prisoners.

1.3 Collect and analyse the available studies on the nature of human rights violations faced by commercial sex workers; causes and remedies; and to evolve comprehensive recommendations for improving their lot.

1.4 Domestic violence against women (dowry death/ rape/sexual abuse/wife battering etc.); to monitor and evaluate the impact of laws; policies and programmes to protect women; reform of laws; to study entrenched attitudes and stereotypes.

1.5 Status of dalit women; special problems/ violence faced by dalit women; evaluate the impact of special protective provisions in the laws.

1.6 Female literacy.

1.7 Study the implementation of Supreme Court guidelines on sexual harassment across different sectors and to make comprehensive recommendations.

1.8 Human rights violations faced by the women in the unorganised sector.

2. Rights of Children:

2.1 Child Labour— to monitor and evaluate the impact of policies and programmes designed to eliminate child labour in hazardous industries; undertake State-wise studies on child labour in specific industries; study the child labour in beedi-rolling, silk industry and such other sectors where no studies have been conducted earlier; to monitor the implementation of Supreme Court guidelines; reform of laws and strengthening of enforcement; to study the child labour projects in different States to see which are working and which are not; identifying innovations in rehabilitation of child labourers; sharing of best experiences between States.

2.2 Child Prostitution— to evaluate the impact of on-going programmes; identification of steps for better rehabilitation of victims and to strengthen enforcement.

2.3 Child Marriages— study the underlying causes, effectiveness of the legislation, weaknesses in enforcement and to make suggestions for better enforcement.

2.4 Female Infanticide and Foeticide— review the working of the Pre-natal Diagnostic Techniques (Regulation and Prevention of Misuse) Act, 1994.

2.5 Education of the Girl Child.

2.6 Rights of Disabled Children.

3. Custodial Justice:

3.1 A systematic study of torture, its implications, methods, attitudes of police personnel and other sections on torture.

3.2 Custodial Violence— causes and remedies.

3.3 Monitor and evaluate the impact of NHRC's recommendations made since its establishment to stop custodial violence — suggestions for future, working of the NHRC/Supreme Court guidelines to check custodial violence in practice.

3.4 Conditions of Juvenile Homes and other Institutions/Homes set-up under different statutes; nature of human rights violations therein.

3.5 Protection of Human Rights in Prisons.

3.6 Application of Forensic Science in the Administration of Justice; studying the conditions of Forensic Science Laboratories so as to streamline the criminal justice system.

3.7 Human Rights and Administration of the Criminal Justice System.

4. Health and Human Rights:

4.1 Iron and Iodine Deficiency related Health Problems—to monitor and evaluate the national programme for the control of anaemia, and in particular maternal anaemia; evolving better delivery systems for the supply of iron/folic acid tablets.

4.2 Quality Assurance in Mental Hospitals—to study the implementation of NHRC's recommendations.

4.3 HIV/AIDS and Human Rights—to study emerging trends in the spread of infection, nature of human rights violations faced by those affected/infected by HIV/AIDS; review the laws, policies and programmes on HIV/AIDS in order to secure the protection of rights of victims.

5. Environment and Human Rights:

5.1 Monitor and evaluate Government programmes to check arsenic poisoning of drinking water and flurosis.

5.2 Study of people affected by mega projects and the implementation of rehabilitation programmes in order to evolve recommendations for the protection of human rights of those ousted by mega projects.

5.3 Study the trends in air/water pollution in different States—right to clean air, handling of hazardous, toxic waste and hospital waste.

5.4 Rights of Workers in Hazardous Industries/Mining etc.

5.5 Tribal Rights and Environment.

5.6 Natural Calamities and Rights of People Affected.

6. Review of Laws and Constitutional Provisions:

6.1 Narcotic Drugs and Psychotropic Substances (NDPS) Act, 1985. Is it draconian? What amendments can be suggested to improve the working of the Act?

6.2 Review of the legislation on manual scavenging with a view to secure its effective implementation, eliminate this scourge and rehabilitate those engaged in this profession.

7. Terrorism, Insurgency and Human Rights:

7.1 Impact of militancy on women/children/minorities/ environment/education and employment /media/civil and political rights as well as economic, social, cultural rights of civilians in Jammu and Kashmir.

7.2 Study the conditions of detention in Jammu and Kashmir; recommendations for improvement.

7.3 Mental Health Institutions in Jammu and Kashmir.

7.4 Role of Civilian Administration in the Protection of Human Rights in strife-torn areas of Jammu and Kashmir.

7.5 Study the underlying causes of human rights violations as a result of insurgency in North East; -nature of State response; use of special laws; violations by non-state actors; practical suggestions/ recommendations for improvement in the situation.

8. Review of International Instruments and Treaties:

8.1 Accession to the UN Convention relating to the Status of Refugees, 1951.

8.2 Accession to the Optional Protocol to the CEDAW.

8.3 Accession to the two Optional Protocols to the Convention on the Rights of the Child.

8.4 Desirability of Accession to the two Optional Protocols to the ICCPR.

8.5 Desirability of Accession to the two Optional

Protocols additional to the 1949 Geneva Conventions.

9. Human Rights Literacy and Education:

9.1 Ascertaining the Status of Human Rights Education in Schools, Colleges and Universities— to evaluate the curriculum in different institutions with a view to evolve standards and to ensure quality.

9.2 Furthering Human Rights Education through Non-Formal/Distance Education Mode — effective ways to achieve this objective, spreading legal literacy on the rights, institutions and mechanisms.

9.3 Impediments to the Universalisation of Primary Education—possible solutions.

10. Bonded Labour—study the underlying causes, effectiveness of legislation; monitor the implementation of Supreme Court guidelines and NHRC's instructions; evaluate the impact of programmes to eliminate bonded labour; rehabilitation of bonded labourers.

11. Status of the Disabled/Aged— gaps in the protection of their Rights.

12. Role of Media in the Protection of Human Rights as well as being a Causative Factor in Human Rights Violations.

13. Role of NGOs in the Protection of Human Rights—response of civil society in areas of terrorism/insurgency.

14. Caste Clashes in Bihar—causes, consequences and remedies.

15. Special Problems faced by Religious Minorities—working of protective provisions in laws; extent of protection afforded by the Police to minorities.

16. Impact of Globalisation/Liberalisation on the Poor/Women/Children.

17. Role of Non-State Actors in Engendering Human Rights Violations (private companies/MNCs/armed groups/underworld/religious leaders).

Human Rights Related to Education at Different Level : Primary, Secondary and Higher Education

Human rights education is a way of preparing the ground for reclaiming and securing our right to be human. It is learning about justice and empowering people in the process. It is a social and human development strategy that enables women, men, and children to become agents of social change. It can produce the blend of ethical thinking, action, and participation of people in the decisions which shape their lives, that is needed to cultivate public policies based on human rights. It opens the possibility of creating a human rights culture for the 21st century. The human right to education entitles every woman, man, youth and child to: The human right to free and compulsory elementary education and to readily available forms of secondary and higher education.

The human right to freedom from discrimination in all areas and levels of education, and to equal access to continuing education and vocational training.

The human right to information about health, nutrition, reproduction and family planning.

The human right to education is inextricably linked to other fundamental human rights—rights that are universal, indivisible, interconnected and interdependent including:

- The human right to equality between men and women and to equal partnership in the family and society.
- The human right to work and receive wages that contribute to an adequate standard of living.
- The human right to freedom of thought, conscience, religion and belief.
- The human right to an adequate standard of living.
- The human right to participate in shaping decisions and policies affecting one=s community, at the local, national and international levels.

Unit-IX

Methods of Teaching Human Rights

Lecture

Much of the literature on anti-discrimination law is dauntingly technical, self-congratulatory or overly polemical. Two useful background collections are *Non-Discrimination Law: Comparative Perspectives* (Hague: Kluwer 1999) edited by Titia Loenen & Peter Rodrigues and *Anti-Discrimination Law Enforcement: A Comparative Perspective* (Brookfield: Avebury 1997) edited by Martin MacEwen.

There is a broader discussion in the two volume *The Law of Human Rights* (Oxford: Oxford Uni Press 2000) by Richard Clayton & Hugh Tomlinson and in Theodor Meron's *Human Rights & Humanitarian Norms as Customary Law* (Oxford: Clarendon 1989). For NGOs see in particular *Activists beyond Borders: Advocacy Networks in International Politics* (Ithaca: Cornell Uni Press 1998) by Margaret Keck & Kathryn Sikkink.

Australian Law

We have noted particular Australian works in the individual guides, for example Bede Harris' cogent *A New Constitution for Australia* (London: Cavendish 2002), George Williams' *Human Rights under the Australian Constitution* (Melbourne: Oxford Uni Press 1999), *A Bill of Rights for Australia* (Sydney: Uni of NSW Press 2000) and *The case for an Australian Bill of Rights: Freedom in the War on Terror* (Sydney: UNSW Press 2004).

Others include Chris Ronalds' *Discrimination Law & Practice* (Annandale: Federation Press 1998), *Discrimination Law & Practice* (Leichhardt: Federation Press 2004) by Chris Ronalds & Rachel Pepper, *Retreat from Injustice: Human Rights Law in Australia* (Leichhardt: Federation Press 2004) by Nick O'Neil, Simon Rice & Roger Douglas, Michael Kirby's *Through The World's Eye* (Annandale: Federation Press 2000), Hilary Charlesworth's concise *Writing In Rights: Australia & the Protection of Human Rights* (Sydney: Uni of NSW Press 2002) and Luke McNamara's *Regulating Racism: Racial Vilification Laws in Australia* (Sydney: Federation Press 2002).

Peter Bailey's *Human Rights: Australia in an International Context* (Melbourne: Butterworths 1990) and Margaret Thornton's *The Liberal Promise: Anti-Discrimination Legislation in Australia* (Oxford: Oxford Uni Press 1990) been largely superseded by *Human Rights in International & Australian Law* (Melbourne: Butterworths 2000) by Stuart Kaye & Ryszard Piotrowicz and by *Human Rights & Australian Law: Principles, Practice and Potential* (Annandale: Federation Press 1998) edited by David Kinley.

An official overview is provided by the Human Rights & Equal Opportunity Commission's 255 page *Federal Discrimination Law 2004* handbook. As noted on the following page of this profile, only the Australian Capital Territory currently has a Bill of Rights enactment, which serves to inform lawmakers and the community about the interpretation of the Territory's legislation rather than establish specific rights directly accessible by members of the public.

New Zealand

For New Zealand see *Rights & Freedoms: the New Zealand Bill of Rights Act 1990 & the Human Rights Act 1993* (Wellington: Brooke's 1995) edited by Grant Huscroft & Paul Rishworth and *Justice, Ethics & New Zealand Society* (Auckland: Oxford Uni Press 1992) edited by Graham Oddie & Roy Perrett.

Other Nations

For the UK and other EU jurisdictions see *Anti-Discrimination Law* (Aldershot: Dartmouth 1991) edited by Christopher McCrudden, *EU Human Rights Policies: A Study in Irony* (Oxford: Oxford Uni Press 2004) by Andrew Williams and *Discrimination: The Limits of Law?* (London: Mansell 1992) edited by Bob Hepple & Erika Szyszczak.

McCrudden and Gerry Chambers co-edited *Human Rights & Civil Liberties in Britain* (Oxford: Clarendon Press 1993).

Rachel Murray's *Human Rights in Africa: From the OAU to the African Union* (Cambridge: Cambridge Uni Press 2004), Randall Peerenboom's *China's Long March toward Rule of Law* (Cambridge: Cambridge Uni Press 2002), Stanley Lubman's *Bird in a Cage: Legal Reform in China after Mao* (Stanford: Stanford Uni Press 1999) and *Human Rights in Contemporary China* (New York: Columbia Uni Press 1986) edited by R Randle Edwards are invaluable. For the beginnings of intervention see Carole Fink's *Defending the Rights of Others: The Great Powers, the Jews, and International Minority Protection* (Cambridge: Cambridge Uni Press 2004).

For Eastern Europe see in particular *(Un)Civil Societies: Human Rights and Democratic Transitions in Eastern Europe and Latin America* (Lanham: Lexington Books 2005) edited by Rachel May & Andrew Milton.

Points of entry to the literature regarding Canada include Christopher MacLennan's *Toward the Charter: Canadians and the Demand for a National Bill of Rights, 1929-1960* (Montreal: McGill-Queen's Uni Press 2003) and Ross Lambertson's *Repression and Resistance: Canadian Human Rights Activists, 1930-1960* (Toronto: Uni of Toronto Press 2005).

UN Declarations

The Universal Declaration of Human Rights: A Common Standard of Achievement (Hague: Nijhoff 1999) edited by Gudmundur Alfredsson & Asbjorn Eide is a somewhat self-congratulatory collection from the human rights professoriat.

There is a more tart account in *Human Rights As Politics & Idolatry* (Princeton: Princeton Uni Press 2001) edited by Amy Gutmann, *NGO's and the Universal Declaration of Human Rights* (New York: St Martins 1998) by William Korey and *White Hats or Don Quixotes?: Human Rights Vigilantes in the Global Economy* (PDF) by Kimberly Elliott & Richard Freeman.

Questions of the applicability of human rights as a particularly 'western' and 'bourgeois' construct are explored in *Human Rights: Cultural & Ideological Perspectives* (New York: Praeger 1979) edited by Adamantia Pollis & Peter Schwab, *Asian Values & Human Rights: A Confucian Communitarian Perspective* (Cambridge: Harvard Uni Press 1998) by William De Bary, *The East Asian Challenge for Human Rights* (Cambridge: Cambridge Uni Press 1999) edited by Joanne Bauer & Daniel Bell, and *Human Rights Fifty Years On: A Reappraisal* (Manchester: Manchester Uni Press 1998) edited by Tony Evans.

For the UN Convention Relating To The Status of Refugees see in particular *The Refugee Convention at Fifty: A View From Forced Migration Studies* (New York: Lexington 2003) edited by Joanne van Selm & Khoti Kamanga, *Managing Displacement: Refugees & the Politics of Humanitarianism* (Minneapolis: Uni of Minnesota Press 2000) by Jennifer Hyndman and *Free Movement: Ethical Issues in the Transatonal Migration of People & Money* (Hemel Hempstead: Harvester 1992) edited by Brian Barry & Robert Goodin. We have highlighted other studies here.

Michael Ignatieff's 2000 *Human Rights As Politics* and *Human Rights as Idolatry* lectures (PDF) considers the 'rights debates'.

Costas Douzinas, in *The End of Human Rights* (Cambridge: Hart 2000) despairs of triumphalist column writers, bored diplomats and rich international lawyers ... whose experience of human rights violations is confined to being served a bad bottle of wine.

There is a more positive view in Richard Falk's *Human Rights Horizons: The Pursuit of Justice in a Globalizing World* (New York: Routledge 2000).

Perceived tensions between human rights and state integrity-evident in claims by authorities in China and Indonesia that strengthened human rights will result in disintegration of the state and thus widespread suffering-are explored in *The New World Order: Sovereignty, Human Rights & the Self-Determination of Peoples* (Oxford: Berg 1996) edited by Mortimer Sellers, *Religion & Human Rights: Conflicting Claims* (Armonk: Sharpe 1999) edited by Carrie Gustafson & Peter Juviler, *Autonomy, Sovereignty & Self-Determination: The Accommodation of Conflicting Rights* (Philadelphia: Uni of Pennsylvania Press 1996) by Hurst Hannum, *Prisoners of Freedom: Human Rights and the African Poor* (Berkeley: Uni of California Press 2006) by Harri Englund and *Hard Choices: Moral Dilemmas in Humanitarian Intervention* (New York: Rowman & Littlefield 1998) edited by Jonathan Moore.

For a detailed philosophical and historical analysis see *The International Bill of Rights: the Covenant on Civil & Political Rights* (New York: Columbia Uni Press 1981) edited by Louis Henkin, *Making Sense of Human Rights* (Berkeley: Uni of California Press 1987) by James Nickel and *The Universal Declaration of Human Rights: Origins, Drafting & Intent* (Philadelphia: Uni of Pennsylvania Press 1998) by Johannes Morsink. *The Evolution of International Human Rights: Visions Seen* (Philadelphia: Uni of Pennsylvania Press 1998) by Paul Lauren and *The Political Economy of Civil Society & Human Rights* (London: Routledge 1998) by Gary Madison.

Treaties and Enforcement

For perspectives on treaty-making powers and limitations under the Australian constitution, of particular relevance for the UN Conventions, see *Trick or Treaty? Commonwealth Power to Make and Implement Treaties*-the 1995 report of the Senate Legal & Constitutional References Committee.

The federal Department of Foreign Affairs & Trade has an online Australian Treaties Library on AustLII (here), which identifies current international instruments.

There is a broader treatment in *The Effect of Treaties in Domestic Law* (London: Sweet & Maxwell 1987) edited by

Francis Jacobs & Shelley Roberts and *Delegating State Powers: The Effect of Treaty Regimes on Democracy and Sovereignty* (Ardsley: Transnational 2000) edited by Thomas Franck.

For questions of enforcement-highlighted in decisions by the Commonwealth Human Rights & Equal Opportunity Commission regarding vilification, privacy and online accessibility-see in particular *Enforcing International Human Rights in Domestic Courts* (The Hague: Nijhoff 1997) edited by Benedetto Conforti & Francioni Francesco, *European Human Rights Convention in Domestic Law-A Comparative Study* (Oxford: Clarendon 1983) by Andrew Drzemczewski and *International Prosecution of Human Rights Crimes* (Berlin: Springer Verlag 2006) edited by Wolfgang Kaleck, Michael Ratner, Tobias Singelnstein & Peter Weiss.

Howard Meyer's *The World Court in Action: Judging among the Nations* (Lanham: Rowman & Littlefield 2002) offers an introduction to the court.

Discussion

Characterisations of human rights-and respect for them in practice, rather than merely as aspirational statements-vary considerably, with disagreement for example about privacy, censorship, freedom of religion and "cruel, inhuman or degrading treatment". In 1943 Roosevelt and Churchill proclaimed that "freedom means the supremacy of human rights everywhere".

Slavoj Zizek bizarrely commented 65 years later in *Violence* (London: Picador 2008) that "universal human rights" are an ideological sham: "effectively the rights of white male property owners to exchange freely on the market and exploit workers and women".

Much of the legislation and debate highlighted throughout this site is predicated on human rights as those rights which which a person is endowed simply because he/she is a human being. They are sometimes characterised as those entitlements without which people cannot live in dignity. Violation of human rights treats an individual as though he or she is not a human being.

Landmark statements of principle such as the 1948 United Nations *Universal Declaration of Human Rights* (UDHR) identifies human rights as being held by all people equally, universally, and forever. Those rights are interdependent, inalienable and indivisible. Interdependence, for example, means that an individual's right to free expression and to participation in government is directly affected by rights to the physical necessities of life, to education, to free association and non-interference by police or other agencies. Inalienability means that those rights are innate: a person cannot lose those rights and cannot be denied a right because it is "less important" or "non-essential."

Human rights are aspirational and practical. Human rights principles provide a vision of a just and peaceful world. Human rights agreements establish minimum standards for how organisations, individuals and societies should treat people. They provide a framework that empowers action by civil society advocates, governments and businesses when minimum standards are not met, as people still have human rights even if national laws and institutions do not recognise or respect those rights.

Rights are not isolated from responsibilities. The UDHR for example specifies that Article 29.

In the exercise of his rights and freedoms, everyone shall be subject only to such limitations as are determined by law solely for the purpose of securing due recognition and respect for the rights and freedoms of others and of meeting the just requirements of morality, public order and the general welfare in a democratic society. As statements of principle, national/ international human rights codes assume that there will be support for those whose rights are abused or denied, a support that frequently leads to conflicts between governments (or with NGOs and international bodies) along with disagreement about expectations and mechanisms.

Human rights are also aspects of markets, with the European Union for example highlighting five 'freedoms': free expression, free movement of goods, labour, capital and services. That is an echo of the US-Anglo declaration of 1941, which identified four freedoms-free speech and expression, freedom of religion, freedom from want and freedom from fear (initially through restrictions on physical agression by states)-and identified the individual as a legitimate object of international concern. Michael Burleigh commented that "our societies stand judged by the degree of tolerance we evince towards the most distressed or weakest members".

Civil, Political and Other Rights

Disagreement about the nature of rights-or merely about the priority to be given to particular rights-has been reflected in the cascade of national and international statements of principle, enactments and agreements.

It is common to differentiate between two classes of rights (sometimes labelled as fundamental and complementary rights)-

- civil and political rights
- economic, social and cultural rights

although distinctions are often unclear and particular rights might appear in either class.

Australian lawyer Peter Bailey commented that:

if civil and political rights can be described as the rights which enable individuals to operate freely within the political system and to be protected from arbitrary action in the administration of the law, including particularly the criminal law, then economic, social and cultural rights can be described as allowing people to own property, to work in fair conditions and to be guaranteed an adequate standard of living and facilities for education and the enjoyment of life and of the culture in which they live or have been brought up.

Equity

The initial articles of the UDHR, a child of the Enlightenment, indicate that:

All human beings are born free and equal in dignity and rights. They are endowed with reason and conscience and should act towards one another in a spirit of brotherhood with entitlement to rights and freedoms without distinction of any kind, such as race, colour, sex, language, religion, political or other opinion, national or social origin, property, birth or other status and without distinction on the basis of the political, jurisdictional or international status of the country or territory to which a person belongs.

Everyone has the right to recognition everywhere as a person before the law; no one should be subjected to arbitrary arrest, detention or exile. Articles 7 and 8 of the UDHR declare that:

All are equal before the law and are entitled without any discrimination to equal protection of the law. All are entitled to equal protection against any discrimination in violation of this Declaration and against any incitement to such discrimination.

Everyone has the right to an effective remedy by the competent national tribunals for acts violating the fundamental rights granted by the constitution or by law.

As a corollary it indicates that all are entitled in full equality to a fair and public hearing by an independent and impartial tribunal, in the determination of rights, obligations and any criminal charge. Those charged with a penal offence have the right to be presumed innocent until proved guilty according to law in a public trial at which he has had all the guarantees necessary for his defence.

The emphasis on equity means it is unsurprising that Article 16 of the UDHR states that:

Men and women of full age, without any limitation due to race, nationality or religion, have the right to marry and to found a family. They are entitled to equal rights as to marriage, during marriage and at its dissolution.

Some states have inferred that equity and just provisions imply civil recognition of same-sex relationships, e.g. the removal of discrimination in access to partner superannuation in Australia.

The UDHR indicates that everyone, as a member of society, has the right to social security and is entitled to realization, through national effort and international co-operation and in accordance with the organization and resources of each State, of the economic, social and cultural rights indispensable for his dignity and the free development of his personality.

Elyn Saks' *Refusing Care: Forced Treatment and the Rights of the Mentally Ill* (Chicago: Uni of Chicago Press 2002)

Liberty

The UDHR indicates that everyone has the right to "life, liberty and security of person", with explicit prohibition of slavery. Article 5 indicates that no one shall "be subjected to torture or to cruel, inhuman or degrading treatment or punishment", although there is considerable disagreement about what is cruel or inhumane and how the article is to be put into effect. Everyone has the right to own property, whether alone or in association with others, and no one should be arbitrarily deprived of property.

Privacy-most traditionally in the form of non-interference-is a salient human right. Article 12 of the UDHR for example states that:

> *No one shall be subjected to arbitrary interference with his privacy, family, home or correspondence, nor to attacks upon his honour and reputation. Everyone has the right to the protection of the law against such interference or attacks.*

Freedom of movement (including a rights-based passport and travel regime) is also important, with UDHR Article 13 stating that everyone has a right to freedom of movement and residence within the borders of each state, along with the right to leave any country, including his own, and to return to his country. Everyone has the right to a nationality and under Article 15 should not be arbitrarily deprived of nationality nor denied the right to change nationality. Everyone has the right to seek and, more contentiously, to enjoy in other countries asylum from persecution.

Thought and Expression

For visitors to this site two critical UDHR articles concern thought and expression of that thought.

Article 18 indicates that:

Everyone has the right to freedom of thought, conscience and religion; this right includes freedom to change his religion or belief, and freedom, either alone or in community with others and in public or private, to manifest his religion or belief in teaching, practice, worship and observance.

That article is reflected in debate about censorship and surveillance, which also draws on articulation in Article 19 of the right to freedom of opinion and expression; this right includes freedom to hold opinions without interference and to seek, receive and impart information and ideas through any media and regardless of frontiers.

Participation and Association

Those rights are complemented by positive and negative rights of association and participation. The UDHR indicates that all have a right to freedom of peaceful assembly and association; no one may be compelled to belong to an association.

Under Article 21 everyone has the right to :

- take part in the government of his country, directly or through freely chosen representatives
- equal access to public service in his country.

The UDHR seeks expression of the will of the people as the basis of government authority through "periodic and genuine elections" on the basis of universal and equal suffrage. That aspiration has not, alas, been met in roughly half the world.

Livelihood

Consistent with aspirations to realisation of "economic, social and cultural rights" the UDHR indicates that everyone has the right to:

- work, to free choice of employment, to just and

favourable conditions of work and to protection against unemployment.

- equal pay for equal work
- form and to join trade unions for the protection of his interests
- rest and leisure, including reasonable limitation of working hours and periodic holidays with pay

And that everyone who works has the right to just and favourable remuneration ensuring for that individual and family "an existence worthy of human dignity". That remuneration should be "supplemented, if necessary, by other means of social protection", because everyone has the right to a standard of living adequate for the health and well-being of himself and of his family, including food, clothing, housing and medical care and necessary social services, and the right to security in the event of unemployment, sickness, disability, widowhood, old age or other lack of livelihood in circumstances beyond his control. A perspective is provided in *Freedom From Poverty As A Human Right: Who Owes What To The Very Poor* (Oxford: Oxford Uni Press 2007) edited by Thomas Pogge.

Education, Culture, Creativity

Article 26 of the UDHR identifies a salient right to education, "directed to the full development of the human personality".

Critics of digital divides hail the UDHR's statement that:

Everyone has the right freely to participate in the cultural life of the community, to enjoy the arts and to share in scientific advancement and its benefits.

Recognition of the significance of intellectual property for economic, community and personal development is evident in the statement that:

Everyone has the right to the protection of the moral and material interests resulting from any scientific, literary or artistic production of which he is the author.

The cultural rights of people belonging to minorities are not explicitly recognised by the Universal Declaration of Human

Rights, which assumes that cultural participation will take place in a single culture of a nation-state. They were belatedly recognised by Article 27 of the International Covenant on Civil & Political Rights in 1996 and by the 1948 Convention on the Prevention and Punishment of the Crime of Genocide, which covers deliberate acts with the intent to destroy the language, religion or culture of a national, racial or religious group on grounds of national or racial origin or religious belief (including prohibiting use of a language in schools or publications and destroying libraries, museums, schools, historical monuments, places of worship or other cultural institutions).

Information Access as a New Right?

UNESCO has ambitiously argued (PDF) that access to information (aka right to information or RTI) is a fundamental human right in the 21st century, in line with the 1948 UN *Universal Declaration of Human Rights*.

Article 19 of the UDHR concerns "freedom of expression and the right to seek, receive and impart information", characterised in 2003 as particularly important in the Information Society since it forms the necessary condition for the realization of other internationally recognized human rights.

It encompasses freedom to hold opinions without interference and to seek, receive and impart information and ideas through any media and regardless of frontiers.

In 1997 the UN's Administrative Committee on Coordination (ACC) issued a Statement on *Universal Access to Basic Communication and Information Services*, foreshadowing a 'Human Right for Universal Access to Basic Communication & Information Services'.

The UNHCR argued in 2003 that:

> *the right to access information would also entail the availability of adequate tools to access information, and has implications for the sharing of knowledge as well.*

Although cited at gatherings such as the 2003 World Summit on the Information Society (WSIS), discussed here, there has been little progress in moving beyond generalities. Debate has centred on:

- political or other censorship as a restriction on human rights, with disagreement between the groups in advanced economies and the rest of the world, along with disagreements within most states
- intellectual property as an incentive for or impediment to development in emerging economies (characterised by some as a North-South IP Divide or disparity between the "Information Rich and Information Poor")
- the most effective mechanisms for bridging a variety of national and international digital divides, including barriers posed by disability, lack of education, inadequate infrastructure, expectations and even lack of a credit card (often a prerequisite for engaging in electronic commerce)

Outside the West there has arguably been less interest in-or merely awareness of-a right for individuals to control what information is collected about them and how that information is used, an extension of the right of privacy that has emerged over the past two centuries and is particularly challenging because of pervasive ICT.

Article 27 (1) of the UDHR has been acclaimed as establishing a global 'right to art'-

Everyone has the right freely to participate in the cultural life of the community, to enjoy the arts, and to share in scientific advancement and its benefits.

In practice it is unclear whether such aspirational statements have much meaning.

Case Study

Protection of Right of Victims in Cases of Industrial Hazards: Uttar Pradesh

The petitioner, Ms. Subhashini Ali, drew the attention of the Commission to the occurrence of a ghastly incident in the factory premises of Jyoti capsules on 4 January 1998 in Kanpur, in which 8 workers had lost their lives. The accident occurred due to an explosion caused by the leakage of an inflammable chemical, hexane. The petitioner alleged that the factory had resumed production without taking due care of safety conditions.

The Special Rapporteur of the Commission investigated the case and stated that the accident was the result of criminal negligence by the factory owner in handling and storing explosive chemicals and that he had failed to maintain safe working conditions in the factory. A major contributory factor was supervisory lapse on the part of the Inspectorate of Factories. The Commission directed the Government of Uttar Pradesh to finalise criminal cases registered against the owner and also ordered that the factory should not be permitted to resume production without complying with all safety requirements. The Labour Department of the Government was directed to investigate the reasons for the supervisory lapse and to penalise the culprits. The District Magistrate, Kanpur was directed to ensure early payment of all financial benefits in case of death and injuries. The intervention of the Commission brought about the award of immediate relief of Rs. 5000/-each to the victims apart from the compensation which was sanctioned to them by the State.

Comment

The Directive Principles contained in Art. 48A of the Constitution direct the State to endeavour to protect and improve the environment.

Principle 13 of the UN Declaration on Environment and Development proclaims that States shall develop national laws regarding liability and compensation for the victims of pollution and other environmental damage. The Public Liability Insurance Act 1991 is in consonance with the spirit of principle 13 of the Rio Declaration, in as much as it aims at providing for public liability insurance for the purpose of providing immediate relief to persons affected by accident occurring while handling any hazardous substance or matters connected therewith or incidental thereto. Under the Act, any person handling any hazardous substance is required to take out insurance policies so that he is insured against liability to give relief in case of death or injury to a person, or damage to any property, arising from an accident occurring while handling any hazardous substance. This Act has been enacted subsequent to the Bhopal Gas leak disaster where MIC leaked from the plant of Union Carbide India Ltd. and caused the death of over 3000 persons and serious injuries to a large number of others.

It is important to mention here that in the case brought before the Commission by Ms. Subhashini Ali, negligence was involved on the part of the factory owner. In such cases, exemplary compensation and damages are to be awarded to the victims. The Supreme Court of India has modified the English rule of strict liability in M.C. Mehta vs. UOI and has laid down the concept of 'absolute liability' in the case of industrial hazards, even though there might not have been any negligence on the part of the enterprise owner. By providing additional relief and ordering the expeditious criminal trial of the culprits, the Commission has kept in mind the constitutional obligations of the State and also the UN Declaration on the Environment and Developments.

Role Playing or Simulation

What is it and Why is it Useful?

Role-playing, or "learning through acting", is a technique that requires participants to perform a task in a realistic situation simulating "real life". This type of exercise is an effective means to take in and absorb the content and substance of new ideas. It facilitates an active understanding of the information and gives participants the opportunity to apply new skills and abilities. The simulation serves as a rehearsal on how to conduct future activities. By recreating models of real situations, which "play out" a problematic scenario, the participants are given the opportunity to see the situation from perspectives other than those they might be taking in reality. Both the participants and the facilitators have an opportunity to see "hidden obstacles" that may arise in dealing with the problem and can then explore alternative ways of addressing them. The participants not only rehearse their own behavior in a particular situation, but also have the opportunity as a group to evaluate how effective the staged resolution of the problem actually was.

Role-playing is one of the effective methods to learn and gain experience. An individual is likely to remember their personal feelings more intensely and for a longer period of time. The role game helps to analyze how people behave in a certain situation, how to evaluate and predict their reactions. Therefore, to gain the maximum effect from the role game, proposed situations should be as close to reality as possible.

How to Conduct a Role-Playing Exercise?

There are three stages to a standard role-play exercise: (1) the set-up, (2) the play, (3) the follow up.

1. *Setting up:* In the set up stage, the training team describes the scenario and assigns roles to the participants. If the participant plays a particular role in reality, it would be more effective to assign a different role to that participant during the role-play exercise.

   Another option is to put together a single page description of the scenario to be worked out by the role-play participants.

   Alternatively, it may be useful to write one-paragraph descriptions of the key role players. A description can include the main objectives and concerns of the person in that role, perhaps can include some key dialogues or a statement to be read by the person playing the role.

2. *The Play Stage:* During the play stage, the participants act out their roles and the play is carried out.

   If the role-play becomes too long, then the facilitators can give the participants a time warning of one or two minutes, and then end the play after that.

3. *The Follow Up:* It is important for all the participants to discuss what happened during the role-play. They may question individual role-players to ask why they

took a particular position, made a certain statement, or undertook an action. The explanation and the resulting discussion is important for the participants to obtain a greater understanding of the social dynamics related to a particular "real life" situation.

Sometimes a role-play session may generate strong emotions (anger, dismay, disagreement), especially if some role-players take the play too seriously, and take extreme positions. The follow-up discussions offer the facilitators an opening to explain that these reactions were caused by the structure of the situation, not by the stubbornness of the individuals playing the roles. It is not necessary to avoid strong emotions; rather, it is an opportunity to reveal the nature of some "real-life" situations, and to encourage participants to be sensitive to the different assumptions, values, goals and positions that may be taken by different persons actually in "real life".

Mock Trials and Appeals

Prejudice, discrimination and other hateful behavior must be considered when discussing human rights. While all human rights violations are not a result of prejudice and discrimination, often they play an integral part in the dynamic. When working with students in the classroom it is very important to consider their experiences and life realities and how this affects class expectations and their attitudes and feelings regarding these issues. It is very important to address the fact that human rights principles and issues are not only applicable in the international setting, that human rights education is also relevant "in our own backyards." It is important that education in human rights can be validating and empowering to students who feel oppressed in some way in our society and also it is important to be sensitive to the fact that this same awareness may possibly be quite frustrating. In working with classrooms it is important to consider:

- All of us harbor some prejudice against others, of which we are often unaware.

- By recalling times when we were targets of various forms of prejudice and discrimination, and listening to the experiences of others, we develop the empathy and commitment that will allow us to work against expressions of prejudice in ourselves and others.
- Given that learning is a lifelong process, and that prejudice is learned, we believe that it can be unlearned.
- Learning participants can recognize their biases only in an environment that is non-judgemental and non-threatening.
- Effective techniques for encouraging change are: role play, experiential activities, and interactive discussions without harmful confrontation.
- Only by empowering and developing the commitment in participants can we significantly diminish hateful behavior and world views in youth and adults, by bringing people together as allies in this struggle.
- A multicultural educational environment (addressing experiences and perspectives from individuals with diverse backgrounds) is a key factor in reducing prejudice.

From a World of Difference Institute in Minnesota

Generally speaking, it is important to reflect on our own biases, be sensitive to the experiences and outlook of students and recognize the need of human rights education in addressing our own society's problems as well as the global view. Aiding in this task is the social action componenet built into Partners in Human Rights Education.

Co-operating Learning

Tips for Using Small Groups

1. Make sure the students have the knowledge and skills necessary to do the work (If they don't, you'll know in a hurry; they won't stick to the task).
2. Make the instructions to the group **very clear**. It is

unlikely that the group will be able to follow more than one or two instructions (even clear ones!).

3. Allow enough time to complete the assigned task in the small group. Think creatively about ways to occupy groups that finish ahead of other groups.
4. Form groups of two to five students. Have only two or three when a complicated written product is the intended outcome. Five is probably the upper limit for small group discussion.
5. In striking a balance between independent and cooperative learning, don't force the issue. Use small groups only for tasks calling for cooperative work (*i.e.*, not independent work around a small table).
6. Make small group work a norm in your classroom, not a radical, once-in-a-lifetime departure from "lecture and recite."
7. Think about how your reward/evaluation strategy impacts upon the use of small groups. Be able to provide group rewards for group efforts.
8. Be explicit in dealing with management issues within the groups. If someone must report back to the class on the group's work, be sure there is a process for selecting the reporter.
9. Be prepared for the noise level which occurs during cooperative learning activities.
10. In forming groups, don't catagorize students. Heterogeneous groups are usually desirable.
11. By all means circulate and observe/evaluate what is occurring in the groups. When you stop to visit a group, don't take it over. Think about your role in such a situation.

Social Activities

The purpose of the Community Action! Fund is to provide Partners in Human Rights Education Project teams and their students with the financial resources necessary to create effective Community Action! Projects. Community Action! Projects provide a unique means of integrating classroom learning about human rights with hands-on activities in the community. Through Community Action! Projects, students can more deeply understand the meaning of human rights in their own lives and the lives of others in their community.

In past years, Partners Project participants have funded their own projects, which limited the kinds of Community Action! Projects students could plan. Through the Community Action! Fund, teams and students can plan and execute creative Community Action! Projects that will benefit their local communities without being unduly hampered by financial considerations. As you begin planning, think about the difference you can make in your own school and community. Write down the goals you want to reach. To make the job easier, make a list of those areas you know best and feel most comfortable working with in the project. If you need to find out more information, utilize your resources-call a community organization that is doing work in the area, talk with other Partners Project teams or Partners office staff, meet with your school administrators, and find out about the facts involved in the issue.

Next, think about the action steps you need to take in order to complete the project. Write down all the things that need to happen for you to reach your goal. Identify the resources and connections you will need to utilize. Make a calendar and assign duties and dates by which activities must be completed. Brainstorm strategies for overcoming any obstacles or impediments that you foresee.

To avoid burnout or frustration, start with smaller steps. Keep your goals in mind and stick with the actions that will help you reach them. Don't forget to ask for help if you need it. You may find that many people in your community will want to help.

Unit-X

Agencies of Human Rights Education

Human Rights Education: Role of Family

Human rights provide meaning for relationship between individuals, as well as for their individual and social lives. The concept of human rights is relevant to families at two levels: (a) the rights of the individual member of the family and (b) the rights of the family with reference to its environment. Indeed, the advancement of human rights within the family, equal rights and responsibilities of individual members of families, gender equality, the role of the males and protection and development of children etc. are issues of central significance to social development. Numerous human rights documents recognize the family as the basic unit of society and its entitlement to protection and support by society and the State. This is reflected in provisions of the Universal Declaration of Human Rights, the International Covenants on Human Rights, the Convention on the Elimination of All Forms of Discrimination against Women and especially and most recently in the Declaration and Programme of Action of the World Summit for Social Development held in Copenhagen in 1995.

The family's welfare, its ability to fulfil basic societal functions and its support by the society and the State are major elements in achieving human rights. The explicit articulation of the rights, functions and responsibilities of families can be a source of inspiration and a point of reference for efforts to support families and create family-friendly societies. Indeed, numerous family issues are human rights issues. Human rights education is a necessary condition in the broad process of social change, social integration and social justice, which are preconditions for development and peace. Families are central to the process of human rights education. The promotion of the enjoyment of human rights within the family by all its members is essential, on the basis of equality and human dignity, and the fostering of respect for human rights in society at large. The family is a vehicle for transforming human rights from the expression of abstract norms to the reality of social, economic, cultural and political conditions.

Issues related to infants and children attract the closest attention from Governments and organizations in the context of the relationship between human rights and families. In this regard, high priority is attached to the family's responsibility for caring for the child. Families, as major educational channels in contemporary society, are the principal means for the transmission of values, culture, attitudes and patterns of behavior. Attitudes toward one's society or culture or toward other social groups are profoundly imprinted during childhood within the family and circle. They serve as communicators and transmitters as well as intermediaries between formal and other institutions of informal education. The well being of families is contingent on the achievement of equal rights, access and opportunities for women as well as protecting the rights of the girl-child. The empowerment of women, equal sharing of responsibilities for the family by men and women and a harmonious relationship between them are critical and necessitates the promotion of attitudes, structures, policies, laws and practices which eliminate inequality in the family.

Families as Educators and Providers of Human Rights Education: Suggested Actions

As the fundamental unit of society, families are important in promoting human rights, particularly their enjoyment within the family in society at large. It is in the family where respect to human rights starts. Intra-familiar relationships, irrespective of gender, age, ability, ethnicity or religion, are a natural learning mechanism of how family members can related to each other and to others outside the family unit. Families should be helped to meet the basic needs of their members with emphasis on the principles of equality, nondiscrimination, the inviolability of rights and responsibilities of the individual, mutual respect and tolerance. Policy makers, legislators, social service personnel, educators, community activities, and all those involved in the process of Human Rights Education must take into consideration this closely and complex interrelation of interactions in the family.

Suggested Action to Further Strengthen the Role of Families as Educators and providers of Human Rights

a. Policies should be adopted to ensure the appropriate protection of labor laws and social security benefits; enact family-sensitive legislation; design and provide educational programmes to raise awareness on gender equality; integrate gender perspectives in legislation, public policies, programmes and projects;

b. It is the responsibility of educational institutions to work in concert with families in the development and nurture of children and young people, consulting with parents as partners in the human rights education process;

c. All public policies must be entrenched in the principles of gender equality, the responsibilities of parents to their children and children's rights to a secure family environment; and

d. The United Nations Decade for Human Rights Education should highlight and accord adequate attention to the important role that families can and should play in promoting the learning and practice of human rights.

Peer Group

In the broadest sense Human Rights is the right of every citizen in this country to be treated with dignity regardless of caste, community, gender and thereby realize their own capabilities and capacities. Access to education is but a part to this right to a life of dignity.

There can be two ways in which the question of human rights can be dealt with in the context of education. One is to state that the education system should facilitate the spreading of an awareness of the importance of human rights and an awareness of the importance of human rights and an understanding of the premises on which they are based as well as the safeguards that are available for the protection of these rights. This can be broadly referred to as Human Rights Education (HRE), and NCERT and UGC documents broadly refer to this. The second is to critically look at the practice of human rights within the education system.

There can be no quarrel with the objective of wanting to strengthen the subject content in relation to human rights wherever it is appropriate in subject areas such as social studies, civics as on. In this context it is probably adequate to integrate the teaching of human rights within the content of what is already being taught rather than introduce an additional subject at the school stage and thereby increase and lad of an already burdened school curriculum. There is considerable potential within existing content areas to do so and it is a matter of how effectively and sensitively this is done.

Of crucial importance to the issue of human rights in relation to education is the practice of human rights within the education system itself. In other words we probably need to first understand the concrete practice of human rights within the education system (and the manner in which the experience of different social groups varies in this context), before we can speak in general of Human Rights Education, the content of this education, whom it should focus upon and so on.

Any one who looks at the schooling statistics in any government document will be struck by the extent to which certain social groups lack even the minimal access to opportunities where they can acquire basic skills of literacy and numeracy, *i.e.*, to the primary stage of education. I am specifically referring to the relatively low enrolment and high drop-out rates from school of children from Dalit communities, officially called the scheduled Castes. What is however important is that these are social groups that have also been traditionally denied a life of dignity in society. Today when we are discussing the role of education in human rights literacy it becomes important to see whether children from communities whose human rights continue to be trampled upon are able to receive education with dignity from schools. The school is of particular importance as these are institutions that occupy public space and profess aims of equity ensuring equality of educational opportunity with social justice.

There are two points of importance that need to be remembered in the context of the education of Dalit children. One is that these children come from communities that have been traditionally denied opportunities for education. The lack of exposure of generations to skills of literacy, numeracy, literature and other forms of knowledge considered desirable is likely to put them at a disadvantage where access to school knowledge is concerned. This would imply that such children are likely to require specific pedagogic supp9rt from the school system. This is integral to their right of education. The other point is that Dalit communities have been denied learning in the past specifically because of the caste to which they belong. There is hence need for special vigilance to see that they do no continue to face social discrimination with in the school.

As mentioned earlier the majority of Dalit Children in both rural and urban areas do not attend schools. Though education documents assure us that schools are available within walking distance to all children in rural areas, this does not even hold if one looks more closely at official statistics. Further, given the spatial segregation of Dalit communities in villages and among them specially those who traditionally remove night soil and the fact that schools are located within the upper caste areas, the question of how socially accessible schools are is also relevant.

Coming to the schools themselves what needs to be seen is the quality of facilities that are available to Dalit children.

One knows that the general quality of primary schools in rural areas is poor. What is the condition of schools that cater primarily to Dalit children by virtue of being located in their habitations? Passing references in a few studies and reports give rise to the suspicion that schools where Dalit children predominate may be in poorer conditions than the average rural schools-the minimal facilities may not be available to ensure that education is received in conditions that maintain the dignity of the individual child. Inadequate inputs in schooling, the poor quality of teaching, and as on-likely to be particularly detrimental to the education of children from these communities-are relatively less exposed to the kind of skills required in the classroom.

Equally important particularly for Dalit communities are the social processes within school and classroom that influence the learning environment provided for children. There is not much research evidence on what it means to be a Dalit child within the Indian classroom especially in the rural areas where the majority of Dalit school children are to be found. Scattered references in a number of studies do indicate that the eduation of Scheduled castes may still not be looked upon with favour by upper and dominant castes in many parts of India.

Within the school it appears that Dalit students continue to experience social discrimination and this can be seen both in the official curriculum, *i.e.*, in the approved content of education and the hidden curriculum of schooling. Scheduled caste communities and the experience of untouchability rarely form part of school knowledge. Textbooks are silent about Dalit communities, even in states where these communities form a significant section of the population. Though untouchability and the maintenance of social distance from certain communities still persists in most parts of India such practices are rarely mentioned in school books or discussed in the classroom.

Dalits who look back upon their often painful experiences in school refer not to their invisibility in textbooks but to the distinct message of social inferiority that is conveyed to them by their teachers (the majority of teachers continue to come from middle and upper castes) and peers. Personal experiences of Dalits educated in the post independence period mention instances of Dalit children being asked to sit separately from their classmates, of being refused drinking water and served in broken teacups, made to dine separately and so on. A number of observers have noted the fact that teachers refuse to touch their slates or copies, or even resort to physical punishment for fear of pollution. Discouragement from teachers (who by and large still belong to the middle and upper castes in rural India) and indifference on their part to the academic needs to Dalit students is also reported in a few studies. Passing reference is also made to friendship patterns tending to remain within caste boundaries in schools.

The point being made here is that children belonging to communities that belong to the lowest of castes in the social hierarchy continues to be discriminated within the school and classroom. While blatant practices of untouchability may be less common than in the past, discrimination continues to exist in school practices particularly in the attitudes of teachers and school authorities as well as in peer behaviour. The inadequate academic support given to dalit children, the prevailing attitudes regarding these communities and the stereotypes that teachers and other members of the school community hold regarding their educability and their destiny impinges on the right of the child to education with dignity.

Given the scenario that exists regarding social groups that suffer from the backlash of caste in society at large, it is unlikely that human rights education in the abstract will bring about any significant change in the education environment provided for children belonging to these communities. What is required is that school practices in relation to discrimination, or the need for social justice within schools, is directly addressed. How this needs to be done is a matter of democratic debate and discussion but one can point to a few areas of intervention.

One is the official content of school education where a conscious effort should be made to critically analyze the manner in which school text books portray socially vulnerable communities both in terms of their visibility as well as the kind of roles they are seen to play if represented. In the context of what is called the hidden curriculum there is need for a multipronged strategy. One is the need to ensure that all children (specially in the rural areas) are entitled to equal access to facilities within educational institutions and the meting of stringent punishment where there is any form of discrimination. The other is in the context of programmes to sensitize and create awareness among teacher educators, teachers and school administrators not only of human rights where these children are concerned but also of the deleterious consequences that social discrimination can have for the development of children and the realizing of their full potential. The special role that the schools can play in reinforcing academic inputs for these children need to be stressed. Similarly within the classroom the raising of awareness of human rights requires that such awareness is linked to critical consciousness of school practices including peer group behaviour in as sensitive a manner as possible. For both teachers and students this can be done more effectively through dialogue and discussion rather than in a didactic manner. Group projects can offer opportunities both for the recognition of underlying attitudes and critically looking at them.

Children especially those from Dalit and Minority communities are in an extremely vulnerable position in the classroom. Protection and support to children in order that they can exercise their rights will be important in efforts to create an educational environment conductive to learning with dignity. In this context the links that democratic and civil liberties organisations forge with schools will be critical.

Religious and Social Organisation

United Nations

The **United Nations (UN)** is the only multilateral governmental agency with universally accepted international jurisdiction for universal human rights legislation. Human rights are primarily governed by the United Nations Security Council and the United Nations Human Rights Council, and there are numerous committees within the UN with responsibilities for safeguarding different human rights treaties.

The most senior body of the UN with regard to human rights is the Office of the High Commissioner for Human Rights. The United Nations has an international mandate to:

> *"...achieve international co-operation in solving international problems of an economic, social, cultural, or humanitarian character, and in promoting and encouraging respect for human rights and for fundamental freedoms for all without distinction as to race, sex, language, or religion."*

Human Rights Council

The United Nations **Human Rights Council**, created at the 2005 World Summit to replace the United Nations Commission on Human Rights, has a mandate to investigate violations of human rights. The Human Rights Council is a subsidiary body of the General Assembly and reports directly to it. It ranks below the Security Council, which is the final authority for the interpretation of the United Nations Charter. Forty-seven of the one hundred ninety-one member states sit on the council, elected by simple majority in a secret ballot of the United Nations General Assembly. Members serve a maximum of six years and may have their membership suspended for gross human rights abuses. The Council is based in Geneva, and meets three times a year; with additional meetings to respond to urgent situations.

Independent experts (*rapporteurs*) are retained by the Council to investigate alleged human rights abuses and to provide the Council with reports.

The Human Rights Council may request that the Security Council take action when human rights violations occur. This action may be direct actions, may involve sanctions, and the Security Council may also refer cases to the International Criminal Court (ICC) even if the issue being referred is outside the normal jurisdiction of the ICC.

Security Council

The United Nations **Security Council** has the primary responsibility for maintaining international peace and security and is the only body of the UN that can authorize the use of force (including in the context of peace-keeping operations), or override member nations sovereignty by issuing binding Security Council resolutions. Created by the UN Charter, it is classed as a *Charter Body* of the United Nations. The UN Charter gives the Security Council the power to:

- Investigate any situation threatening international peace;
- Recommend procedures for peaceful resolution of a dispute;
- Call upon other member nations to completely or partially interrupt economic relations as well as sea, air, postal, and radio communications, or to sever diplomatic relations; and
- Enforce its decisions militarily, if necessary.

The Security Council hears reports from all organs of the United Nations, and can take action over any issue which it feels threatens peace and security, including human rights issues. It has at times been criticised for failing to take action to prevent human rights abuses, including the Darfur crisis, the Srebrenica massacre and the Rwandan Genocide.

The Rome Statute of the International Criminal Court recognizes the Security Council the power to refer cases to the Court, where the Court could not otherwise exercise jurisdiction.

Other UN Treaty Bodies

A modern interpretation of the original Declaration of Human Rights was made in the Vienna Declaration and Programme of Action adopted by the World Conference on Human Rights in 1993. The degree of unanimity over these conventions, in terms of how many and which countries have ratified them varies, as does the degree to which they are respected by various states.

The UN has set up a number of *treaty-based* bodies to monitor and study human rights, under the leadership of the UN High Commissioner for Human Rights (UNHCHR). The bodies are committees of independent experts that monitor implementation of the core international human rights treaties. They are created by the treaty that they monitor.

- The *Human Rights Committee* promotes participation with the standards of the ICCPR. The eighteen members of the committee express opinions on member countries and make judgements on individual complaints against countries which have ratified the treaty. The judgements are not legally binding.
- The *Committee on Economic, Social and Cultural Rights* monitors the ICESCR and makes general comments on ratifying countries performance. It does not have the power to receive complaints.
- The *Committee on the Elimination of Racial Discrimination* monitors the CERD and conducts regular reviews of countries' performance. It can make judgements on complaints, but these are not legally binding. It issues warnings to attempt to prevent serious contraventions of the convention.
- The *Committee on the Elimination of Discrimination against Women* monitors the CEDAW. It receives states' reports on their performance and comments on them, and can make judgements on complaints against countries which have opted into the 1999 Optional Protocol.
- The *Committee Against Torture* monitors the CAT and receives states' reports on their performance every four years and comments on them. It may visit and inspect individual countries with their consent.
- The *Committee on the Rights of the Child* monitors the CRC and makes comments on reports submitted by states every five years. It does not have the power to receive complaints.
- The *Committee on Migrant Workers* was established in 2004 and monitors the ICRMW and makes comments on reports submitted by states every five years. It will

have the power to receive complaints of specific violations only once ten member states allow it.

- The *Committee on the Rights of Persons with Disabilities* was established in 2008 to monitor the Convention on the Rights of Persons with Disabilities.

Each treaty body receives secretariat support from the Treaties and Commission Branch of Office of the High Commissioner on Human Rights (OHCHR) in Geneva except CEDAW, which is supported by the Division for the Advancement of Women (DAW). CEDAW meets at United Nations headquarters in New York; the other treaty bodies generally meet at the United Nations Office in Geneva. The Human Rights Committee usually holds its March session in New York City.

Media

The Bhagalpur blindings provide an object lesson in the crucial contribution that sustained journalistic research can make in creating public awareness of human rights, more so in a traditional society in which entrenched abuses are apt to be overlooked. The reporter must be able to place the abuse in its wider legal, social and constitutional context to enable the reader to realise its implications. Stories on human rights must touch the conscience of the reader if they are to arouse rethinking of traditional norms. This requires skill in presentation as well. But the impact can be more lasting and more valuable to society than other newspaper events.

In Bhagalpur, many residents protested against the suspension of the policemen, arguing that such punishment deterred crime more effectively than protracted legal cases. It took a sustained campaign on the rights of prisoners, together with the impact of pictures of the blinded men, to touch the public conscience and expose similar brutal practices elsewhere.

In recent years, media has reflected and further strengthened increasing awareness of human rights in many areas in which they were overlooked before. Exploitation and ill-treatment of domestic workers, often children, is still routine in many households. But a series of press reports describing the cruel conditions in which they are often kept has pierced the silence and forced the police to intervene.

Special cells have been set up to deal with violence against and ill-treatment of women following sustained exposure of dowry deaths and other crimes.

Bonded labour-workers and children chained to fields or workplace for their lifetimes to repay old debts-is treated as an offence only after the press joined social activists in exposing the evil. Now the police are active, at least in Delhi. On September 10, 2000, it was reported that the "South District (Delhi) police have rescued 19 children from Bihar who were being used as bonded labourers." They were between six and 12 years of age. But investigations into the trauma of the children and the circumstances in which they were bonded in Bihar are missing.

Few countries, if any, have inherited such a wide-ranging legacy of social, cultural, economic and other restrictions on human rights as India. At the same time, India has given itself a Constitution guaranteeing human rights to an extent unequalled for a country of its size and complexity. But human rights abuses persist; in some areas they have increased. The primary reason lies in widespread ignorance of the rights due to every citizen of the country, even fifty years after the Constitution came into force in 1950. India was a signatory to the Universal Declaration of Human Rights adopted by the United Nations even earlier, in 1948.

India has nurtured a free press since it became independent, except for the brief experience of censorship under the Emergency regulations of 1975-76. This provides an opportunity to create widespread awareness of human rights, a social obligation yet to be adequately fulfilled, as evident from India's low listing in the annual UN Human Development Reports. As a developing country, the range of human rights issues requiring media intervention is particularly wide, with a marked social content. This was recognised by the United Nations in December 1986, when the Universal Declaration was expanded to include

Right to Development. Access to education, health services, food, housing, employment and fair distributions of income were mentioned specifically. Measures to ensure that women have an active role in development were stressed.

Few papers have taken up the challenge; it needs study and skill to rouse reader interest in often distant processes of human development. But reports selected by the Press Institute of India for publication in Grassroots, its monthly journal on development reporting, demonstrate that such stories can stand out and have a far more lasting impact than routine news stories, however big their headlines. Kalpana Sharma of The Hindu received a prize for her sensitive treatment of the gradual change in caste relations enabling lower caste girls in a Karnataka village to defy the traditional custom of "sitting in the laps" of upper caste elders, and bring out what this meant for social reform. Latha Jishnu's account of the transformation of a remote backward village in Madhya Pradesh by a locally conceived literacy programme has helped promote literacy in the region. Other reports make such issues as panchayati raj, exploitation of tribals, preservation of forests and water conservation meaningful for the urban reader.

One of the biggest contributions of the press in recent years is to make the right to information a national issue. The campaign for right to information began five years ago with villagers of south Rajasthan demanding access to official files containing details of money disbursed for local development works. They knew that much of the money was misappropriated, but could not prove it without access to the files. Though opposed by the local bureaucracy, they were able to establish corruption in some cases. Taken up by the press, especially local newspapers, the campaign spread to many parts of the country. At the time of writing, four states have passed their own right to information legislation and the Central Government has introduced a Bill in Parliament.

That the press has a role in promoting awareness of human rights, then described as social reform, was realised long before Independence. In 1823, the noted Bengali author, Raja Ram

Mohan Roy, brought out weeklies in three languages to campaign against caste discrimination and sati and for widow remarriage. Social reformers elsewhere followed his example. Nearly a century later, Mahatma Gandhi, the most outstanding exponent of journalism in the service of human rights, entered the field. He focussed on the evil of untouchability but also campaigned for women's rights, basic education, prisoner's rights (long before Bhagalpur), community health, rural employment and other development objectives later adopted by the United Nations.

In 1933, Gandhi brought out the first issue of Harijan, or God's children, his name for untouchable. It marshalled support, including a contribution from Rabindranath Tagore, for the Temple Entry Bill that sought to give untouchables the right to enter temples, the first step in their liberation. That the Bill was defeated in the Central Assembly and officially described as "a serious invasion of private rights" indicates the temper of the times. Largely due to Gandhi's sustained campaign at public meetings and in print, untouchability was abolished and its practice forbidden in 1950 under Article 17 of the Constitution. But, as recounted vividly by the prize-winning journalist P. Sainath in a series of articles in The Hindu, it continues to be practised in many ways. The challenge to eradicate the most deep-rooted denial of human rights in India survives.

School/Educational Institution

Postgraduate Programme in Indian Institute of Human Rights

Postgraduate Programme in Indian Institute of Human Rights Indian Institute of Human Rights Course : Postgraduate Programme in Human Rights Eligibility: Graduation How to apply: Prospectus and admission form can be obtained from institute's counter on payment of Rs.45 by cash or by sending MO/IPO/Bank Draft of Rs. 45 .....

Post Graduate Programme Course in Indian Institute of Human Rights for New Delhi.

Indian Institute of Human Rights Course: Post Graduate Programme in Human Rights Eligibility: Graduation in any discipline How to apply: Prospectus and admission form can be obtained from the institute's counter on cash payment of Rs.45 or by sending MO/IPO/Bank Draft for Rs.45 drawn in favour of institute payable at New Delhi .....

Indian Institute of Human Rights (IIHR)

Indian Institute of Human Rights (IIHR) Course: PG in Human Rights Eligibility: Graduation How to Apply : Prospectus and Admission Form can be obtained from the institute on payment of Rs.45 in cash or via a MO/IPO/Bank Draft drawn in favour of the institute.payable at New Delhi Contact: IIHR, A-16, Paryavaran .....

Three Months online certificate course on Intellectual Property Rights and Information Technology by The Indian Law Institute, New Delhi.

Three Months online certificate course on Intellectual Property Rights and Information Technology by The Indian Law Institute, New Delhi Three Months online certificate course on Intellectual Property Rights and Information Technology in the Internet Age by The Indian Law Institute, Bhagvandas Road, New Delhi-110001, commencing November 6,2006. You need: Rs 3,000 fees.....

LLB with specialisation in intellectual property rights and PGDIPL at Indian Institute of Kharagpur.

Bachelor of Law (LLB) with specialisation in intellectual property rights and Postgraduate Diploma in Intellectual Property Law (PGDIPL) at Indian Institute of Kharagpur. Deadline: Extended to May! 5,2007 for submission at the institute. Notified:Times of India, Mumbai, April 22, 2007. .....

Bibliography

Alderson, J.: *Human Rights and the Police,* Strasbourg, Council of Europe, 1984.

Alston, Philip: *The United Nations and Human Rights, A Critical Appraisal,* Oxford, UK: Oxford University Press, 1992.

Barker, Dan: *Maybe Right, Maybe Wrong: A Guide for Young Thinkers,* Buffalo, NY, Prometheus Books, 1992.

Bautista, Liberato: *Human Rights: Biblical and Theological Readings.* Manila, Philippines National Council of Churches, 1988.

Bernstein Tarrow, Norma: *Human Rights and Education*, New York: Pergamon Press, 1987.

Brownlie, Ian.: *Basic Documents on Human Rights,* Oxford, UK : Oxford University Press, 1993.

Cassese, Antonio: *Human Rights in a Changing World,* Philadelphia, Temple University Press, 1990.

Claude, Richard Pierre, and Burns H. Weston: *Human Rights in the World Community: Issues and Action,* Philadelphia, University of Pennsylvania Press, 1992.

Collins, Michael: *Adult Education as Vocation,* London: Routledge, 1991.

Dias, Clarence J: *Initiating Human Rights Education at the Grassroots; Asian Experiences*, Bangkok, Asian Cultural Forum on Development, 1992.

Donnelly, Jack: *International Human Rights,* Boulder, CO: Westview Press, 1993.

Eide, Asbørn, and Marek Thee: *Frontiers of Human Rights Education*, Oslo, Universitetsforlaget. 1983.

Forsythe, David: *Human Rights and World Politics,* Lincoln, NE, University of Nebraska Press, 1988.

Garcia, Edmundo G.: *The Human Rights Reader,* Manila, National Bookstore, 1990.

Gloppen and Lise Rakner: *Human Rights and Development, The Discourse in the Humanities and Social Sciences,* Fantoft- Bergen, Norway: Chr. Michelsen Institute, 1993.

Graves, Norman J.: *Teaching for International Understanding, Peace and Human Rights.* Paris, UNESCO, 1984.

Hannum, Hurst: *Guide to International Human Rights Practice,* Philadelphia: University of Pennsylvania Press, 1992.

Hatch, Virginia: *Human Rights for Children: A Manual of Activities for Elementary Schools,* Washington, DC: Human Rights for Children Committee, Amnesty International USA, 1991.

Hazon, Winnie: *The Social and Legal Status of Women: A Global Perspective,* Westport, CT: Greenwood Press. 1990.

Hicks, David W.: *Minorities: A Teacher's Resource Book for the Multi-Ethnic Curriculum,* Oxford, UK, Heinemann Educational Books, 1981.

Horace Perera, L.H.: *Human Rights and Religions in Sri Lanka: Buddhism, Hinduism, Christianity, Islam,* Colombo, Lanka Foundation, 1988.

Jabine, Thomas B., and Richard Pierre Claude: *Human Rights and Statistics, Getting the Record Straight,* Philadelphia: University of Pennsylvania Press, 1992.

Kerr, Joanna: *Ours by Right, Women's Rights as Human Rights,* London, Zed Books, Ltd., 1993.

Laqueur, Walter, and Barry Rubin: *The Human Rights Reader,* New York, New American Library, 1989.

Livezey, Lowell W.: *Nongovernmental Organizations and the Ideas of Human Rights,* Princeton, NJ, Princeton University Center for International Studies, 1988.

Mayer, Ann: *Islam and Human Rights: Tradition and Politics,* Princeton, NJ: Princeton University Press, 1991.

Meron, Theodor: *Human Rights and Humanitarian Norms as Customary Law,* Oxford, UK: Oxford University Press, 1991.

Newman, Frank, and David Weissbrodt: *International Human Rights.* Cincinnati, Anderson Publishing Co., 1990.

Ramsey, Patricia: *Teaching and Learning in a Diverse World,* New York, College Press of the Columbia University of the City of New York, 1987.

Reynard, A.: *Human Rights in Prisons,* Strasbourg: Council of Europe, 1986.

Richard B. Lillich and Frank C. Newman: *International Human Rights: Problems of Law and Policy.* Boston: Little, Brown and Company, 1979.

Richard Pierre Claude: *Human Rights Education in The Philippines,* Manila, Kalikasan Press, 1991.

Rosenbaum, Alan S.: *The Philosophy of Human Rights: International Perspectives,* London, Aldwych Press, 1980.

Selby, David: *Human Rights,* Cambridge, UK, Cambridge University Press, 1988.

Selwood, Sara: *Free Expressions: The Amnesty International Art Education Pack,* London, Amnesty International UK, 1991.

Shiman, David: *Teaching About Human Rights,* Denver, Center for Teaching International Relations, 1988.

Sieghart, Paul: *The International Law of Human Rights.* Oxford, UK: Clarendon Press, 1983.

Smith, Lesley: *Dimensions of Childhood: A Handbook for Social Education at Sixteen Plus,* London, Health Education Authority and UNICEF-UK, 1988.

Starkey, Hugh: *The Challenge of Human Rights Education,* London, Cassell Education Ltd., for the Council of Europe, 1991.

Timm, Richard W.: *Training of Trainers in Human Rights.* Bangladesh: South Asian Forum for Human Rights (SAFHR), 1992.

Timm, Richard W.: *Working for Justice and Human Rights: A Practical Manual,* Dhaka, Hotline Asia Oceania, n.d.

Tomaevski, Katarina: *Women and Human Rights,* London, Zed Books, Ltd., 1993.

Vincent, R.J.: *Human Rights and International Relations,* Cambridge, UK, Cambridge University Press, 1990.

Index

A

B

C

D

E

F

□□□